THE MARRIAGE GRID ®

Jane Srygley Mouton
and
Robert R. Blake

McGRAW-HILL BOOK COMPANY

New York   St. Louis   San Francisco   Düsseldorf
London   Mexico   Sydney   Toronto

ACKNOWLEDGMENTS

Acknowledgments for permission to use excerpts from copyrighted material include:

Excerpt from *Who's Afraid of Virginia Woolf?* by Edward Albee. Copyright © 1962 by Edward Albee. Reprinted by permission of the author and Atheneum Publishers.

Excerpt from *Everything in the Garden* by Edward Albee. Copyright © 1968 by Edward Albee. From the play *Everything in the Garden* by Giles Cooper. Copyright © 1963, 1964 by Giles Cooper. Reprinted by permission of the authors and Atheneum Publishers.

Robert Anderson, *You Know I Can't Hear You When the Water's Running.* Copyright © 1967 by Robert Anderson. Reprinted by permission of Random House, Inc.

George R. Bach and Peter Wyden, *The Intimate Enemy.* Copyright © 1968, 1969 by George R. Bach and Peter Wyden. Reprinted by permission of William Morrow and Company, Inc.

Philip Barry, *The Youngest.* Copyright, 1922, 1925, by Philip Barry. Copyright, 1925, by Samuel French. Copyright, 1949 (in renewal), by Ellen S. Barry. Copyright, 1953 (in renewal), by Ellen S. Barry. Reprinted by permission of Samuel French, Inc., who also control performance rights for this play.

Rudolph Besier, *The Barretts of Wimpole Street.* Copyright, 1930, 1958, by Rudolph Besier. Reprinted by permission of Little, Brown and Company.

Henry A. Bowman, *Marriage for Moderns.* Copyright © 1960, 1965, by McGraw-Hill, Inc. Copyright 1942, 1948, 1954 by McGraw-Hill, Inc. Reprinted by permission of the publisher.

William and Jerrye Breedlove, *Swap Clubs: A Study in Contemporary Sexual Mores.* Copyright © 1964 by William and Jerrye Breedlove. Reprinted by permission of Sherbourne Press, Inc.

Lewis John Carlino, *Cages: Snowangel/Epiphany.* Copyright © 1963 by Lewis John Carlino. Reprinted by permission of Random House, Inc.

Paddy Chayefsky, *Middle of the Night.* Copyright © 1957 by Paddy Chayefsky. Reprinted by permission of Random House, Inc.

Ron Cowen, *Summertree.* Copyright © 1968 by Ron Cowen. Reprinted by permission of the author.

John F. Cuber and Peggy B. Harroff, *The Significant Americans.* Copyright © 1965 by John F. Cuber and Peggy B. Harroff. Reprinted by permission of Hawthorn Books, Inc., 70 Fifth Avenue, New York, N.Y. 10011.

Jan De Hartog, *The Fourposter.* Copyright 1947, 1952 by Jan De Hartog. Reprinted by permission of Random House, Inc.

Ruth Dickson, *Marriage Is a Bad Habit.* Copyright © 1969 by Ruth Dickson. Reprinted by permission of Sherbourne Press, Inc.

Leslie H. Farber, *The Ways of the Will.* Copyright © 1966 by Leslie H. Farber. Reprinted by permission of Basic Books, Inc., Publishers, New York.

Herb Gardner, *A Thousand Clowns.* Copyright © 1961, 1962 by Herb Gardner and Irwin A. Cantor, Trustee. Reprinted by permission of International Famous Agency, Inc.

Frank D. Gilroy, *The Subject Was Roses.* Copyright © 1962 by Frank D. Gilroy. Reprinted by permission of the author.

Moss Hart, *Christopher Blake.* Copyright 1947 by Moss Hart. Reprinted by permission of Random House, Inc.

Jane Howard, *Please Touch: A Guided Tour of the Human Potential Movement.* Copyright © 1970 by Jane Howard. Reprinted by permission of the author and McGraw-Hill Book Company.

Sidney Howard, *The Silver Cord.* Copyright, 1926, 1927, by Sidney Howard. Copyright, 1954 (in renewal), by Polly Damrosch Howard. Copyright, 1955 (in renewal), by Mrs. Leopoldine B. D. Howard. Reprinted by permission of Samuel French, Inc., who also control performance rights for this play.

Morton M. Hunt, *The World of the Formerly Married.* Copyright © 1966 by Morton M. Hunt. Used with permission of McGraw-Hill Book Company.

Henrik Ibsen, *A Doll's House and Other Plays,* translated by Peter Watts. Copyright © 1965 by Peter Watts. Reprinted by permission of A. P. Watt & Son.

William Iversen, *Venus U.S.A.* Copyright © 1964, 1966, 1969 by William Iversen.

To Jack and Mercer

PREFACE

Marriage is life's most vital and rewarding, but also its most delicate relationship. Anyone has the choice of taking marriage as it comes or of committing him- or herself to strive to make it even better. *The Marriage Grid* is a framework that can help you to *understand* your feelings and behavior by tracing their causes and probable effects on your marriage. When two people have a genuine desire to enrich their relationship, then this way of revealing the state of their marriage can be a very exciting and challenging one.

You can look forward to several things from studying the Grid. The first is that it provides a basis for seeing yourself, your mate, and your marriage in more objective terms. This is helpful because it tells you what is going on. When you see your actions more objectively you can pinpoint what you want to do to change. Second, it can help you see new possibilities for your marriage, ones you may not previously have given much thought to. So by indicating what needs changing and what may be new ways of relating to your mate, the Grid can provide you with valuable insights for strengthening your marriage.

The conversations in the book illustrate marriage dynamics. Selected from many sources, they have been chosen because each makes an important point in a clear, uncomplicated way. Appreciation is expressed for permission to use them. The concepts underlying these conversations are technical. They are drawn from the behavioral sciences of psychology, sociology, and anthropology, and from therapy and marriage counseling. The reader who wishes to consult original sources is referred to the annotated references at the end of the book.

Gratitude is in order for several individuals. Reginald C. Tillam worked with us day in and day out and we value his contribution most highly. Jerry P. Nims provided a stimulating critique of many of our ideas and their implications for strengthening marriage relationships. R. Anthony Pearson not only offered suggestions but also relieved us of other responsibilities. This gave us the opportunity to fulfill our dream of exploring ways in which marriage could become life's most significant relationship. The assistance of people who evaluated this book against their own marriage experience and made recommendations is gratefully acknowledged.

JANE SRYGLEY MOUTON
ROBERT R. BLAKE

Austin, Texas
February 15, 1971

CONTENTS

THE
MARRIAGE
GRID ®

CHAPTER 1 | THE MARRIAGE GRID

George and Harriet are in a store looking at beds. He wants to keep the fifty-four-inch double they've been sleeping in for years. But her mind is made up. She wants twins.

Harriet. —Now, George, please. Let's stick to facts. First, my back is breaking. Second, my nerves are shattered from sleeplessness. Third, you are a morning person, and I am a night person. I like to read in bed and sleep late. You like to go right to sleep and get up early. For twenty years I have turned out the light for you, and. . . . Oh, this is nonsense. We've been over it all.

George. What about a queen size or a king size?

Harriet. We've discussed that. It won't fit in the bedroom. A fifty-four or twins along each wall is all that will fit.

*   *   *

George. Then let's sell the house.

Harriet. Stop being ridiculous.

George. The house is meant to serve *our* purposes, not the other way around. That damned house. I've been breaking my ass to support it, and now it's going to separate me from my wife . . . I want a divorce!

Harriet. All right.

1

George. You don't care. You don't take me seriously.

Harriet. You have a right to say "I want a divorce" three times a
day. I have a right not to take you seriously. Besides, you
keep looking at it from your point of view. . . . Old cuddly
bears under a quilt . . . a couple of soup spoons nestled in a
drawer . . . old night-night. A very romantic picture. Old
ever-ready. . . . Subconsciously I may be rebelling against
that. I may want the space so that you'll have to make the effort, wade across the Persian Gulf. Get your feet wet. . . . Not
just suddenly decide you might as well since you hardly have
to move to get it.

George. That's damned unfair. I have never taken you for granted.
I have scrupulously concerned myself with your moods and
preferences and responses . . . I could have been like some
husbands who just use their wives . . . bang-bang! Thanks for
the use of the hall. That's what some husbands do, in case
you're interested.

Harriet. Not in our cultural and educational bracket. I've read the
articles too . . . so stop congratulating yourself.[1]

These two have reached an impasse. Which way will they go? Get
twins, keep the double, or start separation proceedings?

Is it a satisfying marriage? The conversation gives just a brief
glimpse of it—but enough to tell you something about these two
people. What you will be reading will add to your understanding of
what is going on between them. But far more important is what
you can learn about your own situation and about what's going on
between you and your mate. You'll come to know not only how,
but also *why* you think about and feel toward your mate as you do.
If you already have a good, strong, and sound marriage, this book
can help you to enjoy it even more. But if your marriage is not yet
what you would like it to be, this book will help you to do something constructive about the situation.

As *The Marriage Grid* is a framework for understanding your
marriage, it applies to you and your mate as well as to George and
Harriet. But back to them for a moment. Used as examples, they
will help you get an overview of what the Grid is all about.

There are two main areas of concern in George's mind. One concern is for *what happens.* In the couple's present situation, this concern focuses on whether they keep their double bed or replace it with twins. One mate's degree of concern about what happens may be similar to or different from the other's. The second main area of concern is for *relationship.* George has some particular degree of personal concern for Harriet as a person. So has Harriet for George. The question that evokes this concern at present is whether the bed decision is going to preserve and maybe strengthen their relationship or is going to detract from it.

The way in which your Concern for What Happens meshes with your Concern for Your Mate is what goes to make up your Grid style.

Concern for What Happens is one scale of the Grid.

Everyone experiences some degree of concern for what happens in his or her marriage. If your concern is high, you want your actions to bring about effective results. You care very much that things turn out the way you think they should. You're strongly committed to arriving at solutions which are sound.

Concern for What Happens isn't always high. Some people no longer care what happens. This may be a temporary state of mind, or it could be a more deep-seated attitude. When concern is low, very little effort goes into practical activities and decision-making. If George had felt no interest in the decision, he'd have had low concern for what happened. It is also possible that a person's concern for what happens might fall somewhere in between high or low.

Concern for Your Mate is the other scale of the Grid.

You have probably noticed by now that the terms "husband" and "wife" are not being used. Take "mate" to mean the other person in your marriage. Other expressions might have been used such as partner, pal, companion, friend, comrade-in-arms, and so on. "Mate" is a handily neutral term which applies to each of you, and isn't burdened with traditional and sentimental meaning. So whichever way you're getting along, use *mate* to mean the other person. Interpret it in whatever way fits. Currently it can mean soulmate, helpmate, playmate, cellmate, inmate, even intimate. If you're constantly road blocking each other, think of checkmate. If you're sleeping back-to-back, use it as an honorary title to convey the sense of "stale"mate.

If your concern is high, you care about your mate very much. You want your behavior to reflect your love and affection. You want your mate to be pleased, satisfied, and fulfilled. For example, no matter what the decision, it seems that George wants Harriet to be happy with it. It is quite a different story if you have a low degree of mate concern. This means you wouldn't lift a finger to help your mate to be satisfied or pleased, as in Harriet's case. She's ready to shove George into a twin whether he likes it or not. And there are degrees for concern in between low and high.

Figure 1 shows the Grid. Concern for What Happens and Concern for Your Mate come together in different ways, depending upon the strength of each concern.[2] The line across the bottom represents Concern for What Happens, while the up-and-down side corresponds to Concern for Your Mate. *1* is low, *9* is high concern, and *5* is halfway between. These numbers stand for noticeable *differences* in your thoughts, attitudes, feelings, and emotions. They do not measure and evaluate you in a computerlike way or like the number of gallons you can put into your gas tank. You may find your own attitudes put into words in one of the paragraphs of the Grid diagram. Then when you look for your mate's point of view on the Grid, you may see differences or similarities between the other person's characteristic approach and your own. Questions of what is "good" or "bad" for your marriage will be taken up again and again throughout the book.

The numbers on the Grid like 9,1 or 1,9 are used for identification of attitudes and behavior. They don't ask you to do arithmetic. The advantage of using numbers for identification in this way is that these numbers have a neutral quality. This can help you and your mate talk about each other. It is much more acceptable to say "that's a 9,1 remark," than to say "all you do is nag." When you talk in Grid language you say the numbers *9,1* as nine-one or *1,9* as one-nine. It is as simple as that.

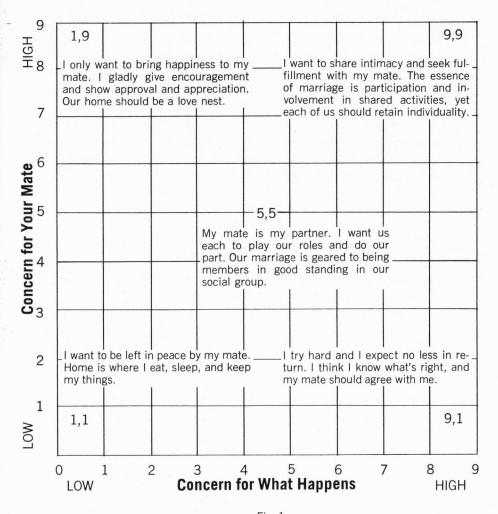

Fig. 1

9,1

Look at the lower right corner. That's 9,1. It means *9* points of Concern for What Happens, together with *1* point of Concern for One's Mate. A husband or wife with a 9,1 attitude is determined to call the shots, to master and *control*. The other mate is expected to comply. The 9,1 attitude is "I know what's right. Don't talk back to me." However, not every mate is disposed to knuckle under, so conflict ensues. When neither mate yields, deadlock, hostility, continued misunderstanding prevail. Here's an example.

Gussie and Jake are at each other again. Both contribute to the hostility by saying things that can't possibly be answered, yet can't really be forgotten.

Jake. Look, it's no use arguing cause I've got the proof of it right here in these repair bills from three years back.

Gussie. Hah! You've got an elephant's memory for every miserable few cents you've ever dropped. Skinflint.

Jake. It's several hundred bucks by now! I'll total it up and show you. Money down the drain. And all because you won't listen. You *never* listen. How many times have I told you . . .

Gussie. You—tell *me?* I take no orders from you, baby. Back off, Jake, you're not boss around here, or anywhere else for that matter. Even the dog doesn't obey you, and you know what a good judge of character he is.

Jake. Lord give me strength to bear this cross. Gussie, my dim light of love, I'm trying to get you to appreciate two undeniable facts and what they mean. You habitually drive with your delicate size-ten foot resting on the brake pedal. Every three months or so a drum burns out and has to be replaced. Y'know, I thought the biggest fool in the world could see the connection between fact A and fact B, but it seems I was wrong.

Gussie. It was a lousy car when you bought it and it's a wreck now.

Jake. Shut up!

Gussie. You haven't got the guts to argue with them and get your money's worth. Instead, you come in here whining and trying to place the blame . . .

Jake. After I get it repaired this time, you're not going to drive it anymore.

Gussie. What?! I'll see you in hell first, it's mine as much as yours.

Jake and Gussie are getting nowhere except into more spattering of each other with insults, recrimination, and threats. Each mate's creativity is devoted to thinking up more and more powerful put-downs, instead of being applied to the car problem itself. "Discussion" in these terms simply widens the breach. It aggravates differences rather than promoting shared understanding. When either you or your mate approach each other with a 9,1 point of view, each puts what is more important to him or her first and foremost, expecting the other mate to come across and surrender.

1,9

The upper left corner is 1,9. Here low Concern for What Happens ties in with high Concern for Your Mate. The desire to "please at any price" is at the very heart of the 1,9 attitude. Through words and actions the 1,9-oriented person sings a melody of "how wonderful you are! May I do this or that for your pleasure or comfort? Nothing is too much, no detail too small, for me to attend to. Your wish is my heart's desire."

Ann is flowing over with 1,9 sentimentality, and Ralph is drowning in it.

Ann. Every moment you can spend with me is heaven. I want to be *with* you—it's the only way I can be happy. You *do* love me, don't you?

Ralph. Why, sure, of course I do.

Ann. I want to be everything and give everything to you. I know you don't want babies right now, but that doesn't mean we can't be as close as two people can possibly be!

Ralph. It's great being married to you, really it is. . . .

Ann. Oh, darling!

Ralph. Don't think I don't appreciate it. . . .

Ann. Then we *do* belong—we're one, we don't have separate lives.

Sure, you have to go to work, but I still feel you're in my heart as I get things ready for you to come home. And when you come, all I want to do is wait on you hand and foot. . . .

Ralph. But I don't want you to sacrifice yourself for me. I'm not some kind of idol. . . . No, let me finish what I'm saying. It's important. Honey, I could *hire* a housekeeper. But I *married* you. Sure, do the household chores and all that, but there's time for you to be yourself, to find some interests. . . .

Ann. But, darling, *you're* my interest.

Ralph. I want to respect you, and I can't if you make me the one reason for your existence. Women who adore their husbands —like you do—sometimes carry it too far. They throw a thousand little ropes around them. We share life together, but each of us is a separate human being. Really, one can only live as oneself; it's unhealthy if you live entirely for me, without any individuality.

Ann. But I'm nothing without you—I depend on you, I want to be part of you!

Can you sense what kind of person Ann is? She is so eager to be loved that she gives herself—mind, body, and soul—to Ralph with almost unthinking sacrifice of herself as a person. The trouble is, he's feeling a need to break free. When either of you approaches marriage from a 1,9 point of view, you are likely to yield that part of personal identity which is based on self, autonomy, and independence in order to be *one* with the other. It amounts to unity by absorption.

1,1

The lower left corner of the Grid is 1,1. Concern is low whichever way you look. Here we have indifference, emotional numbness, apartness from the other person, withdrawal of feeling. The relationship is not much more than going through the motions of being married. This mate is unconcerned.

A 1,1 rule is "even if I *could* succeed, to hell with it." As time goes on, it seems natural, within 1,1 attitudes, to escape. You can do this either physically, by finding other company or contriving to be alone, or by mentally walking out, when you daydream, eye the newspaper, gaze at TV, or retreat behind "leave me alone. I'm tired."

Here's a 1,1-oriented husband. Jim's bedtime habits can tell Mona something. But she's not ready to face facts yet.

Mona. With you it's either working, or watching TV, or going off to sleep. Isn't there anything else you want to do?

Jim. Eh?

Mona. We haven't made it in months. Do I have to wait for a power cut or for the TV to break down before you'll do what's supposed to come naturally?

Jim. You know how it is at the company this time of year, everything's so hectic. It's pressure, pressure, pressure. By the time I get home, I'm worn out.

Mona. But weekends?

Jim. I'm just too uptight. Golf helps me unwind.

Mona. More than I could?

Jim. Oh, come on.

Mona. Look, I'm no spring chicken, but I can still be fun in bed. Your problem is, you've forgotten how to relax. Please step this way.

Jim. I've had a big day. Another time, huh?

Mona. Look, if something's wrong, let's find out! You might need a tonic or something. Or is there something about me? Come on, level!

Jim. I have to feel right about it and—well, if you want to know —I can't stand the sight of those irons in your hair and your face all plastered with that greasy stuff you put on.

Mona. Oh! I hadn't realized. Sorry. Give me five minutes and I'll be your tousle-headed, peach-skinned sex goddess. Then how about lighting my fire?

Jim. Fix some supper, will you? I'm watching Johnny Carson.

It's dead certain that Mona isn't going to get together with Jim tonight. Probably not tomorrow or next week, either. His blandness denotes apathy so deep that it has annihilated whatever passion he might have felt toward her yesterday or last year. He doesn't get mad at her pestering and say, "Drop dead!" To him maybe she's *already* dead as a marriage mate. If she went 1,1, too, that probably would be OK with him. Then she'd leave him alone, which seems to be all he wants.

When both mates adopt 1,1 attitudes, the situation is one where lives are lived in parallel. "Togetherness" is a matter of habit and convenience rather than a real desire to be together. Probably because of their children, their finances, or some other circumstance that's trapped them—as well as for occasional biological reasons —they continue under the same roof.

5,5

In the center is 5,5, the "middle way." The idea is that established *norms* show you the proper way to live. Norms are those rules of life which your friends and associates, or "our crowd," stick to. What are the reasons for their acceptance? There are at least two. When people are guided by what others do, they feel a certainty in their relations. They're not out of their depth; they paddle through marriage while feeling they're in the swim. Second, it's a simple and easy way to live most of the time. You not only act the same, you *think* the same; you pick up the majority opinion of "what is best." You reflect it in your own conversations and attitudes, as well as in your conduct. This saves you the trouble of thinking things out for yourself. It reduces risk from errors of judgment, thought, attitude, or actions.

Wilma and Johnny—but particularly Wilma—show how 5,5 works. They're in bed. Johnny's weary, but Wilma is claiming her "rights."

Johnny. Put the cigarette out and go to sleep.
Wilma. I can't sleep when I'm like this.
Johnny. It's all in your mind.
Wilma. It is not. I feel sexy.
Johnny. It's just nerves. Have a sandwich. Wilma, cut it out. In the morning, in the morning.
Wilma. I'm not interested in the morning. It's not romantic in the morning. It's romantic now.

Johnny. To me it's work.

Wilma. Johnny, when I owe you, you pick the time. But you owe
me, so I pick now.

Johnny. Who are you kidding? I never pick the time. Last night
when we were driving home from Jersey, I offered to pull off
the Pulaski Skyway and get something going, and you said no.

Wilma. I'm a married woman with two children. I am not going to
make love in the back seat of a Volkswagen.

Johnny. Then don't complain to me any more about lack of variety.

Wilma. Johnny, it's Saturday night. We haven't made love in ten days.
We've both worked very hard to make love at least twice a
week and if we don't tonight, there's going to be a lot of pressure on us to catch up.[3]

Wilma's remarks are loaded with "What's proper?"—a characteristic attitude of 5,5-oriented people. One note she strikes is the night-
time norm: sex is the way to *end* the day, not begin it. Another one
is: the place for married couples to make it is in bed, not in the
back seat of a Volkswagen. A "your turn," "my turn," half-and-
half norm is implicit in the couple's bickering. Spontaneity has
been drowned out by protocol. The mechanistic finale occurs when
Wilma sounds off to Johnny about keeping on schedule—"at least
twice a week." Her sex clock is regulated according to "Kinsey
Standard Time." But Johnny is not going to wind her up. Not tonight!

If you are 5,5-ish and have adjusted to the "middle-way," you feel
safe. No one's going to think you're far out. When you do find
you're out of step, getting back in line is the accepted way to keep
from becoming abrasive. Creativity, novelty, *joie de vivre,* lust for
life, and a few other things are not missed. It's nice to read about
adventure, but too risky to live it.

9,9

9,9 is in the upper right area. Both concerns are high. They're integrated too. You are deeply involved in what happens and you want
your relationship to be lively and strong. The very sharing of

thoughts, feelings, and actions which this makes possible serves to enrich your experience of unity with your mate. Joint participation in new, creative, and unanticipated activities can bring pleasure and satisfaction. 9,9 attitudes even enliven routine activities which otherwise might seem humdrum and monotonous. Each mate delights in the other's distinctive qualities. Individual points of view are valued, for within the contrasts are to be found sources of creativity and zest. A marriage in which both parties come to each other with 9,9 attitudes continues to develop in intimacy and love. Freshness charges each successive day, even in situations that otherwise might be run-of-the-mill.

Gary and Jean reveal 9,9 attitudes. He is telephoning to check out an invitation he has extended to an old buddy, Bill.

Gary. Bill just flew in. He'll be here overnight. He's coming to dinner.
Jean. Great! Now we can catch up on Philadelphia. But I haven't been to the grocery this week. We're out of rolls. Would you stop on the way home and pick up a dozen?
Gary. OK. We'll be there about 6:30. But we can have drinks so you won't have to be in a sweat. Can you have the cooking done by then, or would it be better for us to come later?
Jean. It'll take some doing, but come as early as you can and have drinks here. Tell him hello for me.
Gary. Jean says hello, Bill. . . . Bill says hi, Jean. Hygiene! Hey, weren't we going to that meeting on the bond issue? . . . Yes, sure, you can come, Bill, it's about our local sewerage problems . . .
Jean. Come on! That's not so urgent, we can catch next week's meeting when the consultants report. Just bring Bill home, and we'll get an evening started.
Gary. Thanks, Jean. See ya.

Gary and Jean get with it in a spontaneous and happy way to meet this unexpected situation. They react to Bill's visit in a manner that adds to their own pleasure and most probably to Bill's as well. If you are mutually 9,9, each of you has the other's best interests at heart. And while you might not automatically think of yourselves as a team—since each of you is an individual in your own right—you do pull together and share many activities. You also find joy in each other's company, "know" how the other thinks and feels, and take ever-increasing delight in the prospect of more years of life together. Your desire is to make each other's life more complete. Yours is a fulfillment-seeking marriage.

You may have ascertained already that there are eighty-one combinations of concerns represented on the Grid. Adjacent to 9,1 are 8,2 and 7,3. And 1,9 has 2,8 and 3,7 near it. There are 3,3, 4,4, 6,6, 7,7 along the diagonal between 1,1 and 9,9, and so on. But we'll put our main emphasis on the theories in the corners and at the middle of the Grid. The reason is that these are the most distinct marriage styles. They're the ones you see most often. But you might think of a Grid style as you do shades of hair—black, brown, red, blond, and white. Within each hair shade there's a variety—for example, twenty-seven different ways to be a blond—yet on your driver's license the outstanding feature is enough for identification. The five main Grid styles, too, are broadly descriptive. We'll use them in much the same way. While talking about 9,1, remember it's a tinge away to 8,2 or 7,3, or a halftone or so to 6,4, but all these neighboring combinations describe behavior in broadly similar ways.

Grid styles are not pigeonholes for slotting people. Grid theories don't put personality labels on people, such as maintaining that a person is introverted or extroverted, passive or aggressive, manic or depressive. Grid theories don't deal with Oedipus complex or narcissism, or totems and taboos. They have nothing to do with dreams, id, or racial unconscious. Playing with these terms might be fun for self-appointed psychiatrists, but it can provide a horror trip for anyone who's impressionable enough to take such labeling seriously.

Then to what *do* the Grid theories apply? They describe various sets of basic assumptions under which people deal with one another. An assumption is what you take for granted as being true or reliable. Maybe you learned most of your present-day assumptions as you grew up.[4] "I have to be . . . (a tough character or nice girl) . . . to get what I want," illustrates some childhood assumptions that persist. In matrimony they lay down the pathway of your everyday approach. You act on the assumptions you hold even though it may be rare for you to put them into words. The same set of assumptions usually underlies a whole range of attitudes and activities. For example, a 1,9-oriented husband who wants to please his wife may be quite inventive in finding all sorts of ways to show his own affection and his craving for hers. His behavior may not be so simple as to say "I love you and everything you do" twenty-five times a day, but, nonetheless, she will dominate his thoughts and concerns. His wife might say, "I never know what nice surprise Robert will think up next," and yet his core assumptions are remarkably consistent—to please his wife and win her appreciation.

Were you to act without assumptions, your behavior would be random, purposeless; it would *make no sense* in any predictable way.[5] Even so, it is not enough just to *have* a set of assumptions— any old set. Faulty assumptions can ruin a marriage. More reliable ones can enhance your marriage and enrich your life. Each of the sets of numbers used in the Grid describes assumptions about behavior in marriage. When a person acting under any set of assumptions understands them, this Grid knowledge can aid him to predict what the impact of his behavior will be on his mate. We will describe what these impacts are likely to be. Only you can decide whether the impact you have on your mate is good or bad, effective or ineffective, or desirable or undesirable. Thus, learning the Grid framework will help you to understand what kind of actions are likely to lead to what kind of results.

Do you live according to one "dominant" set of assumptions, or do you shift around on the Grid according to which side of the bed you got up on or the kind of situation you happen to be in? Random shifting around is possible, but it's a rare person who doesn't exhibit more consistency in his behavior than that.

Each person's behavior does tend to relate to one of the major sets of assumptions located on the Grid. Yet people aren't so rigid as to act the same way all the time. How does consistency square with the self-evident truth that behavior does shift and change, that it is variable? Some behaviors are just variations on a basic theme. For example, there are many ways in which a 9,1-oriented person might try to gain control and win his point. But what we're talking about here is a shift from one set of Grid assumptions to another.

Here's how it happens. Every person seems to have a "dominant" style and at least one "backup" style. A backup style comes into play when your dominant approach runs into difficulty. It's somewhat like an automatic transmission shifting gears in a car when going up and down hills. This shifting is relatively silent. It is not likely that you catch yourself shifting from dominant to backup as you are doing it. Many times you do an about-face, for example, switching from a hard 9,1 attitude to a soft 1,9 attitude and back again, often without being aware of it.

Let's see how this works.

Dan and Kim are on their way to a party. He is driving, and as they pause at a stop light, he turns to her. He smiles.

Dan. Why're you looking so beautiful, honey?

Kim. For you, of course! Thanks for still noticing after all these years.

Dan. I notice *you* all the time, but I don't notice time passing all that much. There's so much to do, it always seems like "now, next week, next year" to me. You're like that usually, too. What's got you harking back?

Kim. Oh well, I suppose it was meeting Trudy again—remember her when we were in college?

Dan. Vaguely—that mousy little girl who always seemed to be wearing a raincoat?

Kim. She's not like that anymore. You'll see. It's as though she's only been out of college a couple of years, during which time she's modeled in New York. But she's thirty-five. That's the same as me!

Dan. You look like your lovely self when I first met you, plus all the lushness that comes from filling out.

Kim. Ah, Dan, come on!

Dan. Ah, Kim, cheer up! I mean it, you know I do.

Now, an hour later, they are on their way home while the party continues.

Dan. That was a great scene you pulled. What got into you?

Kim. You're so self-righteous. You hypocrite. I saw you. Making

passes at her like a college kid! If you want to play around or
get a divorce, okay, but d'you *have* to humiliate me in public?
Dan. I was talking with her just the same as I would with anyone.
There was nothing to humiliate you. But I was certainly embarrassed when you barged in and tried to cut her down.
Kim. If there's any next time, you'll be more than embarrassed!
Dan. For the life of me I can't see what's gotten into you. Calm
down and tell me what's really bothering you. Honestly, Kim,
it came on me like a bolt from the blue. I had no idea I was
doing anything.

Dan and Kim began their evening on a mutually appreciative
9,9 note. But it seems that Kim saw something at the party which
turned on her wrath. She began berating Trudy and Dan. She's still
on this 9,1 backup as they drive home. Dan, although annoyed, is
holding to his 9,9 as he attempts to get Kim to discuss what she
saw, thought, and felt. If he's successful, the facts are likely to
emerge. Then Dan and Kim can talk through the issues and resolve
the tensions which have arisen between them.

Any style can back up any other. If you're a 1,9-oriented person,
who is normally soft, you may rebel and take a 9,1 pugnacious
posture when sharply challenged. Alternatively, if you approach
marriage in a 9,9 solution-seeking way, you might happen to meet
continued resistance of a kind you can't find any way of creatively
overcoming. You might then slide into a 5,5 approach. Your new
aim is to negotiate a workable compromise under which you and
your mate will be partially appeased and satisfied even though perhaps neither of you feels right about it. Or, when moving away
from 9,9 attitudes, you may pounce on your mate, "calling the
shots" in a 9,1 way. Another possibility could be that ordinarily
you come into discussion with a 9,1 approach, pressing hard to
win. But after a while, when your mate holds firm and you're
against the wall, what happens? You switch from 9,1 to 1,1 and
throw up your hands with a ". . . to hell with it."

In many, if not most, persons' reactions to stress, one can detect
a dominant, a first backup, and, sometimes, a second backup Grid
style and even more. There are no "natural" links between one
Grid style and another in terms of shifting from dominant to

backup. What is characteristic for *you* depends on your history and your current situation.[6]

These forces in your marriage determine the way you act at any particular point:

1. Your most characteristic Grid assumptions and reactions
2. The moment-to-moment reactions of your mate
3. The immediate situation: for example, current finances, your mother-in-law, your health, your children
4. The community you live in, friends who drop in, your job and the organization you work in
5. Influences from the broader cultural scene which are rooted in history, such as ideas of protocol, whether or not it's good to reveal emotions, whether or not one of the mates "should" lead

So let's look a little deeper into influences being exerted upon our daily lives from outside social forces.

Human affairs are never really at a standstill. They never have been. But their rate of change is becoming faster. They probably are in greater flux now than they have ever been before. As a result, old patterns that used to govern human relations are crumbling, but alternative patterns that can replace them are only beginning to be taken up by growing numbers of people.

The current situation is that more and more people seem to want a fuller share of responsibility for their actions. Generally, women are less passive, not so tolerant of being talked at and being told what's good for them as they once tended to be. The classic Pilgrim model wife, walking three steps behind her husband, is nearly extinct.

The authority-obedience marriage dates from an era when people were less well-informed, more patient, and more formally polite than nowadays. Even though the situation was sometimes reversed, the wife was expected to be a homebody, attending only to her lord and master. Thinking and action were taken to be manly qualities; feeling was viewed as woman's specialty. *The fallacy was in separating thinking and emotion as though they were two distinct aspects of human experience.*

Let's look at it in another way. We know every thought stimulates an emotion if the opportunity is provided. Every emotion can promote an insight, too, often creating new awareness of logical ties between different facts. Is there a key for bringing together clear thinking and positive emotion? Can the advantages provided by combining logic and understanding with creativity and feeling be meshed within a marriage?

Yes. The key to doing it is indicated by the meaning of two words, participation and involvement. "Participation" means actively sharing in an experience. "Involvement" means being drawn in and becoming interested and absorbed in the action. Involvement does not necessarily follow from participation, but here is what happens when participation and involvement are merged. Participation helps your mate to understand the situation. It begins to stimulate involvement. These emotions growing along with interest, which stems from the activity, influence further and deeper participation. Under these circumstances, an additional stimulus, such as a sense of duty or obligation, is not needed. The greater the participation, the more the emotional involvement is strengthened. Your mate feels ever more positively engaged in what is now seen as *joint* effort to reach a shared goal. The interplay between thinking and emotion that is brought about by participation and involvement is what brings about full commitment and mutual fulfillment in a 9,9 marriage.[7]

Yet many marriages are not 9,9. They may reflect an authority-obedience pattern whereby, most likely, the husband dominates in a dictatorial rule-the-roost way. In some marriages, it is the wife who controls a henpecked husband. Other marriages are based on accommodation and adjustment in the sense of helping each other while interrelating on a live-and-let-live basis. In others still, suffocating love is the theme. What's being missed, sacrificed, or gained in each of these marriages will be pointed out when particular Marriage Grid style combinations are examined.[8]

CHAPTER 2 | GRID ELEMENTS

How would you describe the *important* qualities in your mate—the feeling, thinking, and action characteristics? These are called "elements" in this book. There are six in all, and they are discussed in chapters that focus on each of the five Grid styles which were briefly described in Chapter 1.

The first three elements are in the solution-seeking area. One of them deals with how *decisions* are made; another with how *convictions* are expressed; and a third with the character of *teamwork*. These form the intellectual side of married life. Marriage is not just for feeling. You're operating a two-person society. This involves such aspects of living as food, clothing, shelter, security, relationships within the extended family and community, career, finances, and the rest. Thus, you can see how important the pragmatic side of marriage is and how much it calls for judgment and action.

The other three elements deal with the emotions of marriage. *Expectations* are not merely what you hope for or think you will get. They result in surprise or disappointment, which can act as emotional boosters or depressants in your relationship. *Conflict* arises when mates' feelings are stirred as a result of basic differences in outlook. And *intimacy* expressed with sexual feelings is marriage's most unique and distinctive experience.

The emotions stirred by expectations, conflict, and intimacy can not be separated in practical life from the thinking stimulated by decisions, convictions, and teamwork. But for better understanding as we proceed, they can be set apart so that each can be examined more thoroughly in its own right.

DECISIONS

When two people live together they are faced with a never-ending series of decisions. These range from minor day-to-day issues of what to eat, to major considerations such as career choices, how to rear children, and whether or not to have Grandma come and live with you.

Why study how couples make decisions? The reason is the fact that decision precedes action. This is true whether you take the action as an individual or as a twosome. If, after reflecting, you do *not* take an action, this implies, too, that a decision has been made. Some decisions determine the course of your marriage for many years. Others, taken singly, are less significant. No one of them, in itself, is necessarily of crucial importance. But they all add up.

The romantic view is "What should be easier to do, for two people who love each other, than agree?" But wise decisions are rarely made emotionally. Where two people are involved in decision-making, each one has a different fund of knowledge and experience to draw upon. In these circumstances, a decision that results from agreement means that two thinking minds have met. In the process, different ideas will have been put forward and challenged in the two-person arena.

What if you don't agree? Marriage is not a "one-mate-one-vote" situation, and, furthermore, there's no one around to cast the tie-breaking vote even if it were. Unless you're content to stay deadlocked, the best alternative you have is reasoning with each other.

Achieving mind-meeting agreement with your mate can be a formidable task, sometimes of mammoth proportions, regardless of the subject—whether sex or tennis. As we will see, much depends on the kind of Grid style employed.

CONVICTIONS

Even if they live together forever, two people can never maintain unequivocally the *same* outlook, or see *everything* eye-to-eye. Also, people vary greatly in the tenacity with which they hold to their thoughts and views. They vary from pigheaded through indecisive to the sort of yielding that resembles a reed bending to every breeze. In a society where people think for themselves, a person who has sound convictions, arrived at by independent judgment, is respected. This person is considered to have character, a sense of self-direction. If a mate lacks conviction, or withholds it, keeps it hidden when it ought to be expressed, or changes it haphazardly, other people see in this conduct insecurity, uncertainty, anxiousness, or indifference to legitimate concerns—even to life generally. Your convictions, then, express the values, opinions, and attitudes you hold. Decision-making comes about when choice must be made from among several alternatives. Many times, convictions form the foundation for making decisions.[1]

TEAMWORK

Two people in marriage have the chance to pull together, mutually supporting each other in pursuing the objectives they've embraced. It's a teamwork situation in the best sense of the word, and there's ample time to learn how to work together effectively. But whether the gains in fuller living which solid teamwork makes possible are realized is another question. When two people really act together in full teamwork, each is able to anticipate the feelings, thoughts, and probable actions of the other. In this way, both are in a position to strengthen the overall effort. Two mates who can work well together in moving toward a shared goal can achieve more than either of them could separately.

But if teamwork is poor, one mate pulls in a sideways or opposite direction to the other. This ensures reduction of their effectiveness. The couple will experience difficulty in accomplishing anything, and so are more likely to live two lives in parallel than together in unison.

EXPECTATIONS

People seldom react to and judge an event entirely by itself, objectively and independently of everything else. Rather, they judge events relative to expectations. When something very unusual has occurred, you will comment, "It was so *unexpected,* I didn't know what to think." *But more often a person has at least a general idea of what he thinks should happen.* If the other person brings you results which are better than had been expected, it's probable that you feel pleasant surprise with accompanying emotions of happiness, maybe even joy. If things turn out just as you expected, neither more nor less, the feeling is a passive registering of the fact. That's why you take for granted it's par for the course. When expectations are set with high-level realism and are held in common, then the decisions that are made usually result in planned action which is capable of fulfillment. Action that takes place without prior thought or expectation-building is likely to be seen as impulsive.

Emotional turn-abouts are typical of marriage relationships where much of day-to-day living is based on differences in expectations regarding what you will or won't think, feel, or do. Under certain circumstances, you and your mate may be joyfully surprised with and proud of each other. Acting in the spirit of the moment with each other's best interests at heart results in spontaneity and delight. At other times, when circumstances are different, you feel sharply taken aback, disappointed with the way you've been treated. Either reaction may be felt with particular poignancy during the early phases of becoming accustomed to each other and then become less acute. Or the surprises or disappointments may increase as you continue living together. Because of the interdependence which marriage promotes, it is probably the one relationship which has the most potential for bringing out these emotions.

CONFLICT
Marriage is a potential battlefield or a Garden of Eden. Conflict can arise at the drop of a hat, or you could be hard put to get a spark out of your mate. Conflict—or the lack of it—lies at the heart of human interaction.

There are occasions when the only alternative is to make your own choice, deciding independently, even though you know the outcome will affect your mate. There is ample time and opportunity for criticism later. At other times, joint action is required. Differences in thought, feelings, or action can produce disagreement. As tensions increase, they can break into open conflict. Conflict is not necessarily "bad." Much depends on how it's met and handled. What makes the conflict "bad" is inability to cope with it constructively and creatively. Then conflict can polarize issues so that the real problem is not probed. Instead, heated arguments lead to bitter words and sour feelings. When disagreement is not brought into the open, unexpressed emotions can fester and infect other areas of the marriage. When conflict is transformed into a lively comparison of viewpoints that leads to deeper thinking, it can provide a basis for mutual understanding and respect which can strengthen rather than erode marriage's foundations.

INTIMACY

How significant is intimacy? Attitudes vary all over the lot. Some think it is a romantic illusion that can never last. Some say, if you have it, okay, but it's not very important. Others feel it is the essence, the center of the whole thing. How can such widely different attitudes be held, and with such conviction?

Here's how. If your situation is sterile, you probably think the value of intimate relations is blown up out of true proportions. If you've never known anything different, there's every reason for you to think intimacy isn't very important. It's not giving you very much now and it never has, so what reason do *you* have for emphasizing it? Maybe you mine other aspects of your marriage for whatever joy you can get from them.

Now let's take a second view. If either you or your mate, in other relationships, have enjoyed fulfilling, intimate experiences, but now, in this union, you're unable to click, probably you will think intimacy is tremendously important. This is because you've experienced a standard of excellence whereby you see how impoverished your present enjoyment really is.

But what if your being together is consistently joyful? There's ecstasy in your relationship. Because you know how rich and completing it is, you probably think loving is a very important aspect of your marriage.[2]

As you read, you may find a close portrait of yourself in this chapter or that, where the Grid style descriptions fit you pretty well. When you find yourself somewhere on the Grid you may wonder, "Am I fixed there for all time?"

No one is really stuck. There's probably no such thing as a permanently inbuilt and unchangeable pattern. What makes your behavior *appear* fixed is that you continue operating on the same Grid assumptions. When assumptions become as embedded as this, they take on the quality of second nature. From the outside, you seem to have an unchangeable "personality." But if you were to study your present assumptions and compare them with alternatives, you might very well decide to reject old assumptions and start building anew. Then your behavior can and will change. Some may find their present patterns very easy to change. For others, it's more difficult. But whether easy or difficult, the possibility is that you *can* change your assumptions, and so your behavior, when *you yourself* see alternative possibilities and want to strive for them.

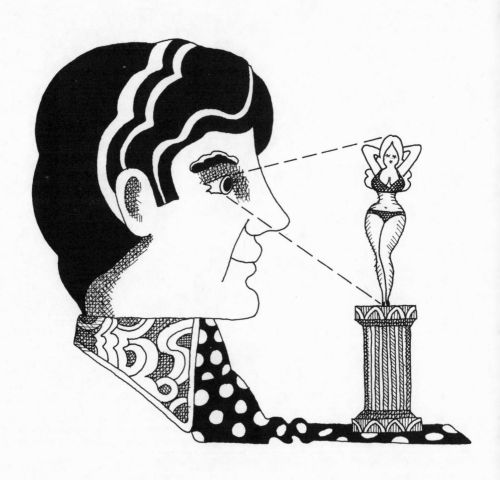

CHAPTER 3 | THE MIRROR

How would you describe the person you're living with?

"Too good to be true," you may think.

Or you may mutter, "Indescribable."

Picturing your mate is more than saying "five feet eight inches, dark and thin," or "short, chubby, and gray," or that your mate has an attractive smile, or comes from Texas. These are surface issues and of no real significance.

When describing someone, you can't form a very clear image if you take a this-is-good, this-is-bad approach. A mirror doesn't pass judgments. Nor does a camera. It shows a view straight through the lens, recording exactly what it sees. Although a camera has intrinsic limitations, it doesn't unwittingly trick itself. Yet *people* sometimes do.

It is possible to describe a person's behavior accurately only when you put yourself to work as a camera. To make your picture, you need to look at your mate when you're in an objective frame of mind. You might not be able to hold your real camera steady when your feelings are worked up. Likewise, you're in the best stance for portraying your mate objectively when you're calm and thoughtful. The goal should be to describe your mate's actions and attitudes precisely. This means tuning out personal preferences and prejudices as much as you can.

Why try to be objective? Why not call it like you feel it? Because you want to describe what your mate *is,* not what you like or dislike about your mate. When you can see and describe your mate accurately, you're well on the way to fuller understanding of the kind that helps develop your relationship.

Something else is important. Are you setting out to picture the person-you-married? No! As far as the marriage record is concerned, that human being may still be one and the same as the person you're living with. But you know that the person-you-married was your *vision* of your new mate through the eyes of romance, anticipation, and desire. That earlier picture, as you now know, probably also had your sentimental distortions built into it. By now, you've been exposed to many more of your mate's quirks, values and beliefs, moods of elation and of despair, loves and hates, and so on. The important person is the one in your life *now.* Furthermore, form your description on the basis of how your mate comes across to you, just you. Let it mirror how you alone see your mate.

After describing your mate you will be asked, "How do you see *yourself?"* When looking into this Mirror, try to see yourself as you *are.* What you see might not be what you would like other people to see in you. But you'll be alone, so be honest with yourself.

The Grid descriptions given in Table 1 provide a beginning by giving the basics—a Grid-style description of each element. When these six elements are put together, they form a paragraph description. Although generally descriptive, these Grid sentences rarely supply a fully accurate portrait of a unique individual's distinctive behavior. Yet they provide a framework that can be used to orient significantly your mate-to-mate discussions about the marriage.

Here is something additional to keep in mind. Because people are so complex, not all the elements of your mate's observable behavior will necessarily reflect the same Grid style. You may find that the sentence you've written about Teamwork is 9,9, but the one you've written about Conflict has a 5,5 quality to it.

The steps to follow are these:

Step 1. Describe Your Mate

A. Read all five Grid style descriptions. They are placed side by side in Table 1 so that you can compare across elements. One of them should stand out as the most descriptive of your mate.

B. On another piece of paper, copy any sentences or phrases in the paragraph that fit.

C. Whenever you can improve the degree of fit, modify or add to the sentence or phrase by writing in your own best description of that aspect of your mate.

D. Keep tailoring the whole paragraph until you can see your mate in it 20-20. When you have finished the paragraph, it will have six tailor-made sentences. One will describe how you see your mate in making *Decisions,* another in expressing *Convictions,* a third for *Teamwork,* and so on through *Expectations, Conflict* and *Intimacy.*

Step 2. Describe Yourself

A. Now look through Table 1 again so see which one fits *you* best.

B. Copy the statements from the Table that fit you precisely.

C. Modify those that don't.

D. Keep tailoring the paragraph until you can see yourself in the Mirror.

In the famous verse which concludes with "To see oursels as ithers see us," Robert Burns implied that what others see in you is what is really true. But that isn't necessarily so. People sometimes see in others what they want to be there. As a result, they may see inner beauty when inner ugliness is more to the point, or vice versa. To possibilities of an observer misperceiving someone else's genuine attributes, add the likelihood of facades which are calculated to throw off the observer. Thus you can be assured that others are not necessarily better observers of an individual than he is of himself. Nonetheless, getting a comparative point of view from your mate is useful, since it's the two of you who interact with each other according to what you observe and interpret.

Table 1
Looking into the Grid Mirror

	Grid Style Descriptions	
ELEMENTS	9,1	1,9
Problem Solving		
DECISIONS	I place high value on making the decisions, even when we think differently.	I defer making a choice and let my mate make decisions because of the importance placed on good relations.
CONVICTIONS	I hold on to fixed opinions, attitudes, and ideas even though it means hurting feelings or rejecting others' views, sometimes even against objective evidence.	I embrace and support my mate's opinions, attitudes, and ideas even when I have reservations.
TEAMWORK	I call the shots and expect support in line with my instructions or "suggestions."	I want to help through supporting whatever my mate has in mind.
Emotional Relations		
EXPECTATIONS	I demand much in a performance way and my expectations are almost always above achievement.	I yearn to be appreciated by my mate and feel hurt if the atmosphere between us gets cold or tense.
CONFLICT	When conflict arises, I either cut it off or fight to win. If my mate loses, that's tough luck.	Conflict rarely arises between us, but if it does, I am eager to make amends to soothe my mate's feelings and to bring happiness.
INTIMACY	When it comes to intimacy, I have definite ideas about when, where, and how, and I am displeased if things don't go my way.	I seek security through intimate relations and feel distressed if there is not a warm response.

1,1	5,5	9,9
Decisions are left hanging, or responsibility for them falls on my mate by default.	I go for workable, even though not perfect, decisions which we can both live with on a give-and-take basis.	I place high value on getting sound decisions through understanding and agreement.
I am indifferent to opinions, attitudes, and ideas, but usually go along with the ones presented, seldom expressing a difference.	I express opinions, attitudes, and ideas in a tentative way so I can accommodate in order to avoid being too different from others.	I have clear convictions but listen for, seek out, and respond to better opinions, attitudes, and ideas by being convinced of a sounder position.
To me, cooperation seems unnecessary.	I want us to cooperate according to what society prescribes for husbands and wives.	I want us to gain the advantages of "two heads are better than one"; otherwise to divide things up according to who is in the best position to do what.
I ask for little and expect less.	I keep expectations in line with performance and therefore am rarely surprised or disappointed.	I have high expectations and am challenged to find ways to realize them.
I avoid arguing and rarely get heated up about anything. Little or nothing seems that important.	I handle conflict by appealing to the wisdom of tradition or by splitting the difference or compromising.	When conflict arises, I seek to understand our feelings and to relieve the emotions that are aroused. I try to identify reasons for differences in our positions and to resolve underlying causes.
I rarely feel involved or aroused by my mate.	I have a friendly, companionable approach and like our intimacy the way it is. We make it on a regular basis.	Intimacy is an expression of my love for my mate which is thoughtful and imaginative in ways that bring richness to our relationship.

Why not give this book, or an extra copy, to your mate to study also? Then your mate can follow Step 1. This means starting by selecting the Grid sentences from Table 1 which fit you best and amending them to make a true Mirror portrait. Then your mate picks an approximate self-description in Grid terms and adjusts it for a still closer fit.

Step 3. Swap Notes

There are any number of ways in which you may compare Grid-style descriptions. You and your mate may informally exchange each other's notes to get a sense of what the similarities and differences are between how you see yourself and how your mate sees you. Sometimes it's more useful for each of you to sit down alone and to compare your self-description with your mate's description of you, on a sentence-by-sentence basis. As you're doing this, you can make notes for use in a later discussion of how the two Mirror-descriptions compare. Then the same can be done with your description of your mate and your mate's self-description.

Step 4. Get Together on Your Findings

Mirror-descriptions are not like final examinations. There is no pass or fail in them. They should be interpreted cautiously. At best, they give you a sense of your character. They are not unchallengeable.

Grid-style descriptions constitute a point of departure for discussion, and this is probably their most interesting and valuable feature. The objective of a discussion is to help each of you gain accurate insight into your personal marriage behavior and to perfect the descriptions. The real purpose is to understand how your mate describes you and for your mate to understand the description you provided. As you compound these sentences you may have some of one Grid style and some of another Grid style in the different sentences. This is because it is unlikely that anyone's Grid style will be completely consistent like pure 5,5 or pure 9,9 or pure 1,1. But beneath these differences you probably have noticed a common theme which is most like one Grid style or another. Coming to at least a tentative conclusion regarding your dominant Grid style and that of your mate can be useful at this point. It will give you a basis for testing what you read throughout the book. It can help you see yourself and your mate more clearly as you talk together.

It should be recognized that each of you is approaching any discussion from the point of view of your personal Grid style. The basic assumptions and attitudes associated with your presently dominant Grid styles will have some bearing on what has been described, what is said now in discussion and how it is said. When one mate describes the other's marriage style, the discussion can be very pointed and personal. After all, both of you are being described by the person who knows the other best! Each knows what the other does and thinks and, maybe, feels, and what the reactions are to a wide variety of situations. Strive for a discussion atmosphere of openness and candor, of mutual respect and appreciation, one that avoids defensiveness or accusation and counterattack.

So, there are several precautions to be taken. One is directed to the person whose behavior is being talked over. If the goal is mutual understanding, try to avoid defensiveness, explaining away, or interrupting to tell the other person, "That's wrong and I'll tell you why." While your marriage style is being described, listen. This might be the first opportunity you've had to see yourself as your mate sees you, and it can be a unique and valuable experience.

The person who is explaining and clarifying a description of his mate needs to keep in mind the objective of the discussion, namely, to help his mate's self-understanding. Be careful not to use this as an opportunity either to flatter or to criticize your mate. Otherwise, it would be of little value to either of you.

What are some of the issues that may arise in your discussion? Among other things, certain distortions in judgment and analysis may enter into assessments. The first is the tendency of people to up-evaluate their own behavior—that is, to see more 9,9 in their concepts than others see revealed in their actions.

Next, there are distortions based upon a person's position on the Grid. For example, a 9,1-oriented person is likely to look at a person who has a high degree of 9,9 in his actions and see "the high concern for the other person" to an exaggerated degree. Thus, a 9,1-oriented person may see more 1,9 than is actually present in the 9,9-oriented person's behavior.

In a similar way, a 1,9-oriented person who is viewing a 9,9-oriented person is likely to magnify the 9 of Concern for What Happens and see more 9,1 in the 9,9-oriented person's behavior than there actually is.

There is a tendency for 1,9-oriented people to see more 9,9 in "everyone's behavior" than is seen by the 9,1-oriented person.

5,5-oriented persons are likely to put 9,9 elements in their self-description, with 5,5 as backup statements. Another 5,5 reaction is "nobody's perfect." Believing this, you think 9,9 as a basis for a marriage relationship may be ideal, ". . . but 7,7 is probably the best anyone could hope to achieve."

Sometimes a person who has drifted into the 1,1 corner is unaware that this has happened. For example, a busy executive who is pumping his energy and effort into his job may, without noticing it, have withdrawn energy and attention from his home. He might not realize that to his wife his behavior looks 1,1; that when she encounters him, he appears disinterested, withdrawn, and apathetic. Thus, some people who are in the marriage 1,1 area are quite oblivious to where they are and why they are there.

If you find wide differences between the descriptions, differences that are difficult to reconcile, it may be useful to consider whether one of you is describing a dominant approach and the other a backup. If this turns out to be the case, you may find that a more complete description can be provided when the paragraph is revised to include a dominant and a backup for every element, if both seem characteristic. In discussing either your own Grid Mirror or your mate's, you may want to discuss "both of you" element by element from Decisions through Intimacy, or you may want to center on one person at a time.

Step 5. Revise Your Descriptions

If you've explored reasons for discrepancies between how you see yourself and how you are seen, you may feel you've gotten as much out of the discussion as you can. Or you may want to clinch the discussion by revising your paragraph again so that it reflects a more valid description based upon this additional information.

Now that you both know where your dominant Marriage-Grid styles are in relation to one another, a new question can be posed. This is: "What to do about it?"

One possibility is that you're seeking no change. Either what you have is good and you're happy with it, or your marriage is not what you'd expected, but you're reconciled to it and want to keep it.

For contrast, let's take the opposite possibility. It could be that the Mirror-picture disturbed you. It's the shock of recognition. You recognize it's accurate. It portrays an unsatisfying marriage. You might begin thinking how to separate from your mate. The current divorce rate shows that many discontented mates pick this option. This solution may feel "right" for the moment. But it's no bed of roses. After the pain of the divorce process and searching for a new mate, there's a good chance of your marrying the same kind of "mistake" as previously.[1] Marital history does tend to repeat itself. So separation is not the easy way out that it looks to be.

Then another thought may come to your mind. Ken's remarks to Evie during a divorce court recess illustrate this third possibility.

Ken. I guess I know now, Evie. I guess I've really known for a long time. Funny—it never surprises you about other people— their marriages—but your own—somehow you can't think of it happening to you. It's always somebody else who gets run down by that taxi—not you. How did we come to this, Evie? Where did we go wrong? We have grown apart—terribly. . . . Do you think I can—change, Evie? I know the kind of guy I am—you're right—I've always needed that little island of safety and security—always—I guess that's what *I* grew up with—that's what I brought into it on my side—afraid to break any of the rules—stick to the game and play it safe— that's what I took along with me. After a while it gets good and safe—and smug. I'd like to be—the person you want me to be, Evie. I'd like to try. We've never really faced it like this —together. I'd like to try.[2]

They're close to the brink, but Ken is holding out hope for turning around their marriage.

There's still a fourth possibility. Your Mirror may not reflect the image of a perfect marriage, but, on the other hand, what you see does not shock your senses. Rather, *what* you see is opportunity for improvement. But you may want to put this question of what to do about it aside for now and pick it up later. The reason is that the next several chapters will give you deeper insight into the Marriage Grid and how your behavior influences your relationship. Then, each of you may see where some Grid assumptions have been causing you to relate to the other on a less than satisfying basis. Also, having come to know the Grid framework and its marriage-style alternatives, you may already see where you could make better contributions to your marriage relationship by changing your customary approach.

Many conversations will be used to provide concrete examples of what the concepts mean. It's quite likely that you hear yourself in some. It's also likely that you'll hear your mate in others. Whenever that happens, don't just say to yourself, "That's me!" or "That's my mate." Jot it down so you'll be able to find the example later, particularly for use in connection with the discussions suggested in Chapter 16 where suggestions are given for enriching your marriage.

CHAPTER 4 | 9,1—CONTROL AND MASTERY

A 9,1 viewpoint is established when high concern for what happens joins with low mate concern. 9,1 is a fascinating marriage style to look at from the outside. This is because of the drama associated with seeing people interacting with intense feelings that are rooted in antagonisms.

Living in the same house with it is something else. One feels pain and frustration so personally when hostility is present in the situation. A husband who takes on 9,1 characteristics is often described as overbearing, dictatorial. A 9,1-oriented wife might be pictured as domineering or as a bitch. These are merely labels. They don't really tell much, so let's listen to real attitudes being expressed.

Edward Barrett is talking with his adult daughter Elizabeth about his concept of himself as husband and father. He also describes his wife's response over many years.

Elizabeth. . . . Oh, Papa, can't you see, won't you ever see, that strength may be weakness, and your sense of justice and right and duty all mistaken and wrong?

Barrett. Mistaken and wrong? What do you mean? . . . No, be silent. Don't answer me. . . . If there were even a vestige of truth in what you say, my whole life would be a hideous mockery. For always—through all misfortunes and miseries—I've been up-

41

held by knowing, beyond a doubt, what was right, and doing it unflinchingly, however bitter the consequences. . . . And bitter they've been—how bitter, only God knows! It's been my heavy cross that those whom I was given to guide and rule have always fought against the right that I knew to be the right—and was in duty bound to impose upon them. . . . Even you. Even your mother.

Elizabeth. My mother?

Barrett. Yes, your mother. . . . But not at first. . . . You . . . were born of love and only love. . . . But the others—long before they came the rift had begun to open between your mother and me. Not that she ever opposed me—never once. Or put into words what she felt. She was silent and dutiful and obedient. But love died out—and fear took its place—fear. . . .

Elizabeth. No! No!

Barrett. And all because I saw the right—and did it.

Elizabeth. Oh . . . oh, dear God, what she must have suffered.

Barrett. She?—She? . . . And what of me? What of me?

Elizabeth. You? . . . Oh, Papa, then you—you still loved her—after her love for you had died?

Barrett. Love? . . . What's love? . . . She was my wife. . . . You—you don't understand. . . .[1]

There are numerous clues here indicating how Barrett's 9,1 style shaped his marriage. His wife seems to have responded in a 1,1 way. She ceased being a mate in any significant sense, except possibly as inmate.

It is tempting to think that 9,1 is primarily a male attribute, as in Barrett's case. But watch out, here comes Zilla Riesling, as described to a confidant by her husband Paul.

Paul. . . . And Zilla—Oh, I don't want to squeal, but you know as well as I do about how inspiring a wife she is. . . . Typical instance last evening: We went to the movies. There was a big crowd waiting in the lobby, us at the tail-end. She began to push right through it with her "Sir, how dare you?" manner— Honestly, sometimes when I look at her and see how she's always so made up and stinking of perfume and looking for trouble and kind of always yelping, "I tell yuh I'm a lady, damn yuh!"—why, I want to kill her! Well, she keeps elbowing through the crowd, me after her, feeling good and ashamed, till she's almost up to the velvet rope and ready to be the next let in. But there was a little squirt of a man there —probably been waiting half an hour—I kind of admired the little cuss—and he turns on Zilla and says, perfectly polite, "Madam, why are you trying to push past me?" And she simply—God, I was so ashamed!—she rips out at him, "You're no gentleman," and she drags me into it and hollers, "Paul, this person insulted me!" and the poor skate he got ready to fight.

I made out I hadn't heard them—sure! same as you wouldn't hear a boiler-factory!—and I tried to look away—I can tell you exactly how every tile looks in the ceiling of that lobby; there's one with brown spots on it like the face of the devil— and all the time the people there—they were packed in like sardines—they kept making remarks about us, and Zilla went right on talking about the little chap, and screeching that "folks like him oughtn't be admitted in a place that's *supposed* to be for ladies and gentlemen," and "Paul, will you kindly call the manager, so I can report this dirty rat?" and—Oof!...[2]

Zilla's a real cat—fur up, claws out, back arched. When she wants to deal out more damage than her tongue's inflicting on the man in the cinema lobby, she tries to unleash Paul on him. It shows she has no real concern for Paul as a mate. He's no volunteer in her majesty's service. He's drafted from the reserve, pulled out of storage for use now as a gun to aim at her adversary. But she's worked Paul over so much that his powder's wet. It would take a far greater spark than *she* can ignite to get him to blaze away at her "enemy." The hostility he feels is exclusively for *her*, even though his surface behavior toward her may seem as 1,1 in its disengagement as Mrs. Barrett's did to Edward her husband.

Neither Edward Barrett nor Zilla Riesling seems to have evoked much positive response from their respective mates. Yet neither seems to lack energy nor the ability to make an impact. Let's examine this in closer detail.

The behavior of a husband or wife who's adopted 9,1 marriage assumptions is motivated by an ever-present wish to boss, to dominate, to have the upper hand. Power is what counts.[3] This means that, when action is needed, but indecisiveness is present, he or she rushes in to fill the breach and to run the show. With this outlook, a person has a "locked-in" sense of direction: we go *this* way, *my* way. No one else is allowed to steer, or even suggest, another course.

One hallmark of the 9,1 orientation is taking over one's mate to make the other person a mere appendage to oneself. Any opinions which present different or contradictory points of view are dismissed. The person rejects these contrasting expressions of tastes, habits, values, beliefs, and aspirations, all the while "demanding" that the other mate adopt his views in their place. Any further disagreement is viewed as insubordination to be brushed aside.

Such core assumptions show up in everyday actions in a thousand different ways.

9,1 assumptions about problem-solving reveal a person whose rightness is self-presumed, first time and every time. If the other mate disagrees, his or her views are likely to be rejected as nonsense, or as being founded on a childish lack of understanding, or as bullheaded "thickness." Proceeding with the confidence of self-righteousness, a 9,1-oriented person might dominate without ever feeling that the other mate is being coerced.

The 9,1-oriented person's approach to agreement is simple and straightforward: "Any way's OK as long as it's my way." It can be captured in a phrase: control the terms of discussion, and you'll control the agreement that results. When you see a problem, leap in. Seize the initiative, fill the vacuum, and announce your solution. That's it. Do you check on whether the solution is acceptable to your mate? Probably not, for you see no reason for doing so. Your mate *should* agree, just as the light should come on when you turn a switch. In order to dictate the decision, you already have the solution laid out—or at least a directed opinion as to what it should be—before discussion begins.

One way to do this is to assume command over the way in which a problem is defined. The question of whether or not your definition of the problem is sound or unsound doesn't occur to you.

You've seen a problem. You tell your mate what it is. Unless already on the defensive, your mate is inclined, more or less automatically, to accept your analysis. You've caught your mate unawares and unprepared to challenge you.

Dinah is unhappy, but Neal quickly puts her in the wrong.

Dinah. If you didn't want to pay so much for that outboard motor and your fishing tackle, we could have an extra TV set to put in the bedroom.

Neal. Look, we can save money not having to rent a power boat. I thought that'd please you—it's what you're always talking about. Money, money, save, save. Besides, don't you realize, we'll be getting something extra, not two of the same thing. Fishing's a lot of fun. Who needs two TVs? The lounge is the place for viewing, not the bedroom. . . .

Neal is trying to trap Dinah into his definitions. Fishing is fun for him, so "we" need an outboard motor; and besides, we're saving money. TV in the bedroom might disturb his sleep, so "we" don't need that—why squander our money on it?

Short-cutting discussion can be effective in getting your 9,1 way, as we see in how Joan engineers a decision.

Joan. Mother called and invited us to come up for Easter. It'll be good for you to have a break. So I told her we'd arrive at her place late Thursday night.

Mel. Oh damn! I was thinking of having a clear three days so as to strip down and performance-tune the Mustang.

Joan. Well you didn't say so, and now we're *committed*.

Your mate's ability to resist is weakened if you allow little or no time for this person to develop an independent attitude or think of alternative possibilities. Your answer to the problem is all packaged, ready for implementation, and your manifest impatience says, "Get with it!"

When your mate is the first to bring up a problem, you're put in a potentially losing position. You're obliged to *respond* to outside influences, rather than continuing along your own lone mental tracks.

The immediate stand you adopt is that nothing your mate says or believes is to be taken very seriously, or even at face value. "Let me tell you why you're wrong," is a good opener. Look under the chips. Another reaction to your mate's initiative is to voice doubt, distress, and suspiciousness. "Nothing *you* do or think is ever right," is the basic attitude. Poke holes into your mate's position. Challenge your mate to "prove" it. Demonstrate an "obvious" weakness in it. Once you get crowbar leverage, you can fragment your mate's view of what the problem is.

Even if it is possible for your mate to prove that another way of looking at it is right, you grasp control by immediately announcing your solution. "Here's the answer. . . ." This is a particularly useful ploy when your mate's definition is self-evidently right and thus difficult to pick on.

A still different way is this. Accept your mate's point of view. Then exercise your control over what's done about it. "It's OK for you to do it." Instead of concurring in its soundness, or acquiescing in a disinterested way, or giving it your full endorsement, take the attitude of a boss giving approval for the decision to be carried out. You authorize action on what's been proposed, rather than agreeing to its soundness. You give your mate responsibility with an implied threat of consequences in the event of failure.

The following picks up Martha and George. Martha is a college president's daughter. She had her decisions made and direction set and was looking for someone to do the donkeywork in giving them practical effect.

> "And I got the idea, about then, that I'd marry into the college. . . . I mean, Daddy had a sense of history . . . and he'd always had it in the back of his mind to . . . *groom* someone to take over . . . some time, when he quit. . . . So, I was sort of on the lookout, for . . . prospects with the new men. An heir-apparent. . . . It was something *I* had in the back of *my* mind. . . . And along came George . . . bright-eyed, into the History Department. . . . You know what I did? I fell for him. . . . And the match seemed . . . practical, too. . . . I had it all planned out. . . . He was the groom . . . he was going to be groomed. He'd take over some day . . . first, he'd take over the

> History Department, and then, when Daddy retired, he'd take
> over the college . . . you know? That's the way it was sup-
> posed to be. . . . And Daddy seemed to think it was a pretty
> good idea, too. For a while. . . . Until he watched for a couple
> of years and started thinking maybe it wasn't such a good idea
> after all . . . that maybe Georgie-boy didn't have the *stuff* . . .
> that he didn't have it in him! . . . You see, George didn't have
> much . . . push . . . he wasn't particularly . . . aggressive.
> . . ." 4

Unfortunately for Martha, her aspirations were higher than
George's ability to deliver. We'll see more of them later and get a
better picture of George and why he didn't measure up.

Why would a 9,1-oriented person want to give answers and cut
off discussion? You may suspect that the decision that could come
after discussion might lead to your losing control. You also believe
hesitancy is for weaklings. Being able to provide an answer, no
matter how complex the circumstances, betokens strength. What you
most want to avoid is an appearance of weakness. Moreover, your
9,1 attitude is one of low concern for your mate as an individual.
So you find no real reason to be interested in what your mate
thinks. Or you genuinely believe that whatever your mate suggests
can't be worth very much. Of course, you may not say that in so
many words. But the message comes through repeatedly: it can be
inferred from your everyday actions and reactions.

You may be wrong, but you're never in doubt. It may seem important to test your convictions, but this tends to be an after-
thought. The finality with which you put these convictions across
tells its own story.

John and Nettie are talking about their son, who's twenty-one.
John comes on with some loaded questions and comments, but
Nettie refuses to budge from her locked-in attitude.

Nettie. If you're saying I have confidence in him you're right. And
    why not? Who knows him better?
John. Is there more coffee?
Nettie. He's exceptional.
John. Here we go again.

Nettie. Yes—exceptional!
John. In what way?
Nettie. I refuse to discuss it.
John. A person who's going to be famous usually drops a *few* clues
   by the time they're 21.
Nettie. I didn't say famous—I said exceptional.
John. What's the difference?
Nettie. You wouldn't understand.[5]

There's a big gap between Nettie's and John's evaluations of their son. For Nettie, it's "My son's wonderful"; for John, it's "The hell with that opinion." The only similarity is the tenacity with which each holds to his own convictions.

The 9,1 ultimate in staying convinced is shown in the following. John is talking to his son Timmy. Nettie isn't around at the moment. Timmy is just back from military service and he and John hadn't got along too well before his induction.

John. I know what the trouble is. You know what the trouble is?
   You're like me. . . . Stubborn. . . . All the Clearys are stubborn. . . . Would rather die than admit a mistake. . . . Is that a
   fact? Yes or no? [6]

John is seeing his own 9,1 attitudes in Timmy. To die, rather than to shift, is the ultimate test of faith. You *can't* do more than that when upholding a conviction. The irony John seems to have noticed is that he, and other Cleary clan members, will hold to *any* convictions they happen to have, all the way to the bitter end.

When 9,1 convictions are riding you, areas you're interested in are kept in the focus of attention so that they can be commented upon—often critically—as a way of propelling and correcting your mate. You believe in keeping a full set of convictions handy. Being asked for an opinion and not having one might suggest that your vigilance had been relaxed. That, in turn, would imply that your mate could get away with something without being caught. So your personal ground rule is to be certain instead of doubtful, tenacious instead of tentative. You feel that to be tentative, to have doubts, or to seem vague about the actual extent of a problem would tele-

Rose. What's this, Swiss loaf, that's not what I told you to get!
Henry. It was something European, wasn't it?—I couldn't remember exactly, that's why I asked you to write it down....
Rose. Stupid! Did you fix that rattle? And where are the green
   stamps?

No matter how hard Henry tries, Rose is one mental step ahead.
Even if he had picked up and followed her rapid-fire directives
word-for-word, she'd probably have a new command ready before
he could take an uninstructed breath.

Now we can turn to the emotional factors in marriage. Where 9,1
attitudes are present the common theme is a lack of sensitivity and
responsiveness, a low evaluation of life's emotional aspects. With
these case-hardened qualities, a person can act without qualms to
achieve mastery.

Arnold and Murray are brothers. Arnold is telling Murray what
he sees to be wrong with him.

Arnold. Murray, I finally figured out your problem. There's only
   one thing that really bothers you—If it wasn't for them other
   people, everything would be great, huh, Murray? I mean, you
   think everything's fine, and then you go out into the street—
   and there they all *are* again, right? The other people; taking
   up space, bumping into you, asking for things, making lines to
   wait on, taking cabs away from ya—The Enemy. Well, watch
   out, Murray, they're *every*where—[10]

The 9,1 quality that Arnold points to in Murray is Murray's
rejection of other people as things that get in his way.
Expectations regarding one's own performance are usually set
high. You apply the same high expectations when dealing with
your mate. You take it for granted that these set standards for the
entire marriage. They operate continuously in that, at any one
time, you believe your mate *should* be doing this and that. From
moment to moment, new thoughts occur and are added to the task
list. Everything's important and must be done quickly. Like Rose's,
your anticipations always run ahead, no matter how much your
mate puts into performance. So, shortfalls between what actually

graph unsureness. To broadcast forceful, positive convictions is an
excellent way to communicate the fact that you're in charge.
   You assume—almost as a "given"—that other people share,
or *should* share, your own thoughts, feelings, and perceptions. "Of
course we wouldn't want that." "Okay, here's what *we'll* do...."
Naturally, whenever you see evidence that your mate is not functioning as an extension of yourself, you're offended. Your mate's
thinking and behavior are at fault. "How can you act like *that?*"
"Why didn't you do it the *right* way?" "Of course we'll vote for...."
"Yes, I already know that." (I know enough about it to have made
up my mind; I need no further input from you.) Another characteristic assumption is that what you see is unalterable. "That's the way
it is, and that's how it's going to be." "If you live with me, you'll
take me as I am, the rough with the smooth."
   A person who has convictions which are clearly expressed and
strongly held, even though oversimplified and occasionally dead
wrong, often comes across as forceful, dynamic, even attractive in
the absoluteness and directness of his views. If these convictions resonate with the other person's, mind-meeting consensus can appear
in a flash, without deliberation or discussion. The conclusion that is
to serve as the basis of joint action can be spontaneously reached,
even though neither of you has a very clear idea of how it came
about or of exactly where to go next.
   Let's say you develop convictions in this way, and when you express them they gain quick and unqualified endorsement from your
mate. Does this have any bearing on how you feel about your
mate? It certainly does. You like your mate more every time it happens. This rates an "A." It reinforces in you the belief that you're
right. The stronger your mate's support of your ideas, the more
warmly your mate is esteemed. Of course, you quickly detect the
differences between heartfelt agreement of this kind and blind endorsement, reluctant compliance, or grunting acquiescence. All of
these last three you despise because they don't say "Amen" with
fervor.
   But what happens when your mate *challenges* your convictions?
This threatens your dominance and puts you into a sternly correc-
tive frame of mind. You use every ounce of effort it takes to make
your view prevail over your mate's. If you win, your feelings toward your mate are likely to become more positive, especially if

your mate says, "Damn it, I was wrong"—or even better—"Damned if you're not right!" If your mate is penitent, cowed, and sorrowful, you tend to be patronizing.

A result of such certainty is that you think life is in black-white, right-wrong, good-bad, all-or-none terms. In giving an opinion, you're pronouncing final judgment. "This is *utterly* right. That is *completely* wrong." You quick-sort your perceptions into judgmental compartments: good or bad, black or white, and so on.[7] "As soon as you said that, I knew you hadn't understood anything I've been telling you for the last ten minutes." "See the mess their garden's in? I want nothing at all to do with them." "You are either for me or against me."

What are the reasons for this either-or thinking? Probably strong convictions would not so quickly appear if the many situations you encounter were considered in their true complexity. In generating the strength you need for feeling secure, you ignore facts that don't fit and select data to support your position. Thus, certainty can be achieved at the expense of oversimplification. With your 9,1 attitudes you don't see the disadvantages. You cut to essentials.

As a 9,1-oriented person, the way you define the basis of teamwork is this. Your mate does just exactly as told. You give the instructions. From then on it's up to your mate, who "surely" knows what you want and *must* follow through. It's typical of you to complain about lack of cooperation, for things seldom get done right. Then you apply pressure in a punitive way.

Here's Bill describing his teamwork with Mabel:

> A man's ... gotta be strong. ... He's gotta be strong and stick to his word. He shouldn't be afraid to put his foot down when it's going to do some good.
>
> The wife ought to do her duty and I don't rightly know how to say what her duty is, except that you can tell when she's doin' it. And you want her to do it right, and not be a sourpuss about it.[8]

You can clearly sense a quality of 9,1 sincerity in Bill. He genuinely believes his mate should see things the way he does and do things the way he says.

Yet not all people respond to this kind of direction. Your mate may be 9,1, too. Here's a 9,1-versus-9,1 situation where lack of teamwork is striking. Who is struck? The child!

> "We don't work together as man and woman. We fight a lot. I'd say no to the child and he'd say yes. Like for example about manners. He says I'm too strict, I'll holler at her not to do something and he'll say 'go ahead.' I'll hit the child and she says she'll tell him and I'll say go ahead and I'll hit her again in front of him. That sort of thing works on the nerves and aggravates you till you can't take it. If I had a home to go to I wouldn't be here, though I know it isn't good for a kid to be brought up without a father." [9]

In that marriage's arithmetic, 1 plus 1 equals 0, or a minus quantity.

Another common reaction to the 9,1 teamwork approach is that your mate adopts a 1,1 attitude of doing only what is spelled out in detail. This may develop after many tongue-lashings for not doing things the way you wanted them done, even though you hadn't previously explained "how" you wanted them. Your mate may fall into the practice of getting you to clarify your every mandate, and that produces a dumbbell, a drag—not a teammate!

Rose is calling the plays in this marriage:

Rose. I'll not drive till you fix that rattle.

Henry. Sorry, dear, but I haven't heard it—where is it?

Rose. You must be deaf. I heard it all the way from Mother's. Use your ears as you go down to the supermarket. Get some cornflakes, a big melon, that spice what's-its-name, frozen vegetables, low-fat milk—low-fat, don't forget—and a loaf of Holsteiner pumpernickel bread. And don't forget the green stamps.

Henry. Could you give me a list, dear, and I'll go look under the hood?

Rose. List? You *heard* me, didn't you? Get over there while your memory's fresh. Oh, and make sure the milk's fresh too.

*   *   *

gets done and your vision of what *should have been* done are frequent. Resenting what you see as perpetual slow motion, you try to prevent future disappointment by cracking a whip over your mate, urging, setting deadlines, and progress-checking as often as you can. Instances where your mate's performance exceeds your expectations and gives you a pleasant surprise are rare. If you *are* surprised and happy about the result, you prefer not to show it. You think that if your mate knew your anticipations had been surpassed, a subsequent slackening-off would ensue. So it's, "Okay, now have you finished the other thing?" Your usual finding, though, is that your mate fails to measure up. You tend to be displeased and disappointed and, in the extreme, to feel hopeless. A 1,1 backup is close behind many a person's 9,1 dominant.

9,1 emotional expectations are on a noticeably different level as compared with performance expectations. While expectations for performance are likely to be demanding, emotions are to be muted and held under rigid control. In the following discussion, Father is trying to surprise Mother with a gift that will evoke more pleasant memories than the ones she habitually broods over.

Father. Wait 'til you see what I've got.
Mother. What'd you get?
Father. You're going to love this.
Mother. What is it?
Father. Okay. If you're not interested . . .
Mother. I am interested! Stop acting like a two-year-old.
Father. Look! A swing!
Mother. A swing?
Father. It's not velvet, but it's red!
Mother. Who's going to swing on it?
Father. We are!
Mother. I'm too old to . . .
Father. Too old? If I'm not too old to push you, you're not too old to swing!
Mother. You'll hurt your back.
Father. I'll be careful. Stop mothering me.
Mother. Who's mothering you? Go ahead and hurt yourself.
Father. It isn't even up yet and you've managed to spoil the whole surprise.[11]

As a 9,1-oriented person, you feel no great need for love talk, and other expressions of tenderness from your mate. In fact, you may find a warm atmosphere of "sweet nothings" pretty gooey going. Insofar as you make comparisons between your mate's emotional expectations and your own, when you see a gap you probably feel indifferent to it. If your mate is continually expressing very warm affection for you, you find this irritating. "Stop pawing me!"

A 9,1 orientation has something uniquely destructive about it in comparison with other Grid positions. It comprises the set of assumptions under which people are most likely to operate when they perceive their security and well-being being threatened. In this sense, it is the primitive and fundamental theory which dictates that "my best defense is to attack"; a theory that is put into effect when survival seems to be in doubt.[12] Survival in modern society is not just a matter of life and limb; conceivably it's a matter of preserving identity or of maintaining status, community approval, or someone else's acceptance and endorsement. Anything you see as a survival issue will appear worth fighting over. The readiness to see any other person as an adversary and to engage in battle when that person seems to jeopardize one's sense of personal well-being is characteristic of 9,1 behavior. For some people, this proclivity is right on the surface and it's their way of orienting themselves toward others most of the time. These are people who have adopted 9,1 as their dominant theory not only in threat or conflict situations but also as a natural reflex. For still others it may be more deeply buried. But for none of us—even the 1,9 person, who seeks security and approval through love and warmth—is the tiger's reaction impossible. Even a person who has settled into 1,1 withdrawal can be provoked into violent reaction under conditions of high stress.[13]

For this reason, 9,1 conflict strategies are examined in much detail. Even though your dominant approach may be some other style, those particular situations which make you "fighting mad" may push you into the 9,1 corner at some time or another.

Within a 9,1 orientation are two major approaches for dealing with unresolved disagreement. One is suppression. The other is battling to win.[14]

First, what does suppression do? Let's see. You are talking with your mate. You get into a disagreement. You can't get through to each other and you can't get anywhere nearer resolution. At some point, you say forcefully, "Knock it off! I've had enough. Not another word." Misunderstanding persists. But you've plowed it under. Your mate's facial twitches or change of color don't matter to you. As far as you are concerned, your opposition is squashed.

For first-strike effectiveness, putting a veto on further talk may create alarm and despondency, which paralyzes your mate's thinking and inhibits initiative. Here is one such 9,1 cut-off with overtones of "your case is lost because my verdict is against you."

Doris. . . . I just said I didn't understand what . . .
Benny. That's enough! If you've no proof that controverts Joel's statement, keep your fat mouth shut! [15]

Here are some phrases that are clues to 9,1 techniques used in suppression:

"This is the way it's going to be." (It's no use *your* proposing anything different, because *I'm* the boss and my mind is made up.)

"It's too late." (I've already got the ball rolling, and there's nothing *you* can do to alter its course.)

"I *forbid* you to do this." (You're my subordinate. Disobedience is a punishable offense.)

"You're not going to do this, and that's final." (You're not strong enough to disobey me, so forget about that idea of yours. Get back into line.)

These attitudes are expressed with finality. For all practical purposes, your mate's avenues for maintaining independence or for escaping your control are barricaded. The only path is the straight and narrow, the one leading in the direction of your own objective. No choice but to toe the line. When both mates take a suppression approach to disagreement, the frustrations resulting from being prevented from speaking one's mind are likely to accumulate as battle fatigue.

The win-lose dynamic is widespread and very much a part of life. It is the most likely reason why a 9,1 backup is evoked. A successful suitor wins the hand of a lady. A successful salesman wins the bid. A successful student wins when he gets a merit scholarship. A persons loses when his girl rejects him for another. You lose when you have a poor hand in a card game. You feel personal defeat when your football team loses. It's almost as though life were a matter of choosing up sides and battling it out. Attitudes about the glory of winning and the horror of losing become deeply implanted. Winning becomes an end in itself, irrespective of what issue is under discussion or of the validity of your mate's position. Winning is equated with strength, and losing is an indication of weakness.

Here's a pair of accomplished battlers. This French couple live and work in America. After an outing, they return home and start tearing into each other.

Nicole. But you like everything American, my dear. Particularly their women.

André. What is that supposed to mean?

Nicole. Nothing, darling, but I do hear Virginia McHenry is quite a piece.

André. So that's it. Nicole, when are you going to stop listening to gossip and eating yourself up on rumors?

Nicole. I did not mean to insult you about American women. You'll jump into bed with anyone.

André. You're the one who sounds like an American wife. Complaining, jealous, shrewish. No wonder they've got a country of rich widows. And you act just like one of them.[16]

As you can see, this conversation contributes little to improving the relationship between the two. Indeed, it was not intended to help. First, Nicole gives André a flick of her tongue-whip, and then he lashes back, and so on. These people are in their twentieth year of marriage, and about the only thing we can say of them is that over this period they have learned to increase the effectiveness of their 9,1 rabbit punches and fishhook humor. Look at it. In one breath she's accusing André of hanky-panky with Virginia McHenry and the next minute she's saying he'll go for any female without regard for nationality! And, of course, he comes back at her. His last word is to tell her that she's become as "shrewish" as a typical American wife. Their conversation, though bitter, is controlled by some kind of governor that keeps it from escalating too far. Other couples are much less inhibited. Fist and fingernails are sometimes the court of last resort.

9,1 fight tactics include weakening your mate and increasing your own strength. Both can tip the balance in favor of getting your own way regardless of your mate's thinking, wishes, and feelings. Let's examine the "weakeners" first. There are several ways of putting the skids under your mate without relying on outright suppression.

You may try to make your mate feel doubtful about the basis for disagreeing. Sharp comments are made, such as, "That's absolutely ridiculous!" "Your logic is all screwed up." "Your facts are wrong." "You can't *prove* it." These assertions are intended to reduce your mate's self-confidence, perhaps to the point of capitulation.

Twisting meaning is another way. Listen to Father and Mother again. They are focusing on "What Might Have Been," which is part of Mother's gunny-sack load of grievances.

Mother. . . . God, I wish we could have another child.
Father. That's all you need . . . having to go through all that again. Could you really do it?
Mother. I suppose not. I wish we'd have had more children when we could.
Father. Not me. One son was more than enough.
Mother. What would enough have been? None?
Father. I didn't mean it.
Mother. Loving one son was all you could handle? It must have been a tremendous exertion for you, raising your only son.
Father. I said I didn't mean it.
Mother. When were you ever here long enough . . .
Father. I was here as much as I could!
Mother. And one son was too much for you. Well you had to have an heir, you know. A prince to inherit the fortune. Who are you going to leave the kingdom to now? A pet dog? A pet charity?
Father. Stop baiting me!

Mother. I'm not baiting you. You just told me that no son would have been . . . enough for you. No sons, a minimal amount of sex . . .[17]

In this case Mother is doing a super 9,1 job of needling Father and then, as he opens his mouth to react, stopping him cold. She has a tricky technique. She tacks negative meanings onto his words, meanings he didn't intend. If she'd wanted to cut to the heart of the matter, she could have saved a lot of words by saying, "You're a worthless lout." Take, for instance, that remark "I'm not baiting you. . . ." She's acting innocent, when, in point of fact, the skills she has used for zapping and toppling him would make any medieval siege engineer proud.

Another weakening tactic is to attribute your mate's opinion to a "bad" source, one which is generally rejected or held in disrepute. You put a plague warning on what's been said. "How superstitious can you be?" "That's not *you* talking—I've heard your mother say the same thing a thousand times."

Cutting people down to size is a third 9,1 tactic. "You've forgotten how to be honest with yourself." "You flunked that subject at school. How could you possibly understand what I'm saying?" "Without me, you wouldn't be anything." "*You* only think about yourself. *I'm* thinking of what's best for both of us." "You're just arguing for the sake of being disagreeable." All of these are classic crack downs.

If all else fails, threats can be used to gain compliance, for example: "How much do you want to bet on whether or not I'm right? C'mon, lay your money down," "Do as I say or you won't get any loving out of me," and so on.

Even 9,1 humor has the quality of a weapon. It has a sharp tang to it. It is the kind of joking that puts down the other person by exposing faults and inadequacies and making him or her look ridiculous. It's not fun humor. The person uses it like a prod in a caustic fashion.

Listen to Wilma and Johnny, whom you've met before.* They're still in bed. She's been complaining about his unwillingness or in-

* Chapter 1, pp. 10–11.

ability to keep to their love-making schedule. He's just made an irritable remark about her nagging.

Wilma. I have done everything but nag. I have suggested, implied, rubbed against you while passing, worn provocative nightgowns, perfumed my underwear. I have tried every subtle way to reach you except showing stag films.

Johnny. Wilma—I get the feeling you're trying to make my virility look impotent.

Wilma. When did that feeling first hit you?

Johnny. The day I married you. I was dynamite with other women.

Wilma. Well, sure. They were lucky just to be there with the holder of the world's championship three second record in intercourse.

Johnny. Out of all the women in the world, I had to marry an equal-time orgasm fanatic! . . .[18]

Notice how Wilma uses her humor, calling Johnny the world champ for three-second sex. Is this a come-on? Is she trying to help him be a four-second performer, or five-, or fifteen- for that matter? Or is her humor a way of telling him, "Look, you're no good in bed!"? It sounds that way and that's what *not* having high concern for your mate means.

A 9,1-oriented person thinks of himself as a winner. He loves to talk of times when he scored over someone else and about his successes. Defeats along the way are likely to be forgotten or at least not mentioned. This sustained self-boosting can be impressive if no serious breakdowns occur which show you up as one who's not always strong and wise. In conflict, you strengthen your position even more through (1) exaggeration, (2) using "marginal" but uncheckable data, (3) quoting others as authority for your views, (4) raising your voice, (5) twisting logic, and (6) dramatic gestures. None of these involves deliberate dishonesty. You act with utmost sincerity and with personal dedication to your righteousness.

Sex is a powerful 9,1 tool, either as a dominant or as a backup, when you want to get your way but need to exercise additional power so as to accomplish your purpose. Some people have resorted to this tactic so as to get married in the first place—in much the same way as Anne Boleyn kept Henry VIII on the boil until he made her Queen of England. She won *that* argument, even though she got the chop later. If one of you is influenced by this kind of pressure, the other can use it to exert a great deal of leverage; at least, while the susceptible mate's desires persist.

So, now that we've examined some of the weapons in the 9,1 armory, let's see how the other mate might react when these are used.

If 9,1 suppression tactics squash opposition, then all is well; at least on the surface. Your mate knuckles under. To you, silence signifies agreement. No matter if the side effects are frustration, hostility, and swallowed anger. If your mate hasn't given in, *you* could instead, but that would mean going to a 1,1 backup. Rather than do this, you probably make an all-out effort to win.

What happens next is likely to be a contest where rules of fair play are put in abeyance. The issue is whether you win or lose, not how you play the game. Sometimes the 9,1-oriented person loses out, but even then defeat doesn't often lead to abdication. Actually, it only looks like defeat. In fact, it's a momentary retreat to lick wounds and to get one's second wind. A stand-off truce period is only a lull.

If one combatant loses a round, or if a stalemate is reached this time, one or both mates may stay uptight and trigger-happy, preparing for the next encounter. The tendency is for conflict soon to break out again on the same or a different topic. For instance, one may discharge frustration with an anger-laden command like "turn off that TV and go to bed." This can start wires of tension twinging within your mate. You, if you're 9,1, expect instant obedience. If you don't get it, you're likely to rush to the TV and switch it off yourself. More tension on both sets of heartstrings. From then on, it might be a switch-on-switch-off game that gets increasingly rougher. Whichever way, you can bet resentment will be stored up in each person's mind.

Another result of a 9,1/9,1 head-on clash can be impasse—a no-win situation for both. Benny and Doris have now reached this point.

Benny. You bitch! You malevolent bitch! *That's* it! Shut up! Shut up!

Doris. I'll work inside.

Benny. No!
Doris. OK, tell you what. A deal, I'll shut up if you shut up. OK?
    Order in the court. Order in the court.[19]

These two are finding that when neither one of them will give in, neither can win. When an impasse like this occurs, both mates retreat from their 9,1 'dominants to 1,1 backups for a while. That's "order in the court." An uneasy truce will reign till they've renewed their energies or until one of them opens up on the other one about whatever their next topic happens to be.

At this point, we have heard enough to know that living with a 9,1-oriented mate can be a nerve-racking business. When conflict is frequent, does the strain of it affect a couple very much? Is a breaking point ever reached?

It depends upon circumstances. A person who is not inhibited in expressing himself may discharge most of the tension he has built up inside during the very process of battling—if his mate will fight back. His cork pops off so easily that there is little danger of pressure accumulating in ways that could be hazardous. Here's an example of a 9,1 explosive reaction. A wife became enraged and started breaking things. Her husband grabbed her and hit her a number of times.

> "He really socked me. He said we couldn't afford it for me to get mad and go busting things like that and he'd bust me one every time I did it. I know it's an awful funny thing to say, but I felt a lot better after that." [20]

One of the striking features comes through in her last sentence. Between breaking things and being batted back and forth, lo and behold, she doesn't exactly like it, but something's made her feel better. Why? The resentment boiling up inside her is out: He knows about it.

However, risk is inherent. What if your mate is sensitive and feels "hurt" in a 1,9 way whenever you are critical? Then the lid is likely to stay on, so that tensions build and build and build. Relief might be gained through hitting the bottle, going home to mother, or unwinding with someone else.

Here's how even sports can provide a couple with the opportunity to be antagonistic. Benny and Doris are playing a ball game that brought them together when they got married a long time ago.

Doris. It was a bad start. Why don't you take your turn over?
Benny. Don't you *dare* condescend to me!
Doris. I'm sorry. We should have played something less competitive. Something we could share more.
Benny. I am not afraid of competition.
Doris. I didn't say you were.
Benny. From the minute you walked in tonight your game has been to assert your supremacy. Well, I'm on to your little tricks and I'm not afraid of competition. I will pit myself against you anyway, anytime, and prove myself your superior. This little display is just another example of your premeditated malevolence. I know what you're up to. I haven't the slightest doubt you planned this whole thing and that you've been practicing with your paddle, secretly.[21]

Even though Doris seems to want to get together, her remarks are more than slightly condescending. They come through to Benny as challenges. He bangs back, but there's a weary note in his response. Some 9,1 / 9,1 couples get so tired that they fight with less and less spirit, slumping toward the 1,1 corner. Like André and Nicole, they become "weary wranglers."

At the beginning of this chapter, Barrett was telling Elizabeth how he operated in a 9,1 kind of way as husband and father, and how his wife retreated into a fear-ridden passiveness. This seems to have been a 1,1 backup that became permanent. At any rate, there was enough 1,1 in it to let him rule the roost and get his way on an authority-obedience basis of teamwork.

What about emotional closeness from intimacy? These are rarely evoked when your mate is 9,1. Louise, who has been married to Quentin for seven years, feels this lack.

Louise. We don't seem—*married.*
Quentin. We?
Louise. You don't pay attention to me.
Quentin. You mean like Friday night? When I didn't open the car door for you?

Louise. Yes, that's part of what I mean.

Quentin. But I told you; you always opened the car door for your-self.

Louise. I've always done everything for myself, but that doesn't mean it's right. Everybody notices it, Quentin.

Quentin. What?

Louise. The way you behave toward me. I don't exist. People are supposed to find out about each other. I am not all this unin-teresting. Many people, men *and* women, think I *am* interest-ing.

Quentin. Well, I—I—don't know what you mean.

Louise. You have no conception of what a woman is.

Quentin. But I do pay attention—just last night I read you my whole brief.

Louise. Quentin, you think reading a brief to a woman is talking to her?

Quentin. But that's what's on my mind.

Louise. But if that's all on your mind, what do you need a wife for?

Quentin. Now what kind of a question is that?

Louise. Quentin, that's the question!

Quentin. What's the question?

Louise. What am I to you? Do you—do you ever *ask* me anything? Anything personal?

Quentin. But Louise, what am I supposed to ask you? I *know* you! [22]

Quentin takes Louise for granted. He knows her. He doesn't have to try to understand her thoughts or feelings. What's on his mind is most important to him, and his automatic assumption is that she is merely an extension of himself.

Here is an instance where a wife gets a happy surprise from her 9,1-oriented husband, and you can sense the relationship between her surprise and the message of affection she receives. Vinnie has been ill and Clarence is greatly relieved that she's better.

Clarence. . . . Good to hear you singing again, Vinnie. Oh!—on my way uptown I stopped in at Tiffany's and bought you a lit-tle something. Thought you might like it.

Vinnie. Oh, Clare. What a lovely ring!

Clarence. I'm glad if it pleases you, Lavinia.

Vinnie. Oh, Clare. I don't know how to thank you.

Clarence. It's thanks enough for me to have you up and around again. When you take to your bed this house is like a tomb. There's no excitement!

Vinnie. Clare, this is the loveliest ring you ever bought me. . . .[23]

This surprise delights Vinnie, but what motivates the gift on Clarence's part are the guilt feelings associated with her recent illness and the manner in which he keeps her under constant pressure. The conversation continues as Vinnie mentions she'd like a diamond necklace next.

Clarence. Good God—if you don't know how I feel about you by this time—We've been married for twenty years and I've loved you every minute of it.

Vinnie. What did you say, Clare?

Clarence. I said we've been married twenty years and I've loved you every minute. But if I have to buy out jewelry stores to prove it—if I haven't shown it in my words and actions I might as well—What have I done now?

Vinnie. It's all right, Clare—I'm just so happy.

Clarence. Happy?

Vinnie. You said you love me—and this beautiful ring—that's something else I never expected. Oh, Clare, I love surprises.[24]

In these conversations, then, we hear a gift creating surprise and also Clarence expressing his affection directly in words. Apparently, these are words which have rarely been spoken before. With the ring he gives her, and with words that show an unexpected depth of feeling, Clarence has unwittingly used surprise as a basis for attracting Vinnie's interest and warmth.

The constant striving to gain and keep control and mastery comes through even in intimate relations. A person with 9,1 attitudes might either be very demanding of sex performance or, at the opposite extreme, might react to the other mate's initiatives as though sex were repugnant. The control-and-master core of it is an attitude which communicates: "It's for *me* to say whether or not; and if so—how, where, when, why, and how long. Or if not, 'Why not?' "

So whether the viewpoint is "for" or "against," consistent bossiness accompanies sex. As we examine some men's and women's 9,1 attitudes, we'll hear different tunes of glory being played. Some are all for proving potency; others are absolutely antisex. Usually though, as a 9,1-oriented husband, you *know* you know how to make your wife feel good. You've got the magic, some special fast-action technique. If she can't take it, or if she can't make it, there's something wrong with *her;* and if so, that's no one's fault but her own. "Naturally," what's good for you is good for her; or, if not, why worry much about it? "That's how women are. . . ."

Here's how 9,1 sexuality might feel if you're on the receiving end. Mabel's attitude is anything but 9,1. She's married to Bill. She's already had seven kids—several of them unwanted—even though she takes precautions.

Mabel. . . . I think I'd have a baby every ten months without that. I put it in at night, and sometimes it bothers me and gets sore, and so I get up and take it out. That seems to wake him up and that's it. . . . He made sure that I knew he was boss when we were first married. I was kind of young, and my ma said I had to give in to him. I didn't like it. He used to hurt me a lot when we first started. But my ma said I had to take it.

Interviewer. Are there a lot of women in the same fix with you around here?

Mabel. Yea, I guess so, most of them, I guess.

Interviewer. Haven't you heard of women who managed to get their husbands to be more considerate?

Mabel. Yea, I guess they're better fixed with money.

Interviewer. What's it got to do with money?

Mabel. Well, I guess when a man's got other pleasures, he ain't so selfish about this one.[25]

You're kidding yourself there, Mabel! When it comes to sex, Bill gets right down to it.

Interviewer. Some of the fellows I've talked to have said that they wished their wives would make more fuss over them. Do you feel that way?

Bill. No, as long as she does her duty, I ain't got no complaints.

Interviewer. Well, you like her to respond to you, don't you?

Bill. She does respond to me.

Interviewer. Did you ever meet a woman that you thought you'd rather marry than your wife?

Bill. No, I looked around a bit when I was in the Army, but she's just fine.[26]

He has a lot of tension to work off, and Mabel is his tension-reducer. She's the "1" on his mate concern.

The following tells something about a 9,1 attitude toward dominance, mastery, potency, power, in the context of sex. A bit extreme? Perhaps. Herb is talking with Jack, a business associate, telling what he thinks about his own maleness.

Herb. . . . Because no matter what your wife thinks, I don't think any man feels that his . . . thing . . . is ridiculous. I think he feels it's a formidable weapon, an awesome . . . thing.

Jack. Is that the way you think of it, something to attack with . . . aggressive . . . battering? [27]

It may be that acting out the attitudes reflected in "formidable weapon, an awesome . . . thing . . . something to attack with . . . aggressive . . . battering" is what evokes the reaction on the female side of "beast . . . animal." Think of long-suffering Mabel! Certainly these attitudes are heavily weighted with self-centeredness, seeing one's mate as an object for target practice.

Let's shift to the wife's side and look at 9,1 from that angle. Control and mastery in the sex area once upon a time were the man's prerogative. Wives were expected to "cooperate" whenever required to, but any enjoyment on their part was strictly incidental. Under these circumstances, the classical 9,1-oriented woman was more or less limited to basing her control-and-master tactics on refusing her husband or putting him on short rations. Skillful withholding communicates rejection at its maximum, but in a way that

a husband can't pin down. This use of one's sexual resources remains with us today. It has won many a vacation to Acapulco and
may ensure a yearly Cadillac trade-in, to say nothing of upping the
carats in the diamond.

In any event, there can be little doubt but that women who
counterassault by belittling maleness are reacting in a 9,1 way.
"You've never been able to take me. I've faked it to make you
think you're good." To Herb, that would mean total disarmament.
But, along with society's pendulum-swing from inequality to
equality, it has become tenable for women to express open 9,1
mastery.

In sum, then, the Mirror of 9,1 is:

Problem-solving Relations. I place high value on making
the decisions, even when we think differently. I hold onto
fixed opinions, attitudes, and ideas even though it means hurting feelings or rejecting, sometimes even against objective evidence. I call the shots and expect support in line with my instructions or "suggestions."

Emotional Relations. I demand much in a performance
way and expectations are almost always above achievement.
When conflict arises, I either cut it off or fight to win. If my
mate loses, that's tough luck. When it comes to intimacy, I
have definite ideas about when, where, and how, and I am displeased if things don't go my way.

A variety of distortions of the situation wherein the 9,1 orientation is basic to the relationship, without its looking that way on the
surface, are presented in the next chapter.

CHAPTER 5 | COVERUPS

Some people who are 9,1-oriented don't seem so. There are several different ways to hide 9,1. One is paternalism/maternalism; another is using deceptive strategies which involve a behavior facade; the third—a form of facade—is Statistical 5,5; and a fourth way is "playing games."

PATERNALISM

Paternalism means maintaining mastery-and-control husband attitudes of a 9,1 kind along with an infusion of security-giving approval. The intention is to obtain willing compliance and dependency. The paternalist gives affection while exacting obedience. His approach with his wife, in words and actions, is "I love you when you're good." But when she's bad? Then affection is switched off and she gets a tongue-lashing, as if she'd been caught playing touch football in her party dress. He loses his temper about many things, yet she never knows for sure what's going to trigger him off next. In between thunderstorms appear interludes of sunshine and warmth.

Thus some marriages take on a unique twist. A person gets his manliness mixed up with his fatherly feelings, and he finds a girl who projects feelings of childish dependency along with her developing womanliness. So his fatherliness draws him toward this girl who, in her present state, responds willingly to being "daddied." He's got himself a lovable child; she's got herself a wise and protective father. The reverse of this situation—whereby a motherly girl ties a little-boy man to her apron strings—is maternalism.

Paternalism has nothing to do with paternity, just as maternalism has nothing to do with childbirth. As marriage styles, both are the same, except that only a man can be a paternalist and only a woman a maternalist.

It seems to be the 1,9 qualities of pure-and-simple personal affection and dependency that evoke paternalistic feelings.[1] Here is how an older man feels. Jerry is explaining to his daughter Lillian why he has decided to marry Betty, his office receptionist, who is twenty-four—younger than Lillian.

Jerry. . . . I'll tell you something, Lillian. It's important to me that a young girl finds me attractive. I didn't know it was so important, but it's important. She needs me, you understand, Lillian? It's been a long time since somebody needed me. My kids are all grown up with children of their own. I am a man who has to give of himself. I—I don't have to justify myself. I've decided to get married, that's all.

Lillian. Nobody said no, Pa.

Jerry. This girl is so sweet, I can't tell you. A neglected girl. She's so hungry for love, like an orphan. She has to know twenty-four hours a day that you love her. She's like a baby. All right, so who's perfect? Apparently I'm attracted to childish women. Your mother, she should rest in peace, till the day she died she was fifteen years old. Oh, but this girl is so sweet, Lillian, I can't tell you. She has such delight in me. Like a baby.[2]

Jerry obviously knows what he's after in his next marriage. He will provide strength-with-affection to which Betty will respond with dependency-with-affection, and she and he will fit together in marriage very much as a heating element fits into a radiator. In other words, she is the missing component he needs.

The pattern of paternalistic marriage is one in which the husband is bossy yet indulgent, as a father might be, while the sweet little girl-wife does as she is told and finds joy in the structured security he provides. Sometimes there is a considerable age difference between the mates—fifteen, twenty-five, even thirty-five years. But attitudes are what color relationships, not ages. A daddy-husband of twenty-two can have a wife-doll of the same age.

Here is a study of paternalism. Torvald Helmer, the husband, is talking with his Nora, who has just arrived home from a shopping trip.

Helmer. And I wouldn't want you to be any different from what you are—just my sweet little song bird. But now I come to think of it, you look rather—rather—how shall I put it?—rather as if you've been up to mischief today.

Nora. Do I?

Helmer. Yes, you certainly do. Look me straight in the face.

Nora. Well?

Helmer. Surely your sweet tooth didn't get the better of you in town today?

Nora. No . . . how could you think that?

Helmer. Didn't Little Sweet-Tooth just look in at the confectioner's?

Nora. No, honestly, Torvald.

Helmer. Not to taste one little sweet?

Nora. No, of course not.

Helmer. Not even to nibble a macaroon or two?

Nora. No, Torvald, really; I promise you.

Helmer. There, there, of course I was only joking.

Nora. I wouldn't do anything that you don't like.

Helmer. No, I know you wouldn't—besides you've given me your word.[3]

Later on, when forgiving her for a misdeed, his explanation of why Nora is so attractive to him reveals another facet of paternalism.

Helmer. You loved me as a wife *should* love her husband. It was just that you hadn't the experience to realize what you were doing. But do you imagine that you're any less dear to me for not knowing how to act on your own? No, no, you must simply rely on me—I shall advise you and guide you. I shouldn't be a proper man if your feminine helplessness didn't make you twice as attractive to me. . . .

Nora. Thank you for your forgiveness.

Helmer. No, don't go. What are you doing out there?

Nora. Taking off my fancy-dress.

Helmer. . . . Yes, do. Try to calm down and set your mind at peace, my frightened little songbird. You can rest safely, and my great wings will protect you. Oh, Nora, how warm and cosy our home is; it's your refuge, where I shall protect you like a hunted dove that I've saved from the talons of a hawk. Little by little, I shall calm your poor fluttering heart, Nora, take my word for it. In the morning you'll look on all this quite differently, and soon everything will be just as it used to be. There'll be no more need for me to tell you that I've forgiven you—you'll feel in your heart that I have. How can you imagine that I could ever think of rejecting—or even reproaching —you? Ah, you don't know what a real man's heart is like, Nora. There's something indescribably sweet and satisfying for a man to know deep down that he has forgiven his wife— completely forgiven her, with all his heart. It's as if that made her doubly his—as if he had brought her into the world afresh! In a sense, she has become both his wife and his child. So from now on, that's what you shall be to me, you poor, frightened, helpless, little darling. You mustn't worry about anything, Nora—only be absolutely frank with me, and I'll be both your will and your conscience. . . .[4]

You might well ask, "What's with *him?*" He doesn't question his own reasons for demanding that his wife continue behaving like a child toward him. If he could ask himself this question, an honest answer might be "I feel strong only when she puts herself under my guidance."

Later, after the climactic moment of Nora's disillusionment, she achieves clear insight into her former 1,9 assumptions and conduct. You can also see how she explains having got into a paternalistic marriage in the first place and how she tried to mold herself to her father's expectations so as to avoid trouble.[5]

Nora. You've never loved me, you've only found it pleasant to be in love with me.

Helmer. Nora—what are you saying?

Nora. It's true, Torvald. When I lived at home with Papa, he used to tell me his opinion about everything, and so I had the same opinion. If I thought differently, I had to hide it from him, or he wouldn't have liked it. He called me his little doll, and he used to play with me just as I played with my doll. Then I came to live in your house—

Helmer. That's no way to talk about our marriage!

Nora. I mean when I passed out of Papa's hands into yours. You arranged everything to suit your own tastes, and so I came to have the same tastes as yours . . . or I pretended to. I'm not quite sure which . . . perhaps it was a bit of both—sometimes one and sometimes the other. Now that I come to look at it, I've lived here like a pauper—simply from hand to mouth. I've lived by performing tricks for you, Torvald. That was how you wanted it. You and Papa have committed a grievous sin against me: it's your fault that I've made nothing of my life.

Helmer. That's unreasonable, Nora—and ungrateful. Haven't you been happy here?

Nora. No, that's something I've never been. I thought I had, but really I've never been happy.

Helmer. Never . . . happy?

Nora. No, only gay. And you've always been so kind to me. But our home has been nothing but a playroom. I've been your doll-wife here, just as at home I was Papa's doll-child. And the children have been my dolls in their turn. I liked it when you came and played with me, just as they liked it when I came and played with them. That's what our marriage has been, Torvald.[6]

Study what Nora is telling Helmer about her childhood upbringing. Nora says, for example, ". . . Papa, he used to tell me his opinion about everything, and so I had the same opinion." What she's saying here is that by giving Papa what he wanted to hear, she avoided the risk of getting a 9,1 lecture or a slap on the wrist. She goes on, "If I thought differently, I had to hide it. . . ." Together these give a pretty good idea of how a 9,1-oriented father can rear a girl to have a 1,9 orientation. He taught her to express agreement but to edit out any convictions that might displease him. If her father had kept her in the house for a few more years, she probably would have remained forever submissive with Helmer, too. As it turned out, she retained enough independence to face him down before flying the coop.

MATERNALISM

Now, let's study the contrasting situation. This is where a woman gets mastery and control over a man who wants the security of love and approval. She is 9,1 in her efforts to achieve what she sees as marriage purposes. Yet, at the same time, she has a motherly attitude toward her husband. So it's "Do as I say, and I'll look after you, dear." To some men who have been mothers' boys, it seems natural for the woman to be the decision-maker.[7] These two features, combined with affection, can be very appealing to a man who is in search of the kind of support he once had and still needs.

Agnes and Michael illustrate this kind of relationship. They're in their first year of marriage. Their ways of interacting are almost the same—but in reverse—of those in Helmer's and Nora's marriage.

Michael. . . . Agnes, I'm scared.
Agnes. But what on earth of?
Michael. Of—of the baby. Aren't you?
Agnes. Good Heavens, no. Why should I? It's the most natural thing in the world, isn't it? And I'm feeling all right.
Michael. You have changed a lot, do you know that?

*   *   *

Agnes. Well, you've changed a lot, too.
Michael. Of course I have. I have become a man.
Agnes. Hah!

Michael. Well, haven't I? Agnes, aren't I much more calm, composed—

Agnes. You're a baby!

Michael. That's right! Humiliate me! Lose no opportunity of reminding me that I'm the male animal that's done its duty and now can be dismissed.

Agnes. Michael!

Michael. Yes! A drone, that's what I am! The one thing lacking is that you should devour me. The bees—

Agnes. Michael, Michael, what's the matter?

Michael. I'm afraid!

Agnes. But I'm not, Michael, honestly, not a bit.

Michael. I'm afraid of something else.

Agnes. What?

Michael. That I've lost you.

Agnes. Michael, look at me—what did the doctor tell you?

Michael. It's got nothing to do with the doctor. It's got nothing to do with you, either. It's got to do with me.

Agnes. But you're going to be all right, aren't you?

Michael. I'd never be all right again, if I've lost you.

Agnes. But what are you talking about? You've got me right here, haven't you?

Michael. But your heart, that's gone. I wish I was lying in that cradle.[8]

It appears that Agnes has been alternately bossing Michael and coddling him. Now that a real baby is coming along, Michael brings up the problem he has—of losing her as a mother to him. His yearnings nearly tear him apart. Sibling rivalry on the half shell no less—father jealous of the child he's sired! [9]

There's an old song entitled "I Want a Girl Just Like the Girl Who Married Dear Old Dad." This is a worthy sentiment, as long as you don't go looking for Mother instead of mate. It's risky to try to equip yourself with an updated replica, so as to have a new "Mom" relationship with the grant of marital privileges. The same goes for the "girl-seeking-daddy-husband" dynamic.

A very deep story is to be told here about fundamental difficulties which people have in relating to a person who has 9,1 control-and-mastery attitudes combined with 1,9 loving attitudes.[10] The first group of ideas is likely to make you feel frustrated, wanting to fight back. The second kind makes you feel secure, warm, and caressed. But these two emotions are like oil and vinegar. They don't mix. So what *do* you do? You may reject your warm feelings and go hostile, or you may swallow your hostility in a dependent approval-seeking way. Then, again, you may strike back and pet-to-mollify in quick succession. Or you may even try to escape from this perplexing marriage in the effort to be a whole person. Another possibility is that—after as much confrontation as it may take—you and the other person begin getting together as equal adults and marriage mates.

FACADES

There are three major kinds of facades: one in which you manipulate the environment of your mate without it being known; in another you try to shape your mate's thinking unobtrusively; and a third is Statistical 5,5, whereby you adjust and accommodate to whatever the tensions are in order to get what you want, even though your intentions remain hidden.

Mrs. Craig is influencing her husband without his knowing it. She's explaining her marriage control system to her engaged niece, Ethel.

Ethel. Well, I certainly shouldn't care to think about marriage at all, Aunt Harriet, unless I were at least in love with the man.
Mrs. Craig. That is your age, Ethel, darling; most girls pass through that. It's what they call the snare of romance; and very few girls get through it successfully.
Ethel. Well, *you* married, Aunt Harriet.
                              *   *   *
Mrs. Craig. . . . And I married to be on my own—in every sense of the word. I haven't entirely achieved the condition yet—but I know it can be done.
Ethel. I don't understand what you mean, exactly, Aunt Harriet.
Mrs. Craig. I mean that I'm simply exacting my share of a bargain.

Mr. Craig wanted a wife and a home; and he has them. And he can be perfectly sure of them, because the wife that he got happens to be one of the kind that regards her husband and home as more or less ultimate conditions. And my share of the bargain was· the security and protection that those conditions imply. And I have *them*. But, unlike Mr. Craig, I can't be absolutely sure of them; because I know that, to a very great extent, they are at the mercy of the *mood* of a *man*. And I suppose I'm too practical-minded to accept that as a sufficient guarantee of their permanence. So I must secure their permanence for myself.

Ethel. How?

Mrs. Craig. By securing into my hands the control of the man.

Ethel. How are you ever going to do a thing like that, Aunt Harriet?

Mrs. Craig. Haven't you ever made Mr. Fredericks do something you wanted him to do?

Ethel. Yes, but I always told him that I wanted him to do it.

Mrs. Craig. But there are certain things that men can't be told, Ethel; they don't understand them—particularly romantic men—and Mr. Craig is inveterately idealistic.

Ethel. But, supposing he were to find out sometime?

Mrs. Craig. Find out what?

Ethel. What you've just been telling me—that you wanted to control him.

Mrs. Craig. That's rather an unprovable thing, isn't it? I mean to say, it isn't a thing that one does or says, specifically; it's a matter of—interpretation. And that's where women have such a tremendous advantage over men; so few men are capable of interpreting them. I know you're mentally deploring my lack of nobility.

Ethel. No, I'm not at all, Aunt Harriet.

Mrs. Craig. Yes, you are, I see it in your face. You think I'm a very sordid woman.

Ethel. No, I don't think anything of the kind.

Mrs. Craig. Well, what *do* you think?

Ethel. Well, frankly, Aunt Harriet, I don't think it's quite honest.

Mrs. Craig. But it's very much safer, dear—for everybody. Be-

cause, as I say, if a woman is the right kind of woman, it's
better that the destiny of her home should be in *her* hands—
than in any man's.[11]

In this instance, Mrs. Craig has outlined how to gain dominance
over a man without his knowing it. Her contention is that all men
are in some way gullible. The less they know of what a woman is
trying to accomplish through them, the better.

Playing a bogus game, with your mate prevented from knowing
the real you, is a tough trick to pull off successfully. The closeness
of living together adds to the difficulty of keeping up a false front
in such continuous physical and social proximity, day and night,
year after year.

Yet some can and do develop and maintain a facade. Beyond
that, many couples learn how to present a two-person false front in
their outside social contacts and community life. Indeed, this is a
lot easier than the task of maintaining facades vis-à-vis each
other.[12]

Let's see what a marriage facade actually is. The word *facade*
came into use in architecture. It refers to the face or front of a
building, which may be something else again from what lies behind
it. This is found when a gleaming new front replaces a drab one in
the downtown shopping areas. If so, this front, the facade, gives a
false impression of what actually exists behind. A marriage facade
is similar in its purpose, although here the facade is one of words,
actions, and expressions.

False fronts may have the same outward appearance as Grid
styles. Let's see how to distinguish the two. Let's call the styles that
have been described in the corners and at the middle of the Grid
"pure" styles. What "pure" means here is straight, unalloyed, arising
naturally from the assumptions each particular style is based upon.
Of course, you might think of 9,1 as a pure, unadulterated S.O.B.,
but the person who adopts this style is a sincere, *authentic* S.O.B.
So are the people whose attitudes are unreservedly 1,9, 1,1, 5,5, or
9,9. They're not deceiving anyone. A facade Grid style, on the
other hand, is a cover for deception, intrigue, trickery. If you put
up a facade, your goal is to achieve, by indirect or by roundabout
ways, something which you think would be unattainable if you were

to reveal your actual intent, or confront the issue directly. A prime example here is when a person is having an affair yet still preserves an air of naturalness and rectitude within a customary Grid style, so as to keep his actions under cover.

A common feature of all facades is that the person who avoids revealing what he is thinking manages to give an outward impression of frankness. To all appearances you're open and aboveboard, but behind the facade you're closed and hidden. Why the stratagem? If you let what goes on behind the scene be seen, your mate might quickly come to understand you, to read your real motives. The facade would then be useless. However, you can't afford to appear to be mysterious, either. If you were seen as being closed and hidden, that would tend to arouse your mate's curiosity and doubts. The facadist's goal, then, is to keep actual motivations and intentions obscured, but to appear to be an open book.

The outer appearance of a facade often seems to be 9,9, or 5,5. Less frequently, it comes over as 9,1, 1,9, or 1,1. If your style shifts around, your mate might wonder what Grid assumptions underlie your behavior. This might be interpreted as statistical 5,5, which will be discussed shortly.

What aims exist behind a facade? There are at least two broad categories of motivation which encourage a person to adopt a facade. One of these is feeling a drive to get power over your mate. You might think at first that this is nothing more or less than a 9,1 orientation. However, the authentic 9,1 motive is to control what happens; the primary objective is to prove your greatness. No attempt is made to conceal intentions. In contrast, as a mate who builds and maintains a facade, you're anything but brash. The goal here is real but *unnoticed* power, whether it be power to influence your mate in any direction that's chosen, or power to keep your mate in ignorance about certain aspects of activity outside marriage, or both. You're seeking to control and influence for selfish ends. In other words, striving for power and the capacity to exercise it, rather than Concern for What Happens, distinguishes the facadist from those mates whose conduct is genuinely based upon 9,1 assumptions.

A second category of distortions has to do with the facadist mate's aim to be accepted and secure in marriage relationships.

Here, too, the facade is used to cover up weaknesses. For example, a 9,1 outer shell of "big strong husband" or "wife with a lot on the ball" may, in truth, cover a deep sense of personal inadequacy. No matter what the actual intentions are, however, the general feature of any facade strategy comprises the clouded and hidden aspects of personal motivation.

STATISTICAL 5,5

By means of Statistical 5,5, a person acts according to what he thinks will gain him acceptance from other people but in a way that helps him bid for control of any situation. He does what he thinks will please everyone. This is likely to cause him to act in different styles with different people or in successive situations. His style, then, is "all over the Grid." This particularly common facade is called "Statistical 5,5."

Glenn and Bonnie are a case in point. Bonnie's father was a wealthy man in the construction business, and she was the oldest daughter. Glenn swept Bonnie off her feet, seeing that, as her husband, the estate would soon pass into his hands, through hers, particularly if he were clever with the rest of the family. Therefore, to Bonnie's mother he is the wonderful, appreciative son she never previously had. His eyes reflect almost 1,9 adoration as he does her bidding and command. To Bonnie's father, he appeared as a hardworking, tough-minded entrepreneur, fully capable of sharp decisions and a person who knew the value of money. He stood up to the old man, who liked it when the son-in-law showed this evidence of being strong. Glenn maintained an unreserved commitment and effort, with a realistically critical approach to every business proposition.

To Bonnie, he has always been a helpful, supporting guy, a give-and-take husband, who goes along to get along, avoiding polarizing issues that might irritate her. But what you haven't seen yet is that now, after her father's death, the estate has passed, and Glenn has it tied up under his total domination and control. Bonnie doesn't even know what it's worth or where the major accounts are. She feels wonderfully secure, though, in the belief that he has their best interests at heart.

Glenn is a Statistical 5,5 because he adapts his behavior to whatever he sees as the requirements of a situation. This causes him to shift his ongoing behavior in what might be viewed as inconsistent patterns. Yet a deeper theme runs underneath it. The goal is to achieve his own purposes, and he will do whatever it takes to reach a goal. What makes it a facade-type style is that his real aims are hidden to everyone except himself and possibly a few discerning observers.

Now let's study Nancy. Her ultimate aim, too, is to manipulate the situation. She goes to any lengths to flatter and to please in order to do this. Nancy is visiting the Winslows, a large family with adult sons and daughters. Richard, one of the sons, is her target, but she wants to make him over as well. First, we're present as she greets the Winslow family.

Nancy. Mrs. Winslow!
Mrs. Winslow. My dear—
Nancy. It was too sweet of you to let me come.
Mrs. Winslow. Not at all. Are you feeling better, dear child?
Nancy. Like a girl again. What a pretty room! What nice-looking people in it! Augusta! It's been centuries! How are you bearing up?
Augusta. The sight of you almost revives me.
Nancy. If I had your looks, seven devils couldn't down me. . . . Honestly, Mrs. Winslow—you don't know what a joy it is to see this idiot again. Hello, Alan!
Alan. Ah! You've recognized me.
Nancy. Two years, and not one wrinkle. . . . How do you do, Oliver?
Oliver. How do you do? We're so pleased that you've come just at this time. It's really the loveliest season of the year, for us.
Nancy. It seems perfect. I may settle here.
Mark. . . . We count ourselves most fortunate, to have such a charming house-guest.
Nancy. How I like your pictures, Mark.[13]

Now, with backstage candor, Nancy explains to Muff what her theory of change is, and how it can be applied to Muff's youngest brother, Richard.

Nancy. . . . People are so stupid! They don't realize that people ac-
tually turn out to be the sort of creatures they treat them as.
Muff. You don't really believe that.
Nancy. I do! Treat a mouse like a lion—he'll grow a mane over
night. . . . I shall treat him as if he were the most important
member of this family. Soon he will believe he is—and at that
moment he will be!
Muff. Simple little formula, isn't it?
Nancy. In a few days I can make him over.
Muff. But that's just what he hates!
Nancy. He won't know it's happening. . . . You don't think I can
do it?
Muff. No, I certainly do not.
Nancy. Any bets?
Muff. Sure—anything you say.[14]

Nancy approaches Alan directly in a 9,9 way.

Nancy. . . . I need help. Will you promise to help me?
Alan. Why, of course. What's the—?
Nancy. It's just that I can't go merrily along and let a sweet boy
like Richard endure the torment he does. .
Alan. Oh—If you don't mind my saying so, I think there are
enough people mixing in Richard's destiny already.
Nancy. In the wrong way, yes. *I* shall—
Alan. It's the interference itself he resents. I'd let him be, Nancy.
Nancy. Before I leave, he'll be on top of the lot of them.
Alan. A pleasant little task you've set yourself.
Nancy. I can't stay long, so there's no time to fool with half mea-
sures. I want a downright blowup as quickly as possible. Can
you suggest a way to get it? [15]

Later, Nancy has a tête-à-tête with Mark. She's transformed her
approach to seem 1,9.

Nancy. Good-morning.
Mark. I call this a day, don't you?

Nancy. Heavenly. Doesn't it make you just want to be kind to everyone?

Mark. It certainly does.

Nancy. I wish someone would be to *me*—

Mark. What?

Nancy.—If only I had someone to turn to—But there's no one—no one.

*   *   *

Mark. I have the honor of being at your service always.

Nancy. I need help *so* much.

Mark. Try to tell me—

*   *   *

Nancy. Well—I *was* going to ask you if you'd mind being kind to Richard for the next few days. . . .

Mark. Why, I wasn't aware that I—

Nancy. I know. *I* meant to make a point of being more than usually so,—whatever he does or however irritating he may be . . . he needs helping hands. . . . You'll help me help him, won't you, Mark? Your kindness will be such a charity. It will make a man of him—perhaps even a business man.

Mark. . . . You can count on me, my dear.

Nancy. That means a great deal to me, Mark, in many, many, ways.[16]

Now Nancy gets to Oliver with a 9,1 jab.

Nancy. . . . You know what? I think you and Mark spoil him with your kindness.

Oliver. Well—He's the youngest, you know.

Nancy. All the more reason for discipline.

Oliver. It's a problem!

Nancy.—Another case of too much money and too much leisure, isn't it?

Oliver. Exactly.

Nancy. At his age, oughtn't he to be thinking of going into business? . . . Do you know what I'd do with him?

Oliver. What?

Nancy.—For his own good, of course.

Oliver. Yes, certainly—

Nancy. First I'd stop his allowance—absolutely! Then if he was still troublesome, I'd tell him that I'd lock up his books and manuscripts until he's shown me he could earn his living like a man.

Oliver. It's what he deserves. 'Might work, as a last resort.

Nancy. I wouldn't suggest it, if it weren't for knowing what a trial it must be for you all—to see one of you who doesn't—you know—measure up— [17]

But Nancy was not so clever. Richard found out what was happening.

Richard. Oh, that's a rotten trick.

Alan. She wanted to help you.

Richard. Whatever she wanted, she was with the rest of them. Using me, meddling, making me over—always making me over.

Alan. You're taking this too hard, you really are.[18]

Richard confronts Nancy.

Richard. . . . Wasn't most of it for the fun you got—managing people—and the satisfaction you felt in being able to make someone over? Think, Nancy.

Nancy. You're telling me odd things about myself.

Richard. I'm telling you true things.

Nancy. Even so—the least I could do now would be to straighten out the mess I've made, wouldn't it?

Richard. And for what motive this time, do you know?

Nancy. I'd have to—in conscience—for the sake of your family.

Richard. No—for your sake. Your sake always. Your sake first. If someone else gains, it's the merest chance. It's too bad, but it's so. . . . All of a sudden you find that people and—and things have got out of your hands. That hurts your sense of superiority, doesn't it? Oh, I know what a terribly precious thing it is to you! So long as you've got it, nothing can touch you, can it?

Nancy. In other words, you think I'm a vain, empty little fool.
Richard. Oh, no, I'm not saying what I think of you, I'm just ask-
    ing what it is you want of me.
Nancy. I don't know what I want.[19]

We have now heard Nancy approaching different people from
four Grid positions, each one selected according to her reading of
that person's characteristics and the requirements of her overall
strategy. With Mrs. Winslow, a conventional 5,5-oriented woman, she
adopted a 1,9 approach, radiating sweetness. With Muff, who has
realistic 9,9 attitudes, her pose was one of frankness and friendly
familiarity, of having nothing to hide. With Alan, who knew her
well and was not blocking her path, she also adopted 9,9. Quickly
pegging Mark as a 9,1 strongman, she manipulated with pseudo-
1,9 admiration and flattery. She saw Oliver was 9,1-oriented too,
but that, in contrast to Mark, he was more likely to be her direct
opponent, than a potential ally. So she went about impressing him
by taking a hard 9,1 line and getting alongside by talking about
how to discipline that young brother of his. With Richard, who was
bobbing between 9,1 rebelliousness and 1,1 hopelessness, she came
on like Super-9,9. But the game is over. He's called her bluff, and
she's retired, defeated, into the 1,1 corner.

So Nancy has shown us a full range of Statistical-5,5 tactics. For
her, now, everything has canceled out to zero. But this isn't an inevitable outcome of a Statistical-5,5 grand strategy. What will be
success in these terms depends partly on skill—which Nancy
possesses—but to a greater extent, on keeping your different approaches in separate compartments, so that no one gets an overview of all your maneuvers. Within one household this is difficult to
do, but when there are several relationships where the people who
are being used rarely come in contact with one another, a skilled
strategist has plenty of opportunities for bringing off successful
coups.

PLAYING GAMES

Many couples work out their tensions and frustrations with each
other through games, maneuvers, and strategies. These are not

games with official rule books. Violating the rules of "fair" play brings no official penalty. The goal of the game is to score points even though the player may not win a prize. It's each person for himself. These are deception techniques. They reduce authenticity between two people. A sound marriage relationship is game-free.

There are so many "games" that entire books have been devoted to detailing their characteristics.[20] One example is given below.

Betty, who is staying with her mother while initiating divorce proceedings since leaving her husband, has begun dating a man who is twenty-nine years older than herself. She comes into the living room as her mother is discussing her choice of dates with Betty's girlfriend and one of the neighbors.

Mother. Well, I won't interfere because she doesn't listen to anything I say anyway. She's always had her own way, and I gave up long ago trying to tell her anything.

*   *   *

(Betty enters)
This is the last time you're going out with that man, do you hear me, Betty! This is the last time she's going out with that man!

Betty passes the time of day with her girlfriend before replying to her mother.

Betty. . . . Ma, Mr. Kingsley's coming over here tonight. He'll be here any minute, so be nice. Hello, Mrs. Carroll, how are you? I didn't see you there. I don't see why he can't come up and call for me just like any other man. So please, the minute I introduce him, don't start telling him stories about Tommy Manville.
Mother. What do you think I'm going to do, kick him in the shins? She thinks I'm going to kick him in the shins.[21]

And everyone laughs except Betty. As a move in her game, whose goal is to get Betty to go back to her husband, Mother is playing "Courtroom." [22] This is but a single example of a variety of games, maneuvers, and strategies which cover up the real intention that motivates the game player.

This chapter has presented ways in which 9,1-oriented people pursue their purposes, without appearing to dominate, in a recognizably 9,1 fashion. Covering up the appearance of control is one of the tools people use in achieving their own ambitions. This leads to deception of one sort or another. The deception is intended to make your mate feel you have a high concern for your marriage, whereas, it is actually a means to your private end. In this way, you can control what happens without really having the best interests of the other person at heart.

CHAPTER 6 | FOREVER ANGER

Now that we have an in-depth view of 9,1 as a marriage style, let's see what is likely to happen when two 9,1-oriented people unite for better or for worse.

The key to understanding what a 9,1-oriented person contributes to a marriage can be found in the approach to participation and involvement. A 9,1-oriented person expects to take over and dominate the marriage, to mold and shape certain responses and to suppress others. The mate isn't valued primarily as someone who has unique thoughts and emotions, special needs and characteristics. The kind of participation wanted is compliance—a nod, some brief words of agreement, or better still, nose to the grindstone.

People who approach marriage in a 9,1 manner cut off many possibilities of sound mutual involvement. Little real back-and-forth discussion develops of the sort that can lead to a logical and emotion-reinforced decision taken by both parties. Prior misunderstandings are likely to be retained. Present prejudices are reinforced, and, often, new ones are created as a result of such a powerfully demanding approach. How could two people, each of whom is driven to win, relate with each other? Both can't win. But there has to be something to hold them together; otherwise they'd burst asunder.[1] Maybe as happy warriors they derive pleasure from fighting.

89

"Outbursts of subtle or open aggression" are common in the "happy warrior" mode of marriage. Mates "attack each other emotionally," continually trying to "inflict fresh wounds." [2] But both have tough hides, or rather, armor-plated eardrums. Conflict ranges over family affairs, across the bridge table, during budgeting, or as mates try to outshine each other while talking with friends. Both know that conflict is ever-potential. An atmosphere of tension underlies their togetherness. Many such couples start fighting while courting and continue fighting forever. Yet neither seems to want to get out.

Here is how one husband describes it.

"You know, it's funny; we have fought from the time we were in high school together. As I look back at it, I can't remember specific quarrels; it's more like a running guerrilla fight with intermediate periods, sometimes quite long, of pretty good fun and some damn good sex. In fact, if it hadn't been for the sex, we wouldn't have been married so quickly. Well, anyway, this has been going on ever since. . . . It's hard to know what it is we fight about most of the time. You name it and we'll fight about it. It's sometimes something I've said that she remembers differently, sometimes a decision—like what kind of card to buy or what to give the kids for Christmas. With regard to politics, and religion, and morals—oh, boy! You know, outside of the welfare of the kids—and that's just abstract—we don't really agree about anything. . . . At different times we take opposite sides—not deliberately; it just comes out that way.

"Now these fights get pretty damned colorful. You called them arguments a little while ago—I have to correct you— they're brawls. There is never a bit of physical violence—at least not directed to each other—but the verbal gunfire gets pretty thick. Why, we've said things to each other than neither of us would think of saying in the hearing of anybody else. . . .

"Of course we don't settle any of the issues. It's sort of a matter of principle *not* to. Because somebody would have to give in then and lose face for the next encounter. . . .

"When I tell you this in this way, I feel a little foolish about it. I wouldn't tolerate such a condition in any other relationship in my life—and yet here I do and always have. . . .

"No—we never have considered divorce or separation or anything so clear-cut. I realize that other people do, and I can't say that it has never occurred to either of us, but we've never considered it seriously.

"A number of times there has been a crisis, like the time I was in the automobile accident, and the time she almost died in childbirth, and then I guess we really showed that we do care about each other. But as soon as the crisis is over, it's business as usual." [3]

Fighting to these two is as natural as breathing or eating. Maybe neither would know what to do without the other as a fellow combatant. Though paying alimony might be no problem at all, emotionally they can't afford to separate. This is the very backbone of many a 9,1/9,1 "happy warrior" marriage.

When that husband says, "Of course we don't settle any of the issues. It's sort of a matter of principle *not* to . . . ," a conclusion you might draw is that the crises they've had have helped to keep them together. But to be held together by the suction of a marital tornado is far different from experiencing the affection for each other that can arise from, and be strengthened by, the routines of daily living. Conflict, in other words, involves a subtle act of cooperation. Both mates agree to be hostile and antagonistic to each other. This cooperation is silent, of course. Its basis may never have been put into words, and each partner would probably deny cooperation existed between them. Yet listen to the following, which shows how one mate draws the other in.

Bruce and Sharon have been married only a short time. But it's been long enough for misunderstandings to emerge. They believe in telling it like it is. Here is their way of putting this into practice.

Sharon. That moustache doesn't suit you. I'd shave it off if I were you.

Bruce. But you're *not* me and never will be, so mind your own business.

Sharon. It *is* my business! When we go out together you become part of my decor. Dress, handbag, shoes, husband, everything in the ensemble's got to look right.

Bruce. Count me out. I'm *me,* and I'll look the way I want to.

Sharon. You're so selfish, you should never have gotten married.

Bruce. I'm an individual, free and independent. Don't try rearranging me like one of your rag dolls.

Sharon. You look awful, and your character's something else. God knows what I saw in you to attract me.

Bruce. I guess He does. You were hungry for a man, that's for sure. And now you've got one, so I don't know what your hangup is.

Sharon. I wound up with a brute.

Bruce. I'm going out.

Sharon. Don't you dare leave!

Is there any way out of this closed circle of conflict? Sure. It is for one of the two to refuse to fight. Then, the mate who is not willing to fight can begin to shift the basis of their discussion by perhaps taking an approach that seeks solutions to their differences. The great difficulty of getting out of a traditional 9,1/9,1 arena, though, is that if one mate refuses to cooperate by not fighting back, the other is likely to escalate provocations until the noncooperative mate finally agrees to argue.

Other kinds of fighting lack the zest that has been described. Some pairs of mates are weary wranglers. One or both eventually tires of banging away so uselessly.

Here's what André and Nicole say as their plight begins to dawn on them.

André. . . . Don't you know you complain about everything, woman? This house, my position, your social duties, the maids, the car, your clothing?
  . . . .   *   *   *

Nicole. . . . What is the matter with us? After twenty years some sort of terrible chasm has opened. We can't even talk to each other anymore. We only seem to want to hurt each other.

André. When one is very young, one is able to give and take a fear-

ful beating. But, even with the strongest, time wears them
thin. Scar tissues develop over the continued wounds. You
see, we don't have to hit each other very hard anymore. Just a
well-directed jab to the scar and the wound breaks open and
the blood pours 'out.

*   *   *

Nicole. André, can we talk?

André. Honestly or dishonestly? We'll only seek justifications. Neither of us really wants to know the truth about ourselves. One
of the great human capacities is to avoid introspection at any
price.

Nicole. You know you tie me up with your words. It's not fair.

André. Please, Nicole, I'm very tired.[4]

So after this feeble attempt to examine their situation, they lapse
back into their old ways. If André's and Nicole's marriage continues on its present course, it's heading for the 1,1/1,1 corner.

Why do some 9,1/9,1 marriages become characterized as happy-
warrior situations and others as weary-wrangling? A basic difference exists in the conflict area. It is between fighting on a
win-lose points-scoring basis and fighting to suppress each other.
Win-lose fighters openly express their feelings and emotions of
anger and aggressiveness. In being antagonistic, they become stimulated and excited, often creating readiness to kiss and make up as
soon as tensions have been discharged. One minute they're grappling, then suddenly they're hugging each other. Fighting and intimacy can be very close, strange as it may seem. Some warriors will
tell you, "It's funny, but we make out a lot better after we've had a
good fight."

Suppression as a 9,1 tactic does not allow the more deeply
embedded feelings to burst out. The loser is put down and deadlocked during combat. Not even the relief from temporary reconciliation is possible. For instance, the one who's got in most of the
jabs during Round 13 might spurn the other's sexual overtures just
for the sake of getting in one more low blow. There's no end to the
suppression campaign. Carrying pent-up hostile feelings into the
next fight means that more and more venom is smeared on the ar-
rows that fly back and forth. Eventually, the burden of anger is so

great that battlers become weary and disgusted with the whole thing. Their marriage has become overpolluted and, hence, lifeless.

Several characteristics distinguish a "happy warrior" from a "weary wrangler" orientation. You get a clue to a key difference through observing temper. In a nutshell, it's this. Happy warriors are hot-tempered; weary wranglers are bad-tempered. What are the distinctions between a hot temper and a bad temper? A hot temper flares up, but it cools down almost as fast and leaves nothing as an aftermath. A bad-tempered person heats up just as fast, but continues to carry resentments far beyond the incident which produced the heat in the first place. Once riled, a bad-tempered person persists in feeling antagonism, and this merges with previous antagonisms to form a more general antipathy toward the other mate. Sometimes a weary wrangler is driven by the compulsion to be destructive. Accumulated resentments of this sort have been referred to as a "slush fund" [5] and as "gunny-sacking." [6]

Over the months and years, most 9,1 / 9,1 marriages evolve into either "happy warrior" or "weary wrangler" twosomes. Yet, in spite of the constant battling, a few of these relationships improve as 9,9 attitudes begin to be adopted. Some move backward, with one or both mates becoming 1,1 or 5,5 as separateness increases. These marriages will be discussed in appropriate chapters.

CHAPTER 7 | 1,9—FEAR OF REJECTION

Take a glance at the upper left corner of the Grid, where the 1,9 orientation is summarized. This is the style whereby craving for affection and approval is the basis for dealing with fear of being rejected. If you are 1,9, you are likely to have priorities other than being admired or looked up to on the basis of your character, accomplishments, or contribution. You are hungry for approval, yet are satisfied if your mate loves you back.

Your Concern for What Happens is overshadowed by a deep desire to help your mate. Security seems to center in togetherness. Your attention focuses on maintaining a conflict-free relationship with your mate from one moment to the next.[1]

Now we meet Willy Loman and his wife. He is a salesman and has just returned from a trip to his territory that he didn't complete. Focus on Linda, as she's the one we want to learn something from.

Linda. Don't you feel well?
Willy. I'm tired to the death. I couldn't make it. I just couldn't make it, Linda.
Linda. Where were you all day? You look terrible.
Willy. I got as far as a little above Yonkers. I stopped for a cup of coffee. Maybe it was the coffee.
Linda. What?

Willy. I suddenly couldn't drive any more. The car kept going off
   onto the shoulder, y'know?
Linda. Oh. Maybe it was the steering again. I don't think Angelo.
   . . .
Willy. No, it's me, it's me. Suddenly I realize I'm goin' sixty miles an
   hour and I don't remember the last five minutes. I'm—I can't
   seem to—keep my mind to it.
Linda. Maybe it's your glasses. You never went for your new
   glasses.
Willy. No, I see everything. I came back ten miles an hour. It took
   me nearly four hours from Yonkers.[2]

There's a problem somewhere. To Linda, it's an article of faith
that she will comfort Willy, encourage him, help him be at ease. So
the problem *must* be outside of him. It's the steering, his glasses, or
something or other. She continues trying to soothe him and make
him feel more comfortable.

Linda. Well, you'll just to have to take a rest, Willy. You can't continue this way.
Willy. I just got back from Florida.
Linda. But you didn't rest your mind. Your mind is overactive, and
   the mind is what counts, dear.
Willy. I'll start out in the morning. Maybe I'll feel better in the
   morning. These goddam arch supports are killing me.
Linda. Take an aspirin. Should I get you an aspirin? It'll soothe
   you.[3]

Notice the reluctance to confront realities which might be unpleasant? Aspirins may soothe headaches but they don't dissolve
troubles away.

Now we can look further into a 1,9 orientation from a husband's
point of view. Calvin, a scholar of ancient languages, has recently
married Harriet. As this conversation takes place, they are settling
into their new home.

Calvin. Do you want me, Hatty?
Harriet. Always. Oh, Calvin—I *do* love you.

Calvin. Of course, my dear. Is anything wrong?

Harriet. Why?

Calvin. You said that so—*combatively.*

Harriet. Perhaps I was hoping you would put up an argument.

Calvin. Do you know, at times you are lovely. . . . There is something about your face—your eyes, I think. "Sad and laughing eyes, whose lids make such sweet shadows when they close."

Harriet. Why, Calvin, you quite take my breath away. Is that from the Greek?

Calvin. No, Hatty—Sanskrit.

Harriet. I wonder if any woman before was ever courted in *all* the dead languages.[4]

His sentimentality is deep but she doesn't sound enraptured by it. One also gets the impression she'd like him to take a different stand from her own, so as to make conversation more zestful.

Now we can look more deeply into 1,9 attitudes.

In meeting the problems of life, the 1,9-oriented person looks for a strong shoulder to lean on, someone who'll initiate action, take the final responsibility, map out the steps, be ready to pick up the pieces if things fall apart. If you vocalized all these wishes they might come out as:

" . . . All I want is everything, including somebody to tell me what to do—so long as he orders me to do what I really wanted to do all the while." [5]

This has the 1,9 flavor about it—to have life's problems solved by someone else in the way you'd like. An ultimate expression of 1,9 identification with and absorption into a mate is observed when your own tastes, habits, values, beliefs, and aspirations are abandoned and in their place you substitute those of the person you love.[6]

Decision-making isn't your cup of tea if you're in the 1,9 corner. As you're saying, *"You* decide," you feel you're offering your mate the gift of choosing. Instead of voicing your preference, you accept whatever you get. Your self-sacrifice is another kind of gift. You don't mind changing around to be accepting. Even if this means being inconsistent, it doesn't really bother you.

But what if your mate or the surrounding circumstances pressure you? How can you avoid being cornered and constrained into making a decision?

If you postpone doing something, your choice can't be criticized, for you haven't made one yet. If you're criticized for not having made a decision, you reply, "But darling, I wouldn't make up my mind without consulting you first!" By procrastinating, you may get a clearer idea of which alternative your mate favors. Or the situation may develop so that the proper decision becomes obvious.

Of course, one of the best ways to stay in your mate's good graces is to second-guess what's wanted. Then you can make the decision that pleases. Or does it? Listen to Jake's second-guessing on a prior event that involves Alice.

Jake. I *know* you've always liked palm trees, so I've bought two for our own front lawn!

Alice. I do, when the palm trees are in Hawaii! But blocking the view from our window—that's something else.

Jake's good intentions shine through, anyway. Maybe Alice will remember his thoughtfulness long after the palm trees have been planted on the town dump.

But the safest way is to ask for help, either getting the other person to make the decision, or at least getting your mate's views so that you can then go along with them and take the decision which these views seem to require.

Sometimes a 1,9-oriented person gets in a corner and can't dodge making a decision. If it turns out to be a wrong one, he feels the guilt, the blame, and tries to make amends. The untenable position Mimi creates for Hal is an example.

Hal. Where would you like us to go for our vacation this year?

Mimi. Anywhere but that fly-infested beach cabin you got us into last year! There was nothing for me to do except try to catch some sleep while you and the kids splashed around outside. And cooking on a portable stove—what kind of vacation d'you call that?

Hal. Oh, I hadn't realized. I'm sorry. I liked it there. But this year I want it to be your extra special vacation, so you tell me where.

Mimi. I like somewhere that's restful and luxurious. But we have to think of the kids, they like the outdoors. They wouldn't be happy in a resort hotel.

Hal. Why don't you read the Sunday supplement and pick out something? You know best; I don't seem to be very good at selecting a place.

Last year's mistake has made Hal ultracautious, so he's wheedling Mimi into deciding.

Does what has been described mean that 1,9-oriented people are spineless, have no thoughts of their own, and lack convictions? Yes, in a way it does. But in another, the answer is No. You might simply support the views of your mate. This is inflating your mate's ego, and it may never be realized that you've not taken a definitive stand.

Arthur and Babs are on their way home from a neighborhood meeting at which various acquaintances were present. The discussion had centered on a topic of local interest which was polarizing the town.

Arthur. You were wonderful. It was amazing, the way the others came around to your point of view, after you'd spoken your mind.

Babs. I couldn't put up with Bill's dogmatism any longer. He didn't understand what was really at stake, and he was misrepresenting our group's position. That's what got me going.

Arthur. I just love to listen to you debating. You're so eloquent.

Babs. Did it get through to you, what I was saying? Did all my points check out? Sometimes I get carried away.

Arthur. It was really marvelous. I wish I could express myself the way you do.

What views, if any, does Arthur have on the controversy? Will Babs ever know that she doesn't know?

Even though your assumptions are 1,9, you may well be an intensive thinker—analytic and smart. This can help a lot in avoiding rejection. You use intelligence for anticipating your mate's thinking, sensing possible bad consequences if this or that were said or done, planning pleasant surprises, and so on. But you avoid fixed conclusions, or becoming definite, or locking yourself "in." This way, you can find some reason for agreeing with almost everything your mate says. Remember, it's not necessary to point out anything you privately disagree with. Probably you see yourself as having positive convictions and expressing them. You think "why be negative?" What you are not seeing in yourself is your reluctance to speak for a point of view when it might be challenged. As a result, gains, possible from your own creative thinking, are likely to be lost.

And yet there are 1,9 ways of expressing convictions. For example, instead of saying, "I saw a washer on sale today. I think it's time we got a new one," you would be more apt to say, "Have you noticed how much noise the washing machine motor is making lately?" The latter expresses a point of view, but in such an indirect manner that if it is picked up and disagreed with, you are not directly turned down.

You don't judge your mate's actions—or lack of them. So you feel little loss of identity in not challenging or arguing with your mate. Your convictions are carbon copies. The "loyal mate" refrain says, "There aren't two sides. The only side is your side and that's where I want to be. . . ." You are "faithful forever." You will cross party lines or change hair style if that's what your mate wants.

1,9 teamwork can be summed up as "Eager to help." As your mate's willing assistant, you are ready and waiting to do whatever's asked.

Hugh. Well, I'll get off to work now, honey, it's going to be a big day. Fridays are always hectic.

Dee. Never mind, it's going to be a lovely evening with the Prestons coming to dinner. You're picking them up and bringing them out here, aren't you?

Hugh. Yes. They don't know this area. Jim's a lousy map-reader. I'll go straight from the office . . . say, that reminds me, could you stop by the liquor store sometime today? I won't have time, what with picking up the Prestons and all.

Dee. Why, of course, darling. What would you like me to get?

Hugh. We're okay for liquor, but the soda syphon's not working, it needs a new bulb. Would you get several, to keep us going awhile?

Dee. Of course! Leave it to me.

Hugh arrives home that evening, bringing the Prestons. Soon afterwards, he comes into the kitchen where Dee is arranging hors d'oeuvres. The syphon's in his hand.

Hugh. Gimme a bulb, sweetheart, and I'll fix this. Our guests are having Scotch and soda. Would you like one, too?

Dee. Bulb? I never knew it lit up when it squirted.

Hugh. Ha-ha, you're in great form tonight, love. I must tell them that one.

Dee. Oh my gosh, the *gas* bulb!

Hugh. Don't say you forgot it.

Dee. I'm *so* sorry! I *meant* to get it but somehow it slipped my mind . . . I'll go right now.

Hugh. I could do that, but it'd take twenty minutes and meanwhile the Prestons are waiting for drinks! Have you got any bottled soda?

Dee. Er . . . no—but ooh, look! Here's some Seven-Up!

Hugh. SCOTCH AND SEVEN-UP!?

How did Dee miss? First, it's obvious that when Hugh made his request she wasn't concentrating. What exactly did need to be done to make the soda syphon work? Dee didn't realize, she was too busy glowing from being asked to help him. His request, which she had tucked unthinkingly into her "Of course, darling" grab bag, got lost.

Warm and hopeful emotions don't substitute for violated expectations. This often is a weakness in a 1,9-oriented person's teamwork. Dee's frantic and unrealistic last-minute suggestions for resolving the mess are par for the 1,9 course, too.

Here's teamwork involving another matter: weight. Nelson's just back from a medical check-up.

Nelson. He really read me the riot act.

Marie. Oh, no, he didn't find . . . ?

Nelson. My ticker's still OK and the chest X-rays are negative. But, my God, my weight.

Marie. But, you don't overeat. You never ask for second helpings. . . .

Nelson. The first's enough to satisfy a grizzly bear! You're overgenerous. Or is it that you can't stand up to me and say, "I'm cutting down your rations till you get back to your healthy weight."

Marie. . . . but I like you to eat well. I pride myself on keeping you well-nourished.

Nelson. He wanted to know about your weight . . . and whether you get a yearly check-up. I told him you're getting chubby, too.

Marie. Oh, how could you say that?

Nelson. Come on, face it, Marie, I've said I would cooperate with a leaner diet and you've promised time and again to get us both on one. But we haven't. Why?

Marie. When you're hungry and irritable you get so cross with me. I feel miserable. I can't stand it. I want you to have what you want. I can't be a policewoman. I'm not built that way.

Nelson. I agree, you're not trim enough! So we both run health risks because you don't want to see me irritable? I mean, you could *tell* me when I'm getting snappish. Sometimes I don't realize.

Marie. I can't bear to see you unhappy—surely it's not dangerous to be a little plump. But I'm glad you reminded me I'm getting fat. I'm the one who needs to diet so you'll keep your eyes on me.

That's the 1,9 idea of teamwork. You do whatever is thought to please your mate without regard for future consequences. In this case Marie may have known in an intellectual way that she was not serving Nelson's best interests. But she also knew his likes and put priority on satisfying them. She measured his pleasure by the spoonful, not by pound after excess pound. Even now, she wants to go on putting feasts before him while she fasts to be lovely for him!

From a 1,9 viewpoint, emotional relations are the be-all and end-all of life and the pursuit of happiness. These assumptions put pressure on a 1,9-oriented person to avoid being rejected. It's in this area that thoughts cluster and conflict-avoiding actions are taken.

If your attitudes are 1,9 you have very modest expectations regarding what your mate ought to be doing in the problem-solving area. Typically, you accept your mate as a "whole person," for better or worse. Even though you might not approve of all characteristics, it seems to you that since they are melded in someone who's lovable, you shouldn't single out any as being in need of amendment. You didn't marry this person with performance in mind. In ordinary conversation, you try to accentuate the positive and shine with cheerfulness. Your anticipations don't lead you to be demanding, so it doesn't take a lot to put you on top of the world when your mate surpasses them. Viewing what you see as accomplishment, you react with pleasant surprise. You're proud of your mate. When your mate's performance is less than you expected, your solicitude tells you the poor dear's not well today. This interpretation sometimes saves you from disappointment.

Let's go back to Willy and Linda, whom we met earlier. Linda is looking on the "bright" side of the dismal picture Willy is painting of his job situation.

Willy. A hundred and twenty dollars! My God, if business don't pick
up I don't know what I'm gonna do!
Linda. Well, next week you'll do better.
Willy. Oh, I'll knock 'em dead next week. I'll go to Hartford. I'm
very well liked in Hartford. You know, the trouble is, Linda,
people don't seem to take to me.
Linda. Oh, don't be foolish.
Willy. I know it when I walk in. They seem to laugh at me.
Linda. Why? Why would they laugh at you? Don't talk that way,
Willy.
Willy. I don't know the reason for it, but they just pass me by. I'm
not noticed.
Linda. But you're doing wonderful, dear. You're making seventy to
a hundred dollars a week.

Willy. But I gotta be at it ten, twelve hours a day. Other men—I
    don't know—they do it easier. I don't know why—I can't
    stop myself—I talk too much. . . .
Linda. You don't talk too much, you're just lively.

*   *   *

Willy. I'm fat. I'm very—foolish to look at, Linda . . . they do laugh
    at me. I know that.
Linda. Darling. . . .
Willy. I gotta overcome it. I know I gotta overcome it. I'm not
    dressing to advantage, maybe.
Linda. Willy, darling, you're the handsomest man in the world—
Willy. Oh, no, Linda.
Linda. To me you are. The handsomest.[7]

This failure of Linda to help Willy sort his clearer thoughts from
the wishful mists is what keeps on shifting him away from harsh
facts which need to be faced. In her concern for Willy to be happy,
she isn't realistic. She can't bear to have him take a straight look at
himself. It might hurt. Yet, in confusing his vision, she's leading
him onto dangerous ground. Pretty soon he'll slip and get hurt.

Always looking on the sunny side, and putting in your own
brighteners when needed, may not exactly be deceitful, but it certainly isn't objectivity. But when you're 1,9, to feel personally accepted is more important. You want to be told you're appreciated
and loved. Your hunger for affection may be at so high a level that
your mate seldom reaches it. You may even sense your mate as
colder than may actually be the case. This has you feeling insecure.
If the affection gap seems wide, you feel rejected and lonely.

Dale feels he is not receiving the appreciation he needs from
Lena. She is struggling to maintain her independence.

Lena. Look, Dale, you seem always to be wanting me to put a co-
    coon around you so that you can live in a kind of heaven
    where there are never any problems, friction, or strain, but
    only praise for you.
Dale. Well surely we can be nice to each other. Kind words help a
    lot, you know.

Lena. Dale, I am not a clock chiming the hours of comfort and se-
    curity for you! I can't tell you all's well at eight o'clock and
    nine o'clock and ten o'clock and so on through the days and
    nights.
Dale. But love means something to you, doesn't it, Lena? Loving
    you and needing you are all one to me. I know you're a strong
    person, I've always put you far above me. I *live* for you.
Lena. I'm married to you but I'm still a separate person. That's a
    fact of nature. Two can be together, but two can never be
    one.

See how Dale feels lost and let down when Lena tries to hold to
a more realistic view of their relationship? How different she is
from Linda in the previous example.

We know 1,9-oriented people aren't fighters. They flinch at the
thought of being in the line of fire. To them, conflict means loss of
affection, warmth, and approval—the main staples in the 1,9 emotional diet. This is what makes conflict seem so devastating. So you
stay away from conflict as though it were the plague. But if it does
arise, you try to pour soothing syrup over it and get back close to
your mate.

One way to stay in agreement is to listen for what your mate
thinks. The theory is that if you keep your thoughts running parallel with your mate's, differences can't arise. Without differences, no
basis for disagreement appears. With no disagreement, there's no
conflict. So you cultivate intuition and empathy. When you're with
your mate, your ears and eyes pick up impressions and filter them
through your 1,9 attitudes. They're like direction-finding antennae.
It's better if you don't have to ask, but can feel out the current
wavelength. If your quivering senses are fine-tuned, you may be
able to anticipate what your mate thinks. If you do seek an opinion, this isn't done in a demanding or provocative way. Your eyes
and tone of voice are all interest. And there's nothing false about it.

Here's how a 1,9-oriented wife slid out from under slippery
choices. Bob invited Virginia to accompany him on a business trip
to New York. She has delayed packing until the day before the
trip.

Bob. You really need new clothes for New York.

Virginia. Do you think so? I could get along with what I have if you don't think we should spend the money for just this one occasion.

Bob. But would you feel OK when we're strolling on Fifth Avenue?

Virginia. I guess so. What do you think they'll be wearing? I don't want to embarrass you by taking the wrong things.

In effect, Virginia has shifted the burden of her dress decisions onto Bob now. If she looks out of place in New York, he can't put the blame on her since she never established her own viewpoint, but instead sought his guidance. If she buys new clothes at his direction, he can't blame her for spending too much money. However, it's probable that no such step-by-step calculation operated in her ever-loving mind. Instead, intuition dictated the response which put the load on Bob.

Another way to stay close is to be agreeable. You give ready endorsement by saying, "You're so right," or something similar. In this way, you avoid saying those most danger-laden words, "I disagree" or "You're wrong." Now and then you may feel like taking an independent viewpoint, but, for the most part, you submerge your own thinking, finding yourself now agreeing with something you might previously have disagreed with. More often, though, if you've had this 1,9 approach a long while, you probably don't subscribe too much to any particular viewpoint, in the sense of digging your heels in. So you find it natural to fall in line rather than confront.

Morrie, in the following discussion, is agreeable in this unconditional way. He and Ethel are a fiftyish couple, whose two grown-up sons have married and left home. For some time now, Ethel, bored and lonely in the daytime when Morrie's at work, has been seeking new and meaningful ways of occupying herself. One evening she broaches the subject with Morrie.

Ethel. I've gotta have some action, Morrie, or I'll go out of my skull. We're too set in our ways. It's a dull life and I'm tired of it.

Morrie. Oh, I hadn't realized. Aren't you feeling well, dear?

Ethel. I feel great, except that I'm bored with everything!

Morrie. Why don't we count our blessings? Good health, kids we're proud of, a lovely home. We'll soon be grandparents, and in a few years I'll retire . . .

Ethel. Ever since Barney got married *I've* been retired for all practical purposes, and I hate it! I don't accept sitting around and waiting to die. In fact, I'm not going to. I've thought it all through, Morrie, and here's what I've decided. First, I want you to finish up with that company you've given half your life to, and take whatever they owe you by way of pension et cetera.

Morrie. That's nice of you, Ethel, but really I don't mind working . . .

Ethel. Good! Cause that's what you're going to do. But not for them. For us.

Morrie. Yes, dear. What do you have in mind?

Ethel. We're going to the Northern Territory of Australia just as soon as we can sell this house and stuff and get your pension money in a lump sum. We'll buy some land out in the boondocks and start developing it as a cattle ranch. I've always dreamed of being a pioneer settler and, hot damn, it's not too late yet!

Morrie. It would be quite a change for us, Ethel, wouldn't it? I mean, we've always lived in the city, and being an industrial chemist I don't know the first thing about ranching, or Australia for that matter . . .

Ethel. Dammit, Morrie, stop mumbling and let's get with it. There's a lot to arrange.

So it seems that Ethel and Morrie are headed for kangaroo country. Whether the decision is likely to be a wise one or not doesn't count for much with him. At present, because it is Ethel's decision, it is the right one. That's what Ethel believes too. In this way, Morrie serves as the pliable 1,9 complement of his 9,1-oriented wife. Probably they get along together quite well. He sees her as decisive and strong and as someone whose ideas might be suprising but had better not be questioned beyond the expression of a few mild doubts. Besides, he feels secure with her and, so, is willing to go along with whatever she feels a strong desire to do. Ethel sees him, probably, as a little slow on the uptake but, on the whole, a good husband who does his best to please her.

By definition, conversation is a two-way affair. The response one mate makes to the other's comments can affect emotions or thinking in a back-and-forth, up or down way. Regardless of the topic, if one of you starts in a bit sharply, it might take only a tactless or sharp reply from the other to provoke irritability or even loss of temper. When a 1,9-oriented person is on the receiving end, he or she feels rejected. This tremor in the relationship is amplified by sensitivity so that it feels like a force 7 earthquake. Personal pain is associated with it. But, unlike a stung 9,1, there is no striking back. The feeling that rejection produces is one of hurt. You wince at what you take to be your mate's coldness, hardness, and lack of appreciation. Yet at the very moment you're feeling hurt, you're also worrying about how you can get back into contact again. "I'm sorry!" seems the best thing to say; it kind of bursts out of you naturally. You're sorry for yourself and you're sorry for having been hurt and offended. Perhaps, deep down, you're sorry at having been so much yourself that you've got out of contact with your mate. "I hate myself—I want to be like you but somehow I can't!" Thus, to you, the inevitability of being only yourself poses an agonizing dilemma, even though the source of this dilemma is to be found in your own individual assumptions and not in the real world.

How does intimacy grow in a 1,9-oriented person's garden of love? You are likely to think of intimacy as the ultimate in marriage. It's something you can give anytime to make your mate happy.

Here's how it is between Mike and Marian.

Mike. Did you?
Marian. Did *you?* You *did,* didn't you?
Mike. Yes, I'm afraid I—Oh, I'm sorry! I *am* sorry. I know how it makes you feel.
Marian. Oh, don't worry about it. I'm sure I'll quiet down after a while.
Mike. I'm *so* sorry, dearest. Let me help you.
Marian. I'd rather you didn't.

Mike. But I . . .

Marian. What good is it when you're just—when you don't really
    want to? You know perfectly well, if you don't really want to,
    it doesn't work.

Mike. But I *do really* want to! I *want* to! Believe me. It *will* work,
    you'll see. Only let me!

Marian. Please, couldn't we just forget it? For now the thing is
    done, finished. Besides, it's not really that important. My ten-
    sion always wears off eventually. And anyhow—maybe next
    time it'll be different.

Mike. Oh, it *will*, I *know* it will. Next time I won't be so tired or so
    eager. I'll make sure of that. Next time it's going to be *fine!*
    . . . But about tonight—I'm sorry, dear.[8]

1,9 describes Mike to a tee. His own enjoyment turned to dust
and ashes as he found he'd failed to synchronize. He certainly was
apologetic when his supplementary offer wasn't appreciated by
Marian who is more in the 9,1 corner. She let him know what was
wrong with him. All the loving warmth of a shark that's missed its
meal. Yet Mike keeps working for her affection and approval by
promising better things next time. He won't be so tired or so eager,
he says. Pick the keynote for their next attempt. Will he be so anxious that love's labors are lost? If he *can't* make it, she'll tell him
he's not a man.

What it does for *you* isn't the key question from a 1,9 point of
view. In love-making you spend your time saying, either out loud
or in your unspoken thoughts, "Honey, is this all right? Honey, am
I doing it right for you, honey, do you like it this way? Tell me
what you'd like me to do!" The objective is to give sex in such a
way as to promote feelings of warm intimacy from your mate.

This approach to intimacy carries with it the notion that somehow you—the 1,9-oriented person—aren't quite love-worthy. It's
as though you say to yourself, "It's by some accident I met and
married this wonderful person, who someday is going to wake up
and leave me. And I'll never find anyone else. If what I've got now
slips away, I'm really lost because I can't face being alone." Thus
you feel the overwhelming importance of maintaining a perfect relationship. To an outsider it often seems incredible! You're always
wondering or asking your mate whether you're still loved. If at

some other time, out of the blue, your mate says, "I love you," you put a question mark on the end: "For real?"

This emotional dependence on the other person is noticeable as Valerie talks with Yale on the telephone.

Valerie. I'll be waiting for you at home and longing for the moment when I'll hear you at the door.

Yale. Why don't you go out and get some fresh air? I've no idea how long I'll be.

Valerie. No, I like to be here making things ready for when you'll be home.

Yale. Can't you occupy yourself any other way? How about cracking a book, going to an association meeting, writing your congressman, or something? Why be forever wrapping your life around my comings and goings? You're not making much of a life either for yourself or for me—you're getting duller by the week!

Valerie. Oh Yale, what a thing to say! I live for you and I love looking after you. Don't you appreciate that? Don't you love me anymore?

Yale. I don't know. I wasn't expecting things to turn out this way. I feel I'm in an intensive-care ward, with you as my nurse. You're stifling me. I'm not a hundred-percent home person the way you are. I've got to get out and run in the grass and smell the trees and bury a few bones . . .

Valerie. Yale, is there someone else?

Yale. No! Dammit, woman, you're not listening to what I'm saying. Now hear this, and hear it good. It was fun when we started, but more and more you're making me feel tied down. I don't have anyone else in mind yet, but I'm getting restless. So my advice to you is: ease up on the wet-nurse bit, get yourself interested in something creative, and generally, try to make yourself into a more interesting person than you've become lately. And stop sobbing into the telephone! I'll see you later.

There's a click as Yale puts down the telephone, and Valerie's on her own. She still hasn't gotten the point of what he's been trying to tell her. She's become so completely dependent on him,

wanting only to serve him and bask in his devotion, that her sentimentality and clinging ways have become more than he can bear.
With all her thought and feeling invested in concern for her mate,
she's been entirely disregarding the practical "what happens" area
of living. As a result, Yale finds no stimulating companionship with
her other than, maybe, in bed. Even the sex bond might not be
strong enough to hold him now that he encounters tedium everywhere else in their relationship.[9]

For your mate—if you're recently married—to have a "willing
slave," in and out of bed, may be novel and fascinating. But unless
both of you are 1,9-oriented, one of you is likely to feel the situation becoming one of being trapped.

Look at 1,9 from a non-1,9's point of view. You're being gently
coerced into giving up any outside interests and goals you've set for
yourself, so as to give full time to your mate's home-based interests
and sensitivities. Sure, your mate is warm and loving, but all that
pleading for reassurance of your love seems excessive, to say the
least. This insecurity begins to irritate you when your mate picks
up "bad" vibrations and becomes upset. Then you are likely to see
you are bound to a mate who has an insatiable love-and-tenderness
appetite. Whatever reassurance you give is not enough. *More* is the
name of this game. As the tender-trap tendrils wind around you
ever more smotheringly, you might feel the impulse to break free
and reestablish independence.

The complete Mirror for 1,9 is:

Problem-solving Relations. I defer making a choice and let
my mate make decisions because of the importance placed on
good relations. I embrace and support my mate's opinions, attitudes, and ideas even when I have reservations. I want to cooperate but prefer supporting whatever my mate has in mind.

Emotional Relations. I yearn to be appreciated by my mate
and feel hurt if the atmosphere between us gets cold or tense.
Conflict rarely arises between us, but, if it does, I am eager to
make amends to soothe my mate's feelings and to bring happiness. I seek security through intimate relations, and feel distressed if there is not a warm response.

CHAPTER 8 | SWEETNESS AND BLIGHT

In marriage, a mate with 1,9 attitudes has the concept of two people getting together and staying together in a loving, untroubled relationship. From the 1,9 viewpoint, this seems the essence of participation and involvement. When people love each other, it's easy to stay in tune. Whatever's necessary will be done naturally. You're together as loving mates, the relationship is all; whatever you enjoy doing together becomes its own reward.

One of your gifts of love is to listen tenderly to your mate. You'd never think of restricting *this* person's self-expression. You're ready to listen to whatever your mate wants to talk about, and, when the conversation lags, you look for a new pleasant topic to keep it going. You want to help keep your mate relaxed and at ease.

But the kind of conversations you like coaxing your mate into have an unworldly quality, even though they're congenial, leisurely, and sociable. They probably do very little to create a suitable atmosphere in which the practicalities of married living can be discussed. Your preference is for sentimental chit-chat, for here is where you find pleasure. It's conversational candy floss. It doesn't help bring about the kind of involvement that contributes to planning and achieving something together. So your characteristic approach causes you to hold back from any kind of initiative.

1,9 / 1,9

For many husbands and wives, it's a pleasure to reconnect with an amiable 1,9-oriented mate after a stress-filled day. A warm and comforting welcome lies in store. Drinks and dinner are enjoyed together, with never a mention, or even a hint, of workaday worries. All through the evening, up to and including bedtime, comfort and joy continue to be lavished upon you. Unless you happen to realize it and intervene on a practical note, plans will stay unmade, bills unpaid, and cherished dreams fade because of your mate's overriding wish to wrap you around with momentary joys. You get swaddled in this until the consequences of neglecting practical matters catch up with you. When these eventually penetrate, the impact can be most unpleasant. You rub your eyes and wonder what's been happening while you and your mate were in that ever-loving trance. Nothing's gotten done!

Now let's look deeper into 1,9 to see how these attitudes really work in a marriage. We can join Steve and Amy. They are caught in the rain and are "helping" each other.

Steve. Put my jacket on, honey, and I'll hold the newspaper over
  your head till we get to the car.
Amy. But, darling, you'll get soaked. It's sweet of you, but I don't
  need it, really. You've only got that light shirt on. . . .
Steve. No, please honey—that lovely dress—you'll catch pneu-
  monia. . . .
Amy. Oh, darling, you put it on. You're *so* wet.
Steve. Hold it a moment please, dear, while I pick up the paper.

He bends to pick up the newspaper, and, as he straightens up, she drapes the jacket around his shoulders.

Amy. There now! Let's run to the car, dear.

Steve peels away the soggy outer pages.

Steve. Just a moment, this'll make an umbrella for you. Now hold it over your head, there's a good girl.
Amy. No, you have it, love.

But as he holds the newspaper above her, the coat slips from his shoulders, falling into a puddle.

Steve. Sorry, dear, did it splash you?

What's going on between Amy and Steve? Each is so concerned for the other that both miss the point of what is happening. Rather than applying their efforts to getting out of the rain, they're both busily trying to prove how lovingly concerned with each other they are. They get drenched, but each stays cheerful in a kind of affectionate martyrdom.

These two epitomize what a 1,9/1,9 relationship's all about. Each party operates with total devotion to the other's comfort and happiness. To both of them, that's what marriage is for. Home is a love nest, a sanctuary, a refuge from what they perceive as the harshness of the outside world. It is a safe harbor. But, turning inward on themselves and attempting to create a capsule paradise, they turn aside from what could be constructive thinking about how to sustain or improve the material and practical bases of married living. They've no awareness of the potential of a planned and worked-for future. Instead, their thoughts and actions are perpetually centered on the other's moment-to-moment situation and in making up little bouquets of tender care. If outside factors from the real world break through the fragile shell of their cocoon, they react with panic-stricken distress rather than resilience.

9,1 / 1,9

One view about "who married whom" is that opposites attract. The idea is that each mate contributes something the other lacks. A submissive, sweet woman falls in love with a strong, harsh man. Or it may be the other way around. A domineering woman falls in love with a soft and gentle man.[1] The mates' characteristics differ, but a kind of jigsaw-puzzle fit is achieved between them.[2] Yet, when such a gap exists between the degrees of concern each has for the other, it becomes easy for the 9,1-oriented mate—the one with the least concern—to rule the marriage.[3]

A 9,1 / 1,9 marriage is one that may be a "completing" experience for each mate, as long as neither of them changes the assumptions and attitudes they initially brought into it. If either does, it's a new ball game right away. Whether they relate to each other better or worse, at least they relate differently.[4] But while they're still respectively operating under 1,9 and 9,1 assumptions, the marriage is a going concern, becuause each can go on supplying the needs of the other.

You get the feeling of a happily married 9,1 / 1,9 couple as Cathleen explains her daily routine to Willa.

Willa. My, how spick and span everything is, so early in the morning!

Cathleen. I always try to get housework finished by 9:30. Craig made a study of everything that needed doing and divided it up day by day and showed me how I could get through quick and easy. So now I know what I ought to be doing at any time of day.

Willa. That's marvelous. My Don could never do that, but, come to think of it, maybe I'll try getting my own household chores better organized. You must have a lot of spare time after 9:30 nowadays.

Cathleen. Oh, no; Craig says time saved is time to be used for a *purpose.* That's why I'm afraid I'll have to be going soon, Willa, I'm due at the YWCA in twenty minutes. It's Flower Arrangement Day.

Willa. Then I mustn't. . . . It's nice you have a creative interest like that.

Cathleen. Craig just loved the floral art he saw in Japan, and when he heard of a class here, he registered me.

Willa. He does keep you busy! But I suppose after lunch you can relax.

Cathleen. I take the same lunch hour as Craig does. After all, if we're partners for life, we should take an equal load of work everyday, as he says. At three o'clock I look at our menu planning board and start. . . .

Willa. You *are* systematic. What's this?—every meal listed through next Sunday?

Cathleen. Craig posts that up every Sunday night. See, here are the index cards for recipes.

Willa. How about that? And when's your *exercise period,* Cathleen?

Cathleen feels secure in her knowledge that she is doing what Craig has planned and approved. Also, she is relieved of the burden of making decisions about what to do and when. This reduces her anxiety about the possibility of doing something wrong. Craig seems delighted to have someone whom he can organize. Theirs is a 9,1 / 1,9 marriage which can be called a happy one.

But not all 9,1 / 1,9 mates get along so well. Sometimes one of them alters assumptions. Let's say the man retains his strength of will but comes to learn respect for others. He now sees his wife differently. He wants to see her stand up for herself, rather than hiding behind easy rationalizations of why she can't deal more objectively with other people. Every time she recoils from life's practicalities—whether this is revealed as inability to break away from a salesgirl to keep an appointment or to deal with their son as a sixteen-year-old—respect is lost. Under these circumstances, rather than building a life in common, by experiencing together, analyzing together, planning together, this "misunderstanding gap" widens and the depth of his unhappiness with her is matched by her sense of self-condemnation and failure. This is what has happened to Dorothy and Joe.

Dorothy. Please, please, please don't. It makes me so miserable.

Joe. And that's why our life is an accumulation of unfinished business. We've never *solved* anything.

Dorothy. But we have a lovely life together.

Joe. What do you mean *"together"?* Have we ever really been together?

Dorothy. Don't say that, *please,* after all these years. . . .

Joe. I want to make something of the years that remain! Up to now we've sacrificed plain talk for playfulness and sex. If we *were* together, we'd get things *done* together.

Dorothy. Oh! I've tried so hard. . . .

Joe. Never to be on time for anything! Something always came up to make you late. I've waited for you in the best places in the world. Thirty minutes in Piccadilly Circus while you "lost" yourself in Simpsons. Forty minutes in the Palm Court while you "couldn't get away" from the Bergdorf Goodman salesgirl. An hour at Place de l'Opéra while you tried to make up your mind about that lousy skirt at Au Printemps . . . and I got too drunk in the Fairmont while you waxed ecstatic about oriental art in Gumps, to say nothing of dinner never on time . . . your not being able to get "started in the morning. . . ."

Dorothy. I *wish* you'd understand—I was either choosing something nice for you, or making myself pretty for you, or taking time to add something extra nice. . . .

Joe. And *"we've"* been unable to get a haircut onto Bill for some months cause he couldn't make the same sounds on his electric guitar if he had a civilized appearance! He had to have a car at sixteen because you're afraid he'll leave home if "we" couldn't treat him like a grown-up. And when I think of that poor girl. . . .

Dorothy. You don't feel for him the way I do. My love doesn't set conditions for him, or for you, either. I want you both to be happy! Won't you please stop blaming him for that accident?

Joe. There you go again. It's always "couldn't be helped," "not our fault." . . . And his grades—"he's just a healthy fun-loving boy . . . who'll get interested later on . . ." and his weight . . . "just baby fat."

Dorothy. I want to die. You're so hard on me. I've lived for you but you've never appreciated me!

Joe. Am I supposed to be grateful for all the failures and futility we've experienced?

Dorothy. Why are you so cruel?

Joe. If you only knew it, I'm being kind. I love you, Dorothy, but we aren't getting it together! I know I have faults too. I'm looking for a better way. I wish you'd join me.

This last statement of Joe's may be more effective for improving their marriage than were any of his previous comments. Although he seems to have a clear "rational" set of ideas regarding Dorothy's inefficiency, he seems to have failed to communicate them to her. By making his points with sledgehammer force, he has only brought about an emotional response of distress. The meaning of what he says, as Dorothy hears it, is that he doesn't love her. Joe seems to have realized that by haranguing her he's creating new problems, rather than solving old ones.

Subordinating personal integrity to a deeper concern for your mate is 1,9. Another characteristic of 1,9 is the absence of personal conviction implied in your acceptance that whatever your mate wants to happen to the marriage is for the best. The 1,9 mode is an easy way of adjusting—and a secure one, as long as your mate picks up and carries the ball by acting in ways that support your particular attitudes.

CHAPTER 9 | 1,1—APATHETIC WITHDRAWAL

Occasionally, a marriage begins with one or both mates close to 1,1. Two people drift together and find it easier to remain together than to separate. More frequently, 1,1 attitudes come to the fore after some other Grid approach has failed to result in a satisfying and meaningful married life. Once gravitated into, the deep-rooted apathy of 1,1 can be as strong and dominant a Grid style as can any other. Its assumptions cause people to abandon effort to support each other in a continuing and ever-renewing way.[1] Sheer time —the years you've lived together—may have something to do with the situation where your low Concern for What Happens comes to coincide with low Concern for Your Mate.

The core assumption is in the attitude "I don't care." A person might be aware of his indifference, even embarrassed by it, or he may not even recognize it for what it is. Yet there's no thought of changing. To create or revive commitment, involvement, and interest, you would need to invest feelings of Concern for What Happens and Concern for Your Mate. When you have become emotionally numb to your husband or wife, it's difficult to think of establishing a warmer, more vital relationship.[2]

"He'll come in and slam down his cap and say, 'Watcha got to eat?' While he is feeding his face, sometimes he'll tell me a thing or two that happened and if anything is going on, I'll let him know." Asked if they ever "just plain talked to each other," she said, "What's there to talk about?" . . . Asked if she wished he would explain why he was so quiet at times, she merely shrugged her shoulders.[3]

The 1,1-oriented person, then, remains in the marriage but ceases being a part of it except in the sense of physical presence. Neutral, indifferent, bland, distant—these are words for describing a person who's traveled down the 1,1 road.

Here's a 1,1 attitude on the part of a wife. Marilyn is telling Betty about her own reactions to a 1,1-oriented husband. According to her, Betty's crazy, for what is there to expect in marriage, anyway?

Marilyn. . . . What do you think life is, a Street and Smith Love Story Magazine? You had a good marriage with George. You paid the rent and you went to bed. What are you looking for?

Betty. I'm looking for more than that, Marilyn.

Marilyn. You want to know what life is? You live, that's all. That's life. You get married, you have kids—you get up in the morning and you go to sleep at night. Frank goes bowling every Thursday, and I manage to get down to Macy's once a week, and that's it, and it's not so bad. I don't know what you mean by happiness. You had a good marriage with George. At least he was hungry for you all the time. It was all over his face. That's more than most of us can say about our husbands.

Betty. Are you having trouble with Frank, Marilyn?

Marilyn. Frank and me? We get along fine. We are perfectly happy. He stays out of my way and I stay out of his. . . .[4]

So, to Marilyn, George seems better than her own husband, particularly as his night-light glows a little above "1" in intensity.

Now, let's look in on a discussion between Martin and Frances. His world came crashing down several months ago when he was retired a decade-and-a-half earlier than normal retirement. Frances and he are talking about the dilemma they are in.

Martin. . . . Two weeks' notice, early retirement, forty percent of what I could have had if I'd lasted till sixty-five. What am I supposed to do now, at fifty? I'm too old to learn new skills, too young to retire, too proud to be unemployed, and too sick of it all to give a damn. I'm through. You might as well start looking around for someone else.

Frances. Come on! I know you feel depressed by what's happened. . . .

Martin. You said it.

Frances. But it needn't be permanent. Try to see early retirement as the company's inability to use you, not *your* inability to use your own knowledge and skills.

Martin. No. . . . This is it. . . . It's the end of the road for me . . . I wouldn't have been bounced out of a vice presidency if I hadn't been out of date and out of touch.

Frances. Are you dropping out on me and on our marriage?

Martin. I can't provide for you the way I used to. I can't face people now this has happened. I might as well sit on the dock. . . .

Frances. . . . And fish?

Martin. Why not? What else?

Frances. Your light goes out only when you switch yourself off.

Martin. What do you mean?

Frances. It depends on how you look at things, Martin. We're living *now:* the past, even yesterday, is dead. This can be the first day of the rest of our lives. Or it can be the last day of the kind of marriage we've had. It's in you if you *will* yourself to it.

Martin. I should start it all over again, even at fifty?

Frances. Of course! Why not? Fifty is what? Is it "old," or is it "young"? It's old to a boy of ten. What is it to a man of seventy?

Martin's 1,1 sense of hopelessness is challenged by his 9,9-oriented wife. This may be just in time to turn him around and get him looking with some confidence toward a future he might make. Other people's 1,1 attitudes, when unchallenged, tend to spread and deepen, becoming ever more permanent. Then gloomy prophecies of your future surely come to pass.

One basic feature underlies all 1,1 attitudes. You're trying to avoid being drawn in: you reject involvement. When 1,1 has seeped into your marriage, you are still in attendance in customary ways. But now you make no significant input. Your lack of contribution might not be noticeable for a while, especially if your mate is still pursuing the day-to-day activities which sustain the marriage. But eventually the slowdown will become evident.

1,1-oriented persons seem not to notice when decisions need to be made. If your mate comes up with a suggestion, your response is "uh-huh." It's the same when your mate makes a decision for both of you and says, "We'll do *this.*" Your "uh-huh" response can be interpreted any of several ways. Perhaps it's taken as agreement. But, really, your grunt means nothing. You don't feel committed one way or the other.

Here's an example of 1,1 indifference. Jack is trying to get Lillian to take a vacation with him. She dodges the issue nicely.

Jack. So what'll I tell my boss? Shall I tell him I'll take the vacation Monday? I'll tell you, Lillian, I'd like to get away. . . . It seems to me it wouldn't hurt us to get away somewheres and relax. I feel there's an awkwardness between us. I don't know.
Lillian. What do you mean, awkwardness?
Jack. I don't know. It seems we never talk or go out. It seems—
Lillian. We went out tonight.
Jack. I don't know what I mean. I come home, and we have dinner, and you tell me about the baby, or your father comes over, or—
Lillian. My father hasn't been to the house in three weeks.
Jack. Listen, I like your father. I wasn't objecting to his coming over.
Lillian. Well, I don't know what you mean by awkwardness.
Jack. Well, maybe, that's the wrong word. I just feel that—
Lillian. We've been married more than three years, Jack.[5]

Lillian not only deflates the decision, but also manages to evade facing the point Jack is trying to make about the distance between them that he feels.

Replying to your mate's query with zero commitment can also be a delaying tactic. You're gaining time to think about how not to be drawn in. What you hope for is that your mate will forget the matter, or that something will occur to solve the problem without your having to get in the same boat with your mate and take an oar.

Listen for 1,1 undertones in this discussion.

Andy. This party invitation came in the mail today.
Pat. When is it?
Andy. In three weeks' time. The card says "Formal."
Pat. I guess the moths got my evening gown. I never feel right in one anyway.
Andy. Oh well, plenty of time. . . .
Pat. Go by yourself if you like.
Andy. Yeah, maybe.

Neither Andy nor Pat could care less. Both have 1,1 attitudes when it comes to deciding what to do—or not do—together. Probably they let fate decide for them, much of the time.

When 1,1 attitudes grip you, you have a feeling that nothing is really worth taking a stand on. Sometimes it's easier to *avoid* saying no than to say no.

Eleanor's watching TV and Fred's dozing off. The first time the doorbell rings, nothing happens. Each waits for the other to get up. Then the bell rings again.

Eleanor. You wanna answer the door?

He pulls himself out of his chair and shuffles off. A few moments later, he's back.

Fred. It's the encyclopedia man again. He wants to come in and talk with us.
Eleanor. You talk with him if you want. I need encyclopedias like I need varicose veins.
Fred. Me too, but—well—you tell him, eh? He's showing them to the kids out front. They want us to buy them.
Eleanor. *You* answered the door.

He goes out again.

Fred. Yes, we *are* familiar with these books. You needn't leave any —OK, I'll take a brochure. Thank you for calling. We'll think it over. Goodbye. . . . Oh, you want to call *again?* Make it one morning next week—my wife's always in.

When he returns,

Eleanor. Couldn't you have set a definite day, so that I'd know when to be out?

So well have they avoided revealing convictions that the departing salesman is as little informed of what they think as when he arrived. Most 1,1-oriented persons become expert in expressing apparently meaningful nothings to their mates as well as to third parties. For instance, if your mate is telling you about the difficulties of budgeting, and obviously waiting for a comment, you can say, "It's terrible the way the cost of living keeps going up and up." If there are child-rearing problems, "Kids these days—I don't know what's come over them." How are things at work?—"Oh, y'know, up and down." In these, and many other ways, you can appear responsive, without your comments tying you to any position or commitment.

Saralee. Who'll win in November?
Clint. It's still early . . . I hope the best man will, though.
Saralee. I can't get a feel for either of them.
Clint. The polls are different all the time.
Saralee. I'm voting for whoever promises most community protection.
Clint. There sure is a lot of crime these days.

Clint is mouthing platitudes in such a way as to be in the conversation as an unknown quantity. He avoids expressing any conviction. The skill is in finding a platitude that means little, yet satisfies your mate. Then you're not called on for further comment.

With 1,1 attitudes, one lacks enthusiasm for joint action. But, all the same, some things have to get done so that you can go through at least the mechanics of living together and have your accustomed personal comforts.

In the final analysis, what *you* do is likely to be decided by how much your mate will do if you don't do anything. Responsibilities for essential activities are shifted over to your mate by your default. When you have a mate who won't put up with this, and demands that you take a share of the load, you grudgingly pick up the very minimum that will be tolerated, beginning with those tasks which, if left undone, would directly inconvenience you.

Roger has just sat down to his customary seven-to-ten shift of TV watching.

Carol. The downspout's clogged, and the rain this afternoon ruined the flower bed.
Roger. Yeah, we'll have to do something about it.
Carol. Why don't you go out and fix it now before it rains again?
Roger. There isn't time. Daylight's nearly gone.
Carol. You can do it early tomorrow.
Roger. Yeah, maybe.
Carol. If you don't, I'll have to pay someone to do it for us.
Roger. We don't have that much money to throw around.
Carol. Great—so when will *you* do it?
Roger. As soon as I can get a ladder. I don't know who'd lend me one.
Carol. Well hire one for a couple of hours! The forecast is for a lot more rain.
Roger. Bet you that blockage washes out after a few showers.

There's no budging Roger tonight, and he can probably put off the downspout assignment night after night until Carol gives up trying to push the immovable object.

Real clues to Grid style are evident in the degree to which you and your mate are open, sharing, mutually supporting, and helpful to each other. But one way of denying the possibility of teamwork is to take the view that men and women are like two separate species.

"Men and women are different. The fellows got their interests and the girls got theirs, they each go their separate ways."

"Men are different; they don't feel the same as us—that's one reason men are friends with men and women have women friends." [6]

These remarks imply, in a 1,1 way, "Marriage is for sharing bed and board, but little else."

Emotional apartness also characterizes the 1,1-oriented person. Feelings are disengaged, in neutral. There's no reason to get stirred up. The person's greatest skill is applied in circumstances where some reaction seems required so as to keep up the appearance that a marriage still exists. So long as the other mate hasn't noticed the drop in emotional momentum, no mention of it is made. But when the secret's out, the 1,1 kiss-off is "take it or leave it."

You've few expectations of what you should receive from your mate in the way of performance and affection. If your mate's conduct sank beneath these minimal standards, you would avoid disappointment by sealing yourself off even more tightly than you presently do. High achievement and warm expressions of affection by your mate don't grab you either. Something's happened to cause you to lose nearly all the concerns you're potentially capable of expressing. Until that's settled—and your self-fulfilling prophecy is that it never will be—you've closed the door on your mate.

Here's how one wife feels. She and her husband have slipped into a 1,1 way of living. She's a bit agitated about it—her expectations are still higher than his. But she doesn't know what to do next now that she's awakened to what's going on.

". . . when I think of us and the numb way we sort of stagger through the weekly routine, I could scream. And I've even thought of doing some desperate things to try to build some joy and excitement into my life. I've given up on Phil. He's too content with his balance sheets and the kids' report cards and the new house we're going to build next year. He keeps saying he has everything in life that any man could want. What do you *do?*" [7]

Phil's attitudes are significant. When he takes inventory on his possessions, he has everything. He has a wife. As an inevitable consequence of having a wife, he has a marriage—at least that seems to be his line of reasoning. It was okay when it began; it can't have changed much since. Even if his wife expressed her dissatisfaction to *him* rather than to a third party, he'd probably say, "I don't understand. Why, we've got it made. We've got everything we need." The relationship is way down, but he's not bothered, since it matches his anticipations of what he should be getting in marriage.

Here's another example of a wife who actually doesn't want to be nudged out of the 1,1 corner. Phillip and Martha have been married a long time. At the moment they're talking while drying dishes. Something caused him to liven up and exchange something more meaningful than their usual barren chatter.

Phillip. Games? Martha, I was trying to share a secret with you. For the first time in our marriage, I was telling you something I really felt.
Martha. Don't be open-hearted and frank with me, Phillip.
Phillip. But aren't you at least interested in what I'm really like?
Martha. If I was interested in what you were really like, I don't think I'd have stayed married to you for twenty years.[8]

Martha's last remark says 1,1 in neon lights. Her earlier one, "Don't be open-hearted and frank with me . . . ," reveals where her expectations are and she's not about to let them be violated by Phillip trying to deepen their relationship.

When there's tension in the atmosphere, 1,1 tactics are to say as little as possible or, if dragged into debate, to escape into vagueness. This is the easiest way to get through a bothersome process.

When your mate is complaining about something or spoiling for a fight, your countermove is either to ignore it or to imply that the displeasure has been noted. But, as far as possible, you see no disagreement, hear no disagreement, and speak none. As a matter of fact, you *feel* no disagreement, since neutrality goes way down deep to the core of your 1,1 attitudes of noninvolvement. The calm, placid, patient exterior does not result from inner peace. It comes from being devoid of emotional commitment and thus untouched by challenge, contradiction, or any of the milder forms of hostile attack.

You probably down-play any issue as unimportant: "It'll work itself out." Or you might suggest a truce, by saying more time is needed for thinking things over. When asked what other people think or would do, you supply an infinite variety of neutral answers: "They didn't say"; "I haven't heard"; "I don't know"; "I wasn't there." When pressed further, you provide equally adept answers: "It's up to you"; "It's your life, not mine"; "Whatever you say"; "I'm no expert. . . ." In all these ways, you evade being caught up in controversy. When there is a choice between dealing with disagreement or getting a blast, you prefer the blast. It's just hot air.

As your mate tongue-lashes you, mentally you crawl into a hole like an armadillo and take the brunt. If anyone suffers, it will be your mate, banging and bruising against the hard outer shell of your apathy. Inside, you don't feel a thing. Words will never hurt you.

Ellen has just pinned Milt to the wall. She has quantitative data plotted on a chart. It shows Milt hasn't touched her for months.

Milt. Ellen, for God's sake. . . . We can talk about this later.
Ellen. You're always saying later. That's a favorite play of yours. No, Milt. Not tonight. These things must be said while they still can be said. . . . When something like this is allowed to happen to a marriage, you can't go on pretending. You want to pretend. Oh, the temptation is great to overlook, to find excuses, to rationalize. But here, Milt, here are the facts. Our relationship has deteriorated to such an extent that I don't feel responsible any more for my own behavior.
Milt. Hon, you're mad at me.
Ellen. It isn't a question of being mad at you. We've gone a long ways from that.
Milt. I see. Just the same I'd like to ask you something, El.
Ellen. Speak. I can't stop you.
Milt. Do you think our marriage is a failure?
Ellen. I do.

Milt. I thought so. I thought that was behind it. Well, before I give you a divorce . . .

Ellen. There isn't going to be a divorce.

Milt. There isn't?

Ellen. We've made a mistake, but we've got to make the best of it.[9]

Nothing gets to Milt. After Ellen has laid it on the line and pointed out the flat state of their relationship, Milt's soggy response is, "Hon, you're mad at me." He just won't pick up the issue she's raised. His attitude is "So you're uptight; we'd better divorce then." Their relationship problem isn't something *he* feels is worth digging into.

A grunt is the best reply of all to your mate's reasoning. "Hmm" means more or less "OK, so what—it's no skin off *my* back." If you'd come straight out with this in words, it would have been taken as an affront, a challenge to your mate to attack you more vigorously. But "hmm" is a deadener. It leaves the other person without any certain way to respond. It's hard to tell from the outside whether you're agreeing, submitting, or going your own sweet way, quite unaffected.

Saluting is done whenever the price of agreeing is less costly than the expense of resisting. The standard salute is, "If you say so, OK." Even when your mate's views are way out and you know they are, you make no attempt to comment objectively. That might start an argument, and arguing is a drag. If X and Y are said to come after Z, well OK. Agreed.

Some 1,1-oriented people wear down their mates so as to end conflict, in much the same way as a skillful angler plays a fish till it's tuckered out. For instance, a husband listens silently to his wife's tirade. Whenever she ceases blasting him or pauses for breath, he says, "And that's not all!" Unless she's completely exhausted, this cue seldom fails to set her going again on something new. She thought he was trying to put *his* point of view across. He prompts her time and time again with this kind of comment. Eventually her batteries go dead. Conflict terminates for the day. No harm done.

Now, let's rake through the ashes where intimacy once glowed, or where it still may flicker once in a great long while. The question "How about it?" directed at a 1,1-oriented person may be more a plea than a suggestion. The answer might be "Let's forget about it."

Sometimes this is the first of the marriage aspects wherein one or both of you notice a drift toward 1,1 beginning. In other marriages where relationships have become predominantly 1,1, sex may seem the only reason for staying married. Or maybe not even that.

> "... the simple truth is George and I have a physical marriage, that's the simple truth, Ma. That's the only time I feel he wants me. The rest of the day I feel he's always trying to get away from me. ... We watched T.V. the whole night. I don't think we said a word. Ma, it's not just last night. It's every night. Then I went to bed. Then he came in around one o'clock. He got undressed and got into bed. I turned over to him and I said, 'George, just hold me in your arms a little,' and he reached over and began feeling my leg. You see, I just wanted him to hold me and talk to me. You know what he was thinking, Ma? He just wanted to get me to sleep so I wouldn't bother him anymore. ..." [10]

It seems that to George, sex is a convenient sleeping tablet to administer to his wife as well as to himself.

The issue facing Margaret is even more extreme. Brick has been putting less and less into his marriage. There's never any action, even though Margaret never gives up trying to arouse him. Listen to how he responds as Margaret tells him of an escapade she *almost* got into.

Margaret ... Why, last week in Memphis, everywhere that I went men's eyes burned holes in my clothes, at the country club and in restaurants and department stores, there wasn't a man I met or walked by that didn't just eat me up with his eyes and turn around when I passed him and look back at me. Why, at Alice's party for her New York cousins, the best lookin' man in the crowd followed me upstairs and tried to force his way into the powder room with me, followed me to the door and tried to force his way in!

Brick. Why didn't you let him in, Maggie?

Margaret. Because I'm not that common, for one thing. Not that I

wasn't almost tempted to. You like to know who it was—
hmm? It was Sonny Boy Maxwell, that's who!

Brick. Oh, yeah, Sonny Boy Maxwell, he was a good broken field
runner but he had a little injury to his back and had to quit.

Margaret. He has no injury now and has no wife and still has a
lech for me!

Brick. I see no reason to lock him out of the powder room in that
case.[11]

Is his jealousy brought to a "I'll kill him" pitch? Nope, it remains zero. She's a "thing" he doesn't love, doesn't own, doesn't
want!

Sex, with or without intimacy, takes involvement. That's when it
becomes something you want. For one of you particularly, without
involvement it's pretty hard to make the machinery work to its
maximum capacity. It's like a good engine with no gasoline! But if
you were to explain it that way to your mate, you'd be up to your
eyeballs in troubles. It's much easier to blame your—"weaknesses,"
shall we say?—on fatigue, or office problems, or you-name-it.

Let's listen to an evening interlude between Beatrice and Eddie.

Beatrice. No, everything ain't great with me.

Eddie. No?

Beatrice. No. But I got other worries.

Eddie. Yeah.

Beatrice. Yeah, you want me to tell you?

Eddie. Why? What worries you got?

Beatrice. When am I gonna be a wife again, Eddie?

Eddie. I ain't been feelin' good. . . .

Beatrice. It's almost three months you don't feel good. . . . It's three
months, Eddie.

Eddie. I don't know, B. I don't want to talk about it.

Beatrice. What's the matter, Eddie, you don't like me, heh?

Eddie. What do you mean, I don't like you? I said I don't feel good,
that's all.

Beatrice. Well, tell me, am I doing something wrong? Talk to me.

Eddie. I can't. I can't talk about it.

Beatrice. Well tell me what—

Eddie. I got nothing to say about it! I'll be all right, B.; just lay off
   me, will ya? . . .[12]

In spite of Bea's efforts to get Eddie involved, Eddie is using the
postponement technique to get Bea to leave him alone. Who knows
whether Bea mightn't buzz elsewhere?

Unwillingness to "make it" to the sexual summit is a common
trait of 1,1 intimacy, except in one respect. If it seems less bother
than refusing, she can fake it, though he can't. She can go through
the motions in an uninspired way.

> "She doesn't really refuse me—just so casual and submissive
> and matter-of-fact—like it's part of the weekly toilet or the
> formal etiquette of marriage. She seems to enjoy certain
> moments—like it was in spite of herself. But there's no *joie,*
> you know, no evidence of anticipation, no pleasant talk after-
> wards. It's like copulating with a well-tuned, delicate machine.
> . . . Pretty soon you don't give much of a damn about it your-
> self. . . . A lot of men I know say the same thing. Sometimes
> they blame themselves and sometimes their wives. But there
> just doesn't seem to be much there for a lot of us." [13]

You could listen to these remarks and not be very certain as to
whether the wife had a 1,1 or a 5,5 attitude. Maybe it's a bit of
both, or maybe there were details which the husband didn't observe. If she keeps her eyes closed during the act, or puffs a cigarette, or watches televison over his shoulder, these are additional
clues that she's in a 1,1 frame of mind. If she takes him through it
with a kind of cool efficiency, adjusting to each gradient like a
smoothly functioning automatic transmission, that would seem
more like a 5,5.

Something may have stirred you up. Late night show? A book?
A magazine? Then a sex link-up may be better than nothing, even
when your attitude is 1,1. Certainly you're not fired up with feelings of intimacy, because intimacy takes involvement—a lot of it
—and you've not got that. Moreover, it would require that you had
your mate's interests at heart, and you couldn't care less. Tension-
reduction sex links you with a body, not with another's mind and

emotions. It's sex when you don't give a tinker's dam how your mate reacts. At least it cools you off and helps you get to sleep.

This is the 1,1 Mirror in its entirety.

Problem-solving Relations. Decisions are left hanging, or responsibility for them falls on my mate by default. I am indifferent to opinions, attitudes, and ideas, but usually go along with the ones presented, seldom expressing a difference. To me, cooperation seems unnecessary.

Emotional Relations. I ask for little and expect less. I avoid arguing and rarely get heated up about anything. Little or nothing seems that important. I rarely feel involved or aroused by my mate.

CHAPTER 10 | WED BUT DEAD

Here's how you approach participation from the 1,1 corner. If anyone is going to be involved, it is your mate separately, not you. If something needs doing, you are not out looking for it. If your mate doesn't do it, it can stay undone for all you care. If you're asked a question or are invited into participation, you give flat uncommunicative "gruntmaster" answers. The next move is up to your mate.

The person you've married has unlimited opportunity to talk. It's not only that you don't interrupt; you hardly ever say anything beyond mouthing a few platitudes. Your mate might think you're being attentive, particularly when points are being made which you seem to be silently accepting. Or your real attitude might show through clearly.

You participate in jointly shared activities with all the zest of a constipated sloth moving through a barbed-wire entanglement. It might seem incredible to your mate how difficult or unnecessary every aspect of the project you're asked to handle can seem—to you at least. If an impatient mate grabs the initiative and takes your share of the load, that's completely OK by you.

Some people are alert to signs that indicate a mental walk-out on the part of their mates. Some even notice when they themselves are drifting toward a 1,1 orientation. Take widowed Mrs. McAfee for example. She is explaining to her friend Margaret her own concepts of argument and fighting in marriage.

Now my Sandy—may he rest in peace—was a fine upstanding man who never refused a fight. I'm sorry for any woman whose husband storms out of the house when she wants to argue with him. Why, Sandy McAfee would rear up on his hind legs at the slightest provocation, and we'd battle for hours at a time. We'd even throw things at each other sometimes, Maggie, and that's a tonic in itself. Whenever I was feeling kind of depressed and stale, I'd have a good zingy fight with Sandy and it would pep me up for days afterward. Now, this Mr. Hughes I've recently met; he's a good arguing man. I'm thinking of marrying him.

The point in this set of remarks relates to the values that Mrs. McAfee associates with staying involved. She's a 9,1 happy warrior widow in search of a new sparring partner. Beyond that, she sees conflict as having the value of stirring a person up and making him feel alive again in comparison with the dullness and deadness of the customarily prevailing boredom.

1,1 / 1,1

There are several routes into a 1,1 / 1,1 marriage. But you end up in the same kind of situation regardless of how you get there. These are marriages of mutual resignation where it is easier to stay in than to get out. If you want to get out of the 1,1 corner while still staying married, it may help if you are clear as to how you got in. This is so because differences may be found in awareness of 1,1 / 1,1 situations.

One throughway into a 1,1 / 1,1 marriage relationship is less bumpy than are others. You glide, slide, and drift into 1,1. The gradual shift can be so slow that the mates don't feel it occurring. They can drift into stagnation with neither feeling that much is changing or has changed.

1,1 attitudes begin seeping in when two people become accustomed to reducing their tensions by backing off from them. Since real problems are left unresolved, each successive back-off leaves a larger pile of decomposing "unfinished business" between the two mates. Yet, no one particular back-off episode is big enough to cause the relationship to snap. Neither mate gets *that* worked up.

There's no panic. But after a thousand or so back-offs, the mates are so far apart in terms of feeling for each other or thinking-in-concert that it takes periscopic vision for them to see one another as live people on either side of the years' debris. They're married people living separately' together.

You might think that mates such as these would want out. Why don't they throw in the sponge, call it quits? Some do. Many don't. These marriages are like old soldiers. They "never die, they just fade away." Sometimes they even look good to outsiders. Neighbors say, "What a peaceful easygoing couple they are." Even from inside, the very people who have become solitary in togetherness more often than not fail to see how close they are to becoming marriage's Rip Van Winkles.

For far more couples than might be guessed, marriage sooner or later loses the emotional beauty and physical magnetism it once possessed. Your mate no longer seems very important. Slowly, but surely, one or both of you begins moving off alone. Rarely does this happen all at once. Usually the drifting away from your mate is slow and gradual. It may take years. But by the time the trip's complete, you're separated, whether or not you "share" a double, twins, or two rooms. It might take some serious crisis or deep tragedy to enliven you to each other again. Even that could be temporary, like waking up in the night. Another jolt to awareness may come when the last child leaves home. You might have assumed you still had something together until that happened. You *did*. You both still had a common focus in child rearing. When the kids are gone, what's left? Yet some 1,1 couples are oblivious of the poverty in their relationship, and maybe that's fortunate for them. Listen to this ritual of small talk. Grover is home from the office. Dolly's been in all day.

Dolly. Have a good day at the office, dear?
Grover. Not bad. The boss said good morning to me when he came in. Dunno what he was leading up to, accounting-wise, but I'm not worried. I'm staying on top of things all right.
Dolly. Of course, dear. Guess what? I have another whole book filled with stamps. Only three more to go, and I'll be able to get that whatnot shelf for the dinette.

Grover. Oh, I thought you'd decided on the electric blanket.

Dolly. No, I'm still a little scared of sleeping with all that electricity. You never can tell.

Grover. I guess you're right, hon. Heard from Georgie?

Dolly. Just a note. He wants more money again. Honestly, that boy!

Grover. Yeah, he thinks money grows on trees. He shoulda gone to the College of Hard Knocks, like I did.

Dolly. Well he's just a boy, dear. He'll learn.

Grover. I guess you're right. Live and learn is what they say. You do anything today? [1]

These two have long been on a downward slide. Now they're in the 1,1 corner without realizing it. In their banal chatter you can hear echoes of other Grid styles that might formerly have been characteristic of them. But now their marriage has become a husk, emptied of vitality, while the rituals and routines remain. And they're comfortable, like an old shoe which fits everywhere because it fits nowhere. Maybe Grover still remembers birthdays and anniversaries and sends a card or buys a present. He takes Dolly's arm when they're on the street. He opens doors. She cooks meals and asks each evening how he got on that day. They call each other "hon" and "dear." But there's almost no trace of liveliness left. And they may have been like this with each other for years.

Let us not call these marriages disease-ridden. They're antibiotic in the literal sense of the word. Continued backing off from what 5,5-oriented people would see as unpleasant conflict has gradually destroyed their life. People become used to each other, as the saying goes. You'll be meeting Myra and George, a 5,5 couple, in the next chapter. Here is a description of Myra after many years on the glide path into 1,1.

> . . . she no longer had reticences before her husband, and no longer worried about not having reticences. She was . . . unaware of being seen in bulgy corsets. She had become so dully habituated to married life that in her full matronliness she was as sexless as an anemic nun.[2]

A quicker plunge into 1,1 occurs when you go through some critical incident that brings you and your mate to a high pitch of emotional intensity. To get heated up to the same level, one or both of you needs to have been seething with frustration for some time over the other's shortcomings. When, suddenly, all this culminates in open aggression—either physical combat or violent verbal infighting—the relationship is ruptured. It is a snap, crackle, or pop that results in a 1,1 relationship from that time onward. Unless some very special effort is made to resolve the conflict fully and put it behind you forever, that aggressive outburst forms a turning point in your married lives. It's likely to be a "point of no return," never forgotten by either of you. Both of you are keenly aware of how different the situation is now than what it was before.

You can hear this before/after quality in the discussion between Jeff and Gregg. They are close friends and are exchanging confidences while on a hunting trip.

Gregg. Years ago I suppose our friends would have described us as an "opposites attract" kind of couple. I'm a strong-willed, ambitious S.O.B. with one aim in mind: success. Betty, when I first met her, was a sweet kid. She adored me, and was very much interested in helping me get ahead. We were both eager to build our lives together and to live for each other.

Jeff. I guess things changed, huh?

Gregg. Well, for all practical purposes we broke up a decade ago although we've stayed together. The first few months of marriage were a ball but soon I found myself getting angry at her because she couldn't seem to get things done. Meals, household arrangements, budgeting—everything she touched seemed to get into a mess. Of course, I used to let her know how I felt, and she got more and more scared of me. The more I blew my stack, the worse she got. It came to a point where she'd scarcely take a drink of water without getting my approval first. And then—the way I was in those days—I'd despise her for being such a weakling. God, I must have given her torment from every direction!

Jeff. Look, I mean . . . if it's all past rectifying, why keep on punishing yourself? If she's left you . . .

Gregg. Oh, we're still together—at least, we're married and living in the same house. I don't get angry at her nowadays, and I don't think she'd be frightened anymore, even if I did. We're dead to each other.

Jeff. What in the hell happened?

Gregg. One time, when we'd both had too much to drink, I read the riot act. I was really going to straighten her out. I gave her line and verse. She listened in a sort of paralyzed way. By the time I'd finished, something had snapped between us like an overstretched rubber band. That was our marriage—ping! She said something and I went berserk, I took my wedding band off and threw it at her. It caught the back of her hand as she brought it up in front of her face—must have stung like hell. She gave a screech, slipped hers off and slung it at me. She buried her head in her arms, but there was no sobbing— at least, not while I was there. I turned and walked away. That was it.

Jeff. And haven't you ever become reconciled, never gotten together to talk it out? How do you mean your marriage just snapped?

Gregg. Exactly as I said. From that day, our marriage went slack. It even seemed more problem-free at first, as though we had no misunderstandings to talk about. Each of us went about life in a new way—independently. No more reliance on each other. Nothing she did seemed to bug me any more. I left her alone—of course, I was kind of ashamed at first. But it got to be a way of life. I give her money every month, and she keeps the household going and spends whatever she wants on herself. I don't want to know, and she doesn't bother me with details.

Jeff. Don't you ever do *anything* together?

Gregg. Oh yes, though not in bed—I've had to go elsewhere for that.

Jeff. Then what *do* you do together?

Gregg. Oh, we keep up appearances. For instance, we go to parties. We have a tacit understanding about not seeming to be at loggerheads. Before, we used to fight a lot—or I'd fight—over what to wear, what time to arrive and when to leave. But not anymore. When we go to one of these parties we start by moving around together and talking with people just as any husband and wife would. Then she drifts into one group and I get into another. From then till we leave, each of us flies solo. I watch what I do and say, never criticizing her, and she extends the same courtesy to me. Then we leave. A pleasantry or two, and we go home. That's it, until the next one.

Jeff. What do you do between parties?

Gregg. When I'm not out getting some temporary relaxation—and Jeff, sometimes I just *have* to—I bring work home or catch up with my professional reading. She's joined a couple of book clubs. Sometimes we watch TV if the same show happens to interest both of us. But she's got one in her bedroom and so have I; so that's another thing we don't have to quarrel over.

Jeff. What do you *talk* about?

Gregg. I might say, "What's the book tonight?" and she'll tell me. She might mention an upcoming TV special and I'll say, "Let's watch it." But usually we stay quiet most of the evening, and then it's just "Been a long day. See you tomorrow." "Goodnight."

Jeff. That sounds . . . well, like death in life. Is there anything to prevent you getting a reasonable divorce or annulment, so that both of you can start afresh?

Gregg. Why bother? I'd say we're as "successful" as many another couple, and probably better than most. At least we know where we stand. She keeps up the house, I give her all the money she wants, we cooperate on social occasions.

How does that rate as a relationship? About zero for emotional fulfillment. For building an estate, avoiding family or social criticism, and for survival purposes generally, it may suffice. The wife is providing the outer forms and keeping to protocol without having to proffer anything of what they lost a decade or more ago. No more double binds for her. The husband is paying for services and as long as their current existence continues undisturbed, it'll do. He has no higher expectation than that. After the snap, both abandoned each other as intimates.

So, the chances are good that, if you've come into a 1,1 marriage by the 9,1 snap-crackle-and-pop route, you're aware of it. Weary wranglers or combinations whereby one mate uses suppression tactics as Gregg did are the usual candidates.[3]

The glide-slide-or-drift route most likely starts at 5,5. Skill in adjusting to one another's negative qualities by backing off instead of confronting issues makes it likely that couples glide from 5,5 into 1,1 on wings of silence.[4]

1,1 / 1,9

Another possibility needs to be examined, which is illustrated in the next conversation. Pam is weeping on the shoulder of her sister Polly who has come to visit after five years. Polly asked Pam an innocent question, "How's Honeymoon Cottage? Do you still enjoy it as much each year as the first time?"

Pam. No. We haven't been there for a long time. He just doesn't seem to care about me anymore. I'm so distressed about it.

Polly. What happened? You always seemed so devoted to each other.

Pam. I still love him, I love him very much. But he's not the same. You'd think I was just a piece of furniture.

Polly. What does he do?

Pam. I do things for him and he doesn't appreciate them. I buy new clothes, dye my hair, and he doesn't even comment unless I ask him what he thinks. He's even forgotten I have a birthday.

Polly. What do you think caused it?

Pam. Oh, I don't know. Perhaps he's sick, or worried about some troubles he has at work. But I'm so scared he doesn't love me anymore.

Pam is baffled and hurt. She is unable to understand her mate's behavior. Although he might be sick, she's really sensing he's rejecting her. In this case, we don't know whether from Pete's standpoint it was a snap, crackle, and pop into 1,1 or a 5,5 glide path. We do know he's in the bottom-left corner of the Grid and that it's painful for Pam. It's possible to see a very significant thing about a 1,1 / 1,9 marriage from the 1,9 point of view. The 1,9 person is hurt. High mate concern meets no response. It's just the kind of ignoring that can't be ignored, that can't be excused and that can't be accepted. Pam will go on feeling hurt for as long as Pete stays in his 1,1 no-care position.

1,1 / 9,1

Another pattern is seen when one mate remains 9,1 while the other turns into 1,1. Tim is in 1,1 after a 9,1 snap, crackle, and pop session. You see the distinctiveness of his kind of 1,1 in contrast with the more passive 1,1 examples we've had. He takes action to get away from Patti's 9,1 shrewishness.

Tim. Let me rest after the day's work. I'll take the trash out after
supper.
Patti. Why not now? You've got time! You got nothing else to do.
Tim. Yes, darling . . . later. . . . Excuse me . . . I'll be back.
Patti. Where are you going?
Tim. Out.
Patti. If you're late there'll be no supper.
Tim. Yes, darling.
Patti. Did you look at the bills?
Tim. No.
Patti. Don't you care?
Tim. Yes.
Patti. Why didn't you look?
Tim. I'm going to, later.
Patti. Later, later, later! You'll drive me crazy with that word. Why
do you use it?
Tim. I don't like the word "now."
Patti. What's wrong with the word "now"?
Tim. I'll tell you later!
Patti. Get out of here. Don't come back. No supper for you, now
or later, till you learn to move your lazy ass. Scram!
Tim. Yes, darling. . . .

The likelihood is that Tim's a lively fellow once he gets away from the house. At least his movement is nimble to get out of her line of fire. We saw the converse relationship (husband 9,1 and the wife 1,1) in Barrett's description of how he and his wife got along.* The difference is that she probably came into 1,1 from a 1,9 slide.

* Chapter 4, pp. 41–42.

Her love was terrorized into extinction. After that, only resignation was left.

It's said we live in a society in which feelings of alienation are high and getting higher. Young people feel alienated from their parents; college students from the Establishment; union members from their companies; and so on. Marriage Grid 1,1 is alienation between mates. It's present when the human basis for the relationship has gone. The husk remains but the meat and juice of marriage have disappeared.

1,1 attitudes represent a shrinking away from the other mate and a general belief that a deeper, more vivacious, and mutually rewarding relationship is either not possible or not worth having. Is it inevitable that marriages drift in this direction? Can the proposition *the longer the worse* be changed to *the longer the better?* Yes. How you can make your marriage more satisfying will be examined in a later chapter.

CHAPTER 11 | 5,5—SECURITY THROUGH STATUS

For a majority of couples in America today, marriage neither vibrates with vitality nor does it sound the hollow ring of emptiness. It's somewhere midway between these extremes. If your marriage is like this, you might have expected to get more out of it when you started out than you know you're getting now. Yet what you're getting is enough to make staying together enjoyable and worthwhile.

One key feature of the 5,5 marriage style is awareness of *social cadence*. Themes, rhythms, and tempos resonate through the part of society to which a person feels himself belonging. You accept them as your own. The most reliable ones—those which specify sound behavior and conduct—are formulated by the people you associate with or admire from a distance.

The Taylor family is at supper. Floyd, a lawyer, and his wife Stella are talking with their daughter Jeri, a college graduate, who is now a schoolteacher. They mention her romantic interest in Danny, a boy of unknown background and education.

Floyd. I don't know anything about this Danny. Tell me who he is and what he does.
Stella. What do you know about this young man, Jeri?
Jeri. I met him only recently. He moved here last January and he works in the camera department at Kenworth's. He's nice! He likes music, sports, bowling, just the same as I do.

Floyd. I don't want to run your life for you, Jeri, but do you think you ought to be seen so much with him? You don't seem to date anyone else nowadays.

Jeri. Well, I like Danny a lot. He's taking me to the country club dance Saturday.

Floyd. Stella, why don't you talk to her?

Stella. Jeri, why don't you date some of the nice boys you meet at the parties your father and I take you to? And there are those young lawyers from Dad's office. We could easily invite them here one evening.

Jeri. I don't really like them as much as Danny.

Stella. But we have to live up to our position, remember. This is a small town, and who you're seen with affects our reputation as a family. Surely it's no harder to like a boy from another good family than it is to like this Danny person?

Floyd. What your mother means is that we don't think you should go out with him.

Jeri. But Saturday's all arranged! I invited Danny to the club myself.

Floyd. Then you'll have to uninvite him.

For Floyd and Stella, the whole issue is not what Danny might do to Jeri, but what Jeri's date with Danny might do to their status in the town.[1]

This example comes from what is routinely thought of as the middle class. Yet, 5,5 adherence to norms and role behavior can be found in all walks of life and all economic groups. The significant feature in finding security is copying the behavior and life-style of other people whom you respect. Generally, you try to live by what you take to be *their* standards instead of establishing standards of your own which would provide you with more truly personal criteria of self-esteem.[2]

A second major source for a 5,5-oriented person's outlook, opinions, and actions is "established authority." Those whom you've selected as your authorities might be positioned high up in the organizations to which you belong or give allegiance. Other status figures to whom you refer for calibrating your own conduct and actions don't have any official rank or position but are well-known and widely revered. These are men and women who have disseminated knowledge and leadership. What they say carries weight. It is taken at face value in a second-nature kind of way. The very fact that they occupy secure niches makes them safe and trustworthy. They are your sources of information as to what, in general, you should be doing, thinking, saying, and feeling, whether the topic is inflation, war, young people, crime, welfare, pollution, or whatever.

Ned's wife, Deirdre, needles him in a 9,1 way about his 5,5 reliance on others to mold his thinking.

Ned. It seems to me that kids nowadays probably aren't too different from the way kids were two thousand and more years ago. Why, Aristotle was complaining about their lack of respect and how they wanted to go against society, even in his time. Maybe there's too much attention given to them.

Deirdre. Yes, Jack Dawson writes good editorials in *This Week's News.*

Ned. Well, I've been thinking a lot about the problem, what with Bill going to high school next year.

Deirdre. I'm sure Jack Dawson will appreciate that.

Ned. Huh?

Deirdre. If he knew you were *thinking* about the same issues in the same way, he'd be glad to have this proof of how closely in touch he is with the man-on-the-street.

Ned. But I think he's right.

Deirdre. The editorials in *This Week's News* are the most talked about.

Ned. Okay, okay. So what's wrong with agreeing with them?

Deirdre Not a thing, apparently. All the girls at the office do.

Ned. With whom?

Deirdre. With each other.

Ned. Are you kidding me again?

Deirdre. Is there any reason to?

Ned. No, of course not.

Deirdre. Then of course I'm not.

Deirdre is giving pretentious Ned a lesson that she will probably repeat again and again to little avail. Basically, he hasn't enough self-assurance to begin comparing his own judgments against those of recognized authorities.

Something about the way society operates makes these community-packaged prescriptions easy to dispense. That something is called *roles*. The use of the term *role* here is not far different from its use on stage and in films. When you play an onstage role you're conforming to the expectations an author has put into the script. Other people's expectations will write you a lifetime script if you adhere to them. Because of the way it's organized, society prescribes roles for husband, wife, father, mother, teenager, boy-child, girl-child, boss, subordinate, professor, student, and so on. What society doesn't tell you is how to fit some of these roles together in the individual life you're leading.

Here's a wife's description of 5,5 mutual accommodation and of the way each mate is tied into role routines.

> The children are a lot of fun, keep us pretty busy, and there are lots of outside things—you know, like Little League and the P.T.A. and the Swim Club, and even the company parties aren't always so bad. . . . We laugh at the same things sometimes, but we don't really laugh together—the way we used to. But, as he said to me the other night—with one or two under the belt, I think— "You know, you're still a little fun now and then." . . .
>
> Now, I don't say this to complain, not in the least. There's a cycle to life. There are things you do in high school. And different things you do in college. Then you're a young adult. And then you're middle-aged. That's where we are now. . . . I'll admit that I do yearn for the old days when sex was a big thing and going out was fun and I hung onto every thing he said about his work and his ideas as if they were coming from a genius or something. But then you get the children and other responsibilities. I have the home and Bob has a tremendous burden of responsibility at the office. . . . He's completely responsible for setting up the new branch now. . . . You have to adjust to these things and we both try to gracefully. . . . Anniversaries though do sometimes remind you kind of hard. . . .[3]

The wife's remarks suggest that this couple is departing 5,5, gliding into 1,1. But each party is accommodating by playing an assigned cluster of roles as mate.[4] Note a related trend: As marriage intimacy diminishes, they begin putting more into family and community roles, some of them new. These other roles expand or crowd in to fill what would otherwise be a widening void between husband and wife.

Now we can investigate how the core assumptions that underlie this 5,5 approach work their way into everyday married life.

The words *equal, eclectic,* and *workable* summarize three key considerations 5,5-oriented people keep in mind when considering and dealing with problems. "Equal" has in it the 50–50 notion— equal shares, equal burdens for both. Anything can be divided into his/her halves. "Eclectic" denotes readiness to shop around for ingredients to put into the solution. It is presumed that any single ingredient which is selected as being good will combine well with all others. Everything is mechanical, stirred up together in a neutral mix-master. If you prepared food this way you might mince and blend apples with liver if you thought both were necessary for a balanced diet. "Workable" is the idea that the first practical solution you come up with is *the* solution; there's no need to spend further time on improving it or devising another. The question, "Is there any better solution?" doesn't occur to you. You see an end to your problem and isn't that enough?

5,5 decision-making has a ring of analysis and judgment about it. You weigh facts and data on pro-and-con balancing scales until the right choice seems obvious. Even the decision not to decide has this character. If things don't seem to be in balance yet, you don't make a move. Social wisdom is relied on as gospel.[5] Homey truisms, common sense, and group acceptability are taken to provide a sound basis for everyday living. This approach enables routine choices to be made easily since the boundaries of what's acceptable are defined by what others do and think and feel and believe, whether or not contradictions arise between what's done one day and what's done the next. A 5,5-oriented mate tends to become a kind of "marital bureaucrat" seeking to administer halfway reasonable solutions as a basis for living together with another.

Many feel that 5,5 compromise and adjustment on little decisions is far less significant than the same approach applied to decisions of greater magnitude. There is an obvious truth in this, yet certain unstated consequences merit mention. One is that the same 5,5 compromises and accommodations, which become habitual ways of reaching small-scale decisions, tend to expand and expand as life goes on and to become standard practice for making the larger decisions as well. The other is that little decisions made many times are not really little. They can accumulate and create far larger problems which themselves are manageable only by further 5,5 compromise and accommodation.

Here is an indication of how reliance on what friends think influences decisions made in a 5,5 home. Claudette and Ron have long looked forward to the joys of foreign travel. They are trying to decide on their dream trip. Just what are the dimensions of this dream?

Claudette. Yes, it's finally within our reach. You've saved up six weeks' vacation and we can afford it at last. We don't have to be the Never-Been-Anywheres anymore. Won't Europe be wonderful? You *do* want to go over there, don't you?

Ron. Yes, I'd love to see London, Paris, Rome, Madrid, and maybe Scandinavia or Greece.

Claudette. Of course, how *far* we go depends on how we go. Ship and plane fares cost about the same. I rather prefer going by ship. It's far more relaxing than plane travel. And you *meet* people.

Ron. But the ship takes about five days each way. That's nearly two weeks. We may get there fresher but we'd miss seeing some wonderful and famous places. I want to be able to tell the folks here about countries they've never visited.

Claudette. But spending all this money at one time, I think we ought to make the most of it. I want to see as much as possible, but it's nice to make new friends along the way. You know, people of our social standing we could keep in touch with for years to come. On ships you can move around and you have time to choose and get to know people as friends. Not like a few hours in a flying barn. And not like on a half-day tour.

Ron. Well, either way's OK with me, dear.

Claudette. But it's your vacation, too, I want us to agree.

Ron. How about us going by ship and flying back? With a package deal it doesn't cost too much more, and we'd get the best of "three possible worlds." We'd make a lot of shipboard friends, have additional time for seeing places really worth talking about later on, and arrive fresh as daisies.

The weighing factor in this decision is almost completely status-based. "Places to talk about. . . ." "The chance to meet 'important' people."

Making decisions can be greatly simplified by adopting roles. The stresses and strains of doubt are eliminated. If a decision is based on the appropriate role with its prescriptions of what's acceptable, there is little reason to challenge the validity of the choice. Roles help you to neatly parcel out your activities for compatibility. If both believe, for instance, "Because he is a *husband,* he should never operate the vacuum cleaner," the question "Who should vacuum?" is not something to argue over. Many daily activities in a 5,5/5,5 marriage are related to the accepted roles of husband and wife.[6] Shopping for groceries, choice of furnishings, and maintenance of the general decor, for example, may be wifely responsibilities. The wife's judgments and those of her "authorities" set the rules in that area. The husband takes charge of home repairs, selecting the new car, and negotiating the trade-in. Under the 5,5 division-of-labor concept, his choices in that area are accepted.

Role prescriptions are not so cast-iron rigid that they can never change. But any change authorized by respected sources will be picked up quickest.

Roles exist throughout the fabric of society and any one person can play a large number of them. A man may simultaneously or in close succession operate as husband, father, son, bank president, organization member, alumnus, boss, and so on. A woman may function as wife, mother, daughter, scheduler, bridge player, house cleaner, cook, chauffeur, hostess, etc., in the course of a day. Every adult is cast in a number of situations.[7] But here's the 5,5 point. Whether or not you are "playing" a role—as distinct from enacting one you've created for yourself—depends on whether or not you accept society's role prescriptions with little question. If you're 5,5, you conform to them as though the requirements were final. Not much ad-libbing, free wheeling, or experimenting comes into play. Tradition, the media, and group membership provide a script for operating as husband or as wife.[8]

The package includes appropriate *attitudes, convictions, beliefs,* and *values.* It lays out vacations and trips, sports and hobbies, social club and political party, and, beyond that, you name it. Security comes from knowing how to act and from being aware of what's expected of oneself according to the rules of the roles. This relieves 5,5-oriented individuals from the risk of exercising personal judgment. Little or no initiative is required for finding out what is currently the right thing to do. The most you might need to do is to improvise occasionally in situations where the rules give no guidance.

Here is an example showing how people who think in a 5,5 way can become prisoners unwittingly controlled by the concepts of friends. Richard and Jenny are having a discussion about their financial situation.

Richard. The thing I don't like about being—about not having money . . .

Jenny. We're not *star*ving.

Richard. No, we eat, but if we didn't belong to the, the club we'd eat a lot better.

Jenny. Yes.

Richard. If we didn't try to live like our friends we might put something away sometime.

Jenny. Um-hum.

Richard. Friends we didn't have, by the way, until we moved here, took this place. . . .

Jenny. But *friends.*

Richard. Oh, yeah, well, you find them. We don't live right.

Jenny. Oh God!

Richard. We don't!

Jenny. Poor baby.

Richard. You live in a forty-thousand-dollar house and you have to smoke bad cigarettes to get the coupons so you can afford a good vacuum so you can clean it; you belong to the club so you can pay back dinner invitations from people you wouldn't even know if you hadn't joined the club in the first place, and you *joined* the club, *and* learned how to play tennis, because you decided to move into a neighborhood where everybody belonged to the club.[9]

What has happened to this pair? Society dictates their life. It tells them how to pick associates, what they should be doing, and how they ought to do it. In a certain sense, they have probably achieved more and been more successful in material terms than if they had not gotten into the rat race.[10] In another sense, they have mortgaged their souls to society and are unable to escape its demanding conformities.

Another hallmark of a person expressing convictions based on 5,5 assumptions is the notion that whatever his membership group embraces is correct. He has the idea that majority opinion carries the weight of facts, data, and logic. It's equated with rationality even though it may only reflect a fashionable notion. The presumption is that whenever a number of people agree, the conclusion they support must be the right one. This "Fifty million Frenchmen can't be wrong" outlook is an example of the persuasive power of social consensus. For a 5,5-oriented person, social norms have the certainty of facts.

However, the key to 5,5 convictions is not simply that they are based on social consensus, for persons with other Grid orientations may behave in conventional ways also. The clue is in what lies *beneath* stated convictions. If you as an outside observer try digging below the surface to determine *why* a 5,5-oriented person does what is done and believes what is believed, you are likely to find his tenets shallow. Little nourishing mental soil is to be found in which the seeds of opinion from outside can root and compete with others for survival.

A particular problem arises when a 5,5-oriented person notices a discrepancy between his own thoughts or actions and those of his fellow group members. The problem is one of picking up the cadence again to get back into social rhythm. A second problem is in doing what is normal or average. Thus, he is likely to be comforted if his opinion goes along with the majority of a poll or if his child's behavior falls in the range for what is normally expected.

Since the opinions and attitudes expressed by authorities and status figures constitute a vital source of ideas, public media—the carriers of these opinions—have become far more important in molding thought than ever before. Widespread watching of TV gives the 5,5 appetites much food for "what to think." A 5,5-oriented person likes to quote attitudes and convictions that seem up-to-the-minute but are not way out. "I read it in the paper yesterday. . . ." "The ten o'clock news. . . ." He feels no personal loss if his opinion is challenged. He can reference its origin, while disowning it with "Well, you can't believe everything you read" or "Newsmen are only human." This use of public opinion allows him to take either side of an argument and shift back and forth depending on how the scales in a discussion are balanced. But try to get a straight answer to the question, "What do you *really* think?," and you find yourself fenced in with hedges.

There are few absolutes for a 5,5-oriented person. For every rule there's an exception. It is unlikely you'll hear terms such as *always* and *never*. He's cautious to protect himself with conditional phrases that provide outs should his position be rejected. He may "always be in doubt but he's never wrong."

5,5 teamwork is based on division of labor. Who labors on what is governed by social convention. The idea is that each person is capable of doing certain things for the marriage. So you divide these up as equally as possible, and in this way each of you supports the other. If you tried to do more things together, you might find yourselves quarreling over who does what and how. With smoothly adjusted roles you don't clash. The motto is "separate but equal." The most likely version is that the husband has a job and the wife keeps house and takes responsibility for caring for the children. He looks after the car and the lawn while she cleans and straightens inside. If they have two cars, the husband drives to work and the wife runs an all-purpose taxi service.

Good common sense characterizes this idea of teamwork. It avoids sidestepping of responsibility and duplication of effort. It permits each to do what he does best. But look deeper. Many feel that this kind of teamwork shows how marriages of today are breaking down. Activities are so separate and self-contained that many times a day you might wonder, "So I'm married. For what?" The 5,5 kind of teamwork does tend to separate mates, having them work apart rather than helping them join together in shared pursuits. It creates an unshared world for each where the other tends to become a guest, sometimes uninvited. It works against the notion that "two heads are better than one."

Here's how the approach to practical tasks within marriage begins to give the entire relationship the atmosphere of a chore. Maurice has just sent the children to bed early, as punishment for what he termed their "bad manners and lack of respect."

Dianne. Maurice, I know you don't worry much about how the children behave, except for a fit of bad temper now and then. I hate to say it, but I do think you overdid things this time.
Maurice. Please, will you stop picking at me? I'm tired. Really, I can't be expected to do two jobs: working at the office all day and controlling the kids when I get home. It's obvious they're getting out of hand when they fight with each other and me too over something as trivial as a TV program.
Dianne. If I'm going to teach them manners, you shouldn't jump in and make a scene. I was going to talk to each of them before they went to bed, about flying off the handle. Now you've created such a bad example, it'll be hard for me to explain why they can't carry on like you did.

Dianne feels Maurice is overstepping his bounds and invading her territory. She'll thank him to leave her responsibilities alone.

Specialization of effort is not in itself exclusively a 5,5 idea. Under many conditions, specialization is a valid concept because it permits people to do whatever they are best qualified to do. Specialization does avoid the wastefulness of unnecessary duplication. It is 5,5 when it becomes a mechanical basis for marriage activities where opportunities for real sharing and joint achievement are sacrificed.

Having the "right" emotions is an important part of a 5,5 marriage. Displaying too intense an emotion could expose a person to criticism. The solution lies in finding criteria of judgment concerning what is appropriate. Role prescriptions are a useful source of guidance for emotional relations. From them one learns what one should feel—what's safe and what's enough. For instance, men are never supposed to cry and ladies never shout. Nonetheless, placing limits on one's feelings can deny a person many experiences of life's potential richness. Such is the case when you withhold full commitment to an idea, an objective, or even your mate so as not to be disappointed in the event something goes awry.

When it comes to expectations, a 5,5-oriented person is likely to keep in tune with the *status quo,* taking things as they are.

Arnold is describing himself to his brother Murray:

Arnold. . . . I am willing to deal with the available world and I do not choose to shake it up but to live with it. There's the people who spill things, and the people who get spilled on; I do not choose to notice the stains, Murray. I have a wife and I have children and business, like they say, is business. I am not an exceptional man, so it is possible for me to stay with things the way they are. I'm lucky. I'm gifted. I have a talent for surrender. I'm at peace.[11]

The 5,5 quality in Arnold's self-description is seen in his endorsement of the *status quo,* in spite of its admitted imperfections, and in his readiness to cooperate with it on its terms rather than exerting influences that would improve it.

So, too, in marriage you have only moderate expectations for yourself. By the same token, you don't expect the moon from your mate. Most of the time you feel neither delighted nor despairing as you react to what your mate does. As long as things are in equilibrium, everything's okay. If your anticipations were higher than what your mate could easily fulfill, after a while you would probably shift your expectation level down a few notches. However, performance *above* expectations is something to be proud of and tell your friends about.

In emotional relations, you feel neither suffocated by excess affection nor deprived by sensitivity to a lack of it. Your consistent theme is the normal, usual, and proper degree of intimacy between married people. You don't want to set a bad example for the kids

or scandalize the neighbors. Mostly, you occupy the zone of passiveness, of being accustomed to each other, although feelings of
friendly companionship or tinges of disappointment and insecurity
do sometimes arise. Wide swings away from moderation and stability
are rare.

When expectations are shifted to meet what's possible, life feels
predictable and sound. If you think ahead, this is in terms of
known milestones of life. For example, when the husband is in an
organization where seniority counts, 5,5 mates' plans can take into
account predictable raises up to a retirement date twenty years distant. Charles has his life pretty well on schedule and he's modestly
proud of what he's doing and where he's going.

Nancy. Would you be interested in this Extension Course on Life
   Planning that's being advertised?
Charles. No, I don't think so. We're all set, the way things are.
Nancy. Even so, we've not really plotted anything out in detail. I
   mean, can you tell me where you're going to be five or fifteen
   years from now?
Charles. The best guarantee of where I'll be is to stay with the
   company. I'm steadily moving up the ladder. Five years from
   now I'll be one promotion title from where I am presently,
   and I figure my present chances of being three ahead in fifteen
   years' time are about seventy-five percent. There's the retirement plan, I get sick benefits, and so on. The fringe benefits
   here are wonderful from a security point of view. And in addition, we have endowment policies for the kids' college education, and a lot of life insurance. What could we gain by a
   Life Planning course?
Nancy. I guess you're right. I hadn't realized how much you had
   planned ahead.

While all is very rosy right now, who knows whether the road
Charles is traveling will be smooth all the way? Whether it is or not,
he will probably adjust his speed to the hills, curves, and detours so
that all's well that ends well.

Heated conflict between 5,5-oriented mates is unlikely. The reason is that while you're trying to exert influence, you also want to

avoid losing. There are several ways to get around to a no-lose situation.

The fact that "everybody's doing it," is a powerful argument to a 5,5-oriented person. This is often expressed as "What do the neighbors think?" Of course, when no one else seems to be doing it, that becomes just as powerful a factor in the other direction.

This example shows how dependent 5,5-oriented people are on others to resolve disagreement. George and Myra are having a party for their son Ted and his friends. The young people begin to disappear into the cars out front and George tries to coax the rest to stay in the house.

George. Say, if any of you fellows are thirsty, there's some dandy ginger ale.
Guests. Oh! Thanks!
George, to his wife. I'd like to go in there and throw some of those young pups out of the house! They talk down to me like I was the butler! I'd like to—
Myra. I know, only everybody says, all the mothers tell me, unless you stand for them, if you get angry because they go out to their cars to have a drink, they won't come to your house anymore, and we wouldn't want Ted left out of things, would we? [12]

George is caught between the desire to control the young people's behavior, which he thinks is inappropriate, and the fear that they will reject his efforts. Myra goes to the community for her attitudes of "everybody says . . ." and "all the mothers tell me. . . ." This community reference library provides an easy resolution to conflict situations between 5,5-oriented husbands and wives.

Another situation comes up when you feel a need to act but can't pick up any cadence or indication of which way to go. The social clues as to what is considered acceptable are either non-existent or invisible. What is one to do? If you can, you sit tight, avoiding commitment to any point of view until the circumstances become entirely clear. In effect, you're buying time so that you can listen and pick up a wavelength. Often you can conduct your own private opinion poll to get a feel of what others think or would do.

You "market research" several points of view, testing each under hypothetical or neutral conditions and measuring the reactions they provoke.

If references to roles, rules, or to authoritative sources do not produce easy agreement, the 5,5 tactic, par excellence, is to split the difference. 5,5-oriented people don't relish win-lose conflict in the way that 9,1 happy warriors do. Rather, a win-lose situation is seen as a trap—structured so that someone will be victor and someone will be vanquished. To a 5,5-impregnated mind, that's too much to risk. Besides, other people might get to hear of a husband-wife fight, and, if that happened, the damage would seem several times worse.[13] The preferred solution is for each partner to gain and lose the same amount. It's the idea of "give and take."

Many tactics which have this no-win, no-lose quality are germane for relieving conflict. The major one is compromise. For example, maybe the husband has taken one position, the wife another, and neither wants to abandon his position so completely as to move all the way across to the other mate's. To show reasonableness and flexibility, the husband might propose an intermediate position on middle ground. It doesn't fully solve the problem, but it wasn't intended to. The aim is to find a solution that's sufficient to relieve the pressure or move each mate forward to the safe limits set by what the other will tolerate. Give-and-take compromise provides each person with something of what he wanted, even though not all. Both can live with this part-way solution. Both feel they have been treated fairly. Each feels good about having been "big enough," that is, flexible enough to bend away from his previous convictions and reach an accommodation.

Laura is trying to find some such position which will be acceptable to her husband. Wilbur has put in overtime at the office the past week. On Saturday morning he settled down in the hammock after a late breakfast to read the paper.

Laura. Wilbur, have you forgotten? The grass is high. It looks real shaggy.

Wilbur. I've been under pressure all week and now I want to relax. Give me a break, I'm not my usual peppy self.

Laura. I know it's been tough on you, but we're the last ones on

the block to get started this weekend. I'm ashamed. If the
mower wasn't so heavy I'd push it myself.

Wilbur. But the way I feel now, long grass looks OK. It might even
be good for the roots to let it grow longer before fall.

Laura. You know how everyone around here starts mentioning
property values whenever someone's let his garden get untidy.
I know you're tired, dear, but how about you mowing the
front while I clip? The shrubs hide the back well enough, so
let's let it go for another day or so.

Even when Wilbur wants to forgo the cutting ritual just once in a
while, he doesn't stand much chance against Laura who is backed
up by the neighbors.

Here's still a different way to get around a problem which is
causing friction, yet without really getting to its causes.

Clarence is fifty, Vinnie is about the same age. They have been
married twenty years and have a son going off to Yale. The following conversation tells something of her 5,5 attitude toward keeping
track of household expenses and avoiding conflict between Clarence and herself.

Clarence. We can't go on month after month having the household
accounts in such a mess.

Vinnie. No—and Clare dear, I've thought of a system that will
make my bookkeeping perfect.

Clarence. I'm certainly relieved to hear that. What is it?

Vinnie. Well, Clare, you never make half the fuss over how much
I've spent as you do over my not being able to remember what
I've spent it for.

Clarence. Exactly. This house must be run on a business basis.
That's why I insist on your keeping books.

Vinnie. That's the whole point, Clare. All we have to do is open
charge accounts everywhere and the stores will do my bookkeeping for me.

Clarence. Wait a minute, Vinnie.

Vinnie. Then when the bills came in you'd know exactly where
your money had gone.

Clarence. I certainly would.—Vinnie, I get enough bills as it is.

Vinnie. Yes, and those bills always help. They show you where I
    spent the money. Now, if we had charge accounts every-
    where—
Clarence. Now, Vinnie,—I'm not so sure that—
Vinnie. Clare, dear, don't you hate those arguments we have every
    month. I certainly do. Not to have those I should think would
    be worth something to you.
Clarence. Well, I'll open an account at Lewis and Conger's—and
    one at McCreery's to begin with—we'll see how it works out.[14]

What can be noticed here is dependence on a mechanical system
rather than upon systematic household financial management. By
letting the stores send bills, which can then be collected together
and totaled against payments, it becomes obvious how household
money is being spent. But this will not permit useful control to be
exercised on spending, or joint consideration of the wisdom of buying this or that or of how appropriate is a particular purchase in
the context of current financial resources. The latter would most
likely lead to arguments regarding how much to spend and what to
spend it on.

So 5,5 approaches to conflict have several underlying themes.
One has you and your mate looking outside for a standard which
tells you what is right. If you fail to find one or if you find non-har-
monic cadences, the civilized way of handling conflict is to compromise, going half-and-half so as to keep a fair balance, or to find
some administrative way to get around the potential sore spots.

A well-known marriage manual sums things up this way:

In human relations we may sometimes take a lesson from the
oyster. Were there no irritating grain of sand that found its way
into the oyster's shell, there would be no pearl. The oyster
makes it possible to get along with the grain of sand by
smoothing over its rough edges until it is no longer irritating.[15]

Are *you* someone's pearl by now?

When two people marry but neither invests really deep emotional
involvement or creative effort in the male-female relationship, it is
likely that both of them have a 5,5 orientation toward intimacy.

Marriage is viewed as a practical way to fit into society, and sex in marriage is seen as the "usual" thing. Intimacy is more closely related to companionship than to passion.

An attitude toward the depth of emotions possible between a husband and wife can be seen in the following:

> Why take an unnecessary risk? Intimacy looks . . . like an investment in a high-risk stock: nice if you win, disastrous if you lose, and therefore best left alone.[16]

This is not to imply that sex is wholly *absent*.[17] Performed in the right way with the right frequency it can be a pleasant feature of marriage.

Remember Johnny and Wilma? * Wilma is loaded with 5,5 notions, though she can crack a 9,1 whip too. "It's not romantic in the morning. . . . It's what you do in bed, nowhere else. . . . It's Saturday night, so let's do it. . . . Twice a week is about right. . . ."

Here's another example of sexual attitudes whereby each mate automatically takes what others are reputed to do as the correct standard for themselves. These two are on their honeymoon.

Grace. What, *again?* Is it safe? I've heard it can soften your brain.
Clem. No, you must be thinking of something else. We're married, it's good for us. Why, the pastor almost said so in those counseling talks.
Grace. He didn't say how often, though.
Clem. Well, that's not his bag really. But Kinsey did. Or what amounts to the same thing, he figured the averages. At *least* three times a week . . . c'mon now.
Grace. Please. . . . I'm trying to think. I used to read Kinsey when my parents were out. Wasn't it *twice?*
Clem. Well, I'm no expert, I guess. It's between two or three. Anyway, did he study *how* they did it? You know, the usual ways?
Grace. Man on top, mainly. Sometimes they reversed. It's mentioned how long it takes—around five minutes, I think.

---

* Chapter 1, pp. 10–11; Chapter 4, pp. 58–59.

Clem. Looks like we're pretty typical, 'cept I'm sure not wasting time! How about trying it another way?

Grace. No. I don't want us to turn into a couple of perverts. The regular way's all right. "A place for everything . . . ," remember?

Spontaneous? Hardly. They have a kaffeeklatsch about it first. Boring and dull? Not exactly either. They are finding sex is an interesting part of marriage!

5,5 sex is the kind where you're guided by what others do—including where, how, how much, and how long. But how do you learn what is "right?" The law prohibits sex as a spectator sport and you can't take lessons in it at Arthur Murray's. So mostly it is learning by experience. Sometimes you listen to and learn from others as to which way is acceptable and why. You want to be adequate, so you pick up all the tips you can. You read treatises and manuals. There are plenty of books that tell you the answers to many of these perplexing questions you feel a need to be informed about. After a period of adjustment to one another, you can settle down on a "this is the right way" kind of schedule.[18]

Here, then, is the complete Mirror for 5,5.

Problem-solving Relations. I go for workable, even though not perfect, decisions which we can both live with on a give-and-take basis. I express opinions, attitudes, and ideas in a tentative way so I can accommodate in order to avoid being too different from others. I want us to cooperate according to what society prescribes for husbands and wives.

Emotional Relations. I keep expectations in line with performance and therefore am rarely surprised or disappointed. I handle conflict by appealing to the wisdom of tradition or by splitting the difference or compromising. I have a friendly, companionable approach and like our intimacy the way it is. We make it on a regular basis.

CHAPTER 12 | MARRIAGES IN THE MIDDLE

As a marriage style, 5,5 gains in adjustment, predictability, and security what it sacrifices in spontaneity, commitment, and "life." It's a stable style, and a person living consistent with its assumptions can find practical ways of accommodating and of compromising to keep the *status quo* intact.

5,5 / 5,5

The ultimate in this kind of mutual adjustment is a marriage between 5,5-oriented people. Each is ready to make a go of it by meeting the other halfway, with neither presupposing high standards of what would constitute a truly gratifying, enriching, and deep marriage relationship.

Under the doctrine of "keep things in balance," a 5,5-oriented mate has a trade-out approach to participation and involvement. The ethic that is stressed is "fair shares." But then you reason, "If I'm to get help for putting through the project I have in mind, I should offer some inducement." After all, the proposition that you'll wash the car if your mate will vacuum inside and empty the ash trays might not be very appealing if your mate feels like doing something else or even nothing at all. So it seems necessary to add some tinsel to many a proposition so as to make a deal, especially if your mate doesn't see so much need to keep in step and follow

171

the beat of the social drum as you do. Maybe you realize that the overpowering approach of 9,1 and the directionless suggestions of 1,9 both have serious pitfalls. You see certain things that ought to be done. The best people are doing them already. You want your mate to join in with you in working toward your objectives, and you feel that the quality of cooperation greatly depends on how you approach your mate. You strive to balance your concern for what happens with your concern for your mate on the personal level. How does all this translate into an approach to marriage? It adds up to a readiness to bargain, to induce your mate to conform, stressing "What would other people think if we didn't cooperate on this?" Each mate pulls an oar according to a rhythm which ticks away on the community metronome.

A marriage founded on 5,5 assumptions moves along at a steady tempo, not at fire-alarm speed but not like a funeral cortege either. The mates have learned to adjust to one another. This means that often they skirt around their mutual blocks and frustrations rather than getting to causes and removing them. They compromise their differences instead of resolving them. They have learned to share a meadowland of agreement and not to venture too far into the underbrush of disagreement. Getting along comes at the expense of narrowing their convictions, outlooks, and activities so as to remain mutually acceptable.

Here is a sum-up of 5,5 marriage principles: "Love one another, live moderately, work together towards a common goal, show patience and consideration for each other's needs and desires, respect each other as individuals during the good times and the bad, and you'll make a go of it." [1]

In essence, it's "not too much or too little" intimacy, thoughtfulness, achievement, or any other marriage-related possibility. Let's see how this works out on a day-to-day basis. First we'll look in on George and Myra, who are getting the day started.

George. How about it? Shall I wear the brown suit another day?
Myra. Well, it looks awfully nice on you.
George. I know, but gosh, it needs pressing.
Myra. That's so. Perhaps it does.
George. It certainly could stand being pressed, all right.
Myra. Yes, perhaps it wouldn't hurt it to be pressed.

George. But gee, the coat doesn't need pressing. No sense in having
the whole darn suit pressed, when the coat doesn't need it.

Myra. That's so.

George. But the pants certainly need it, all right. Look at them—
look at those wrinkles—the pants certainly do need pressing.

Myra. That's so. Oh, Georgie, why couldn't you wear the brown
coat with the blue trousers we were wondering what we'd do
with them?

George. Good Lord! Did you ever in all my life know me to wear
the coat of one suit and the pants of another? What do you
think I am? A busted bookkeeper?

Myra. Well, why don't you put on the dark gray suit today, and stop
in at the tailor and leave the brown trousers?

George. Well, they certainly need—now where the devil is that gray
suit? Oh, yes, here we are.[2]

George and Myra provide a clear example of how two mates
with 5,5 orientations get along. They're comfortable enough with
one another. The peaks are chipped off and the valleys filled in. It's
a prairie kind of marriage, flat, with maybe a few gentle rolls in it.
You can sum up the quality and character of their way of living as
George himself does one afternoon. In bed with food poisoning, he
has time to reflect.

. . . he beheld, and half admitted that he beheld, his way of
life as incredibly mechanical. Mechanical business—a brisk
selling of badly built houses. Mechanical religion—a dry,
hard church, shut off from the real life of the streets, inhu-
manly respectable as a top-hat. Mechanical golf and dinner-
parties and bridge and conversation. . . .[3]

If George hadn't eaten a questionable clam, he might never have
had that insight.

So much for George and Myra for their life. Let's look into
5,5 from the standpoint of another husband. He is talking to his
son, giving his views on marriage.

. . . You're forced to find things in common. For instance,
your mother and I are very interested in various types of food
—a good roast beef, leg of lamb smothered in onions, yankee

pot roast with lots of little baby baked potatoes and gravy, and there's always something to talk about: Who's getting married. Who died. Who just had a baby. How much we should give. Marriage is a wonderful thing if you can enjoy your wife for whatever she is.[4]

Food and small talk serve to keep these two in touch with each other. Their interaction is conventional and stereotyped. Maybe neither has ever sought more than this. Certainly they don't seem to have infused each other with insight to any depth. What these illustrations so far amount to is a surfacey quality of mechanical reasonableness, accommodation, and adjustment between two people, each of whom keeps to the rhythms of their environment and one another. In a 5,5 marriage, you and your mate don't yearn after firsthand adventure. The peaks of living are what you read about or view on TV. You can almost feel you're "there" in the crunch of a football tackle, in the day-to-day variety of a serial drama, in the poignant climax of a romantic movie. All in all—in real and vicarious experience—life seems complete.

The 5,5/5,5 marriage pair is probably among the most durable of all combinations.[5] There are several reasons for this. The most important is that neither mate makes high demands on the other. Thus the kinds of friction that might otherwise create strain and produce a rupture simply don't occur. The social tools of adjustment, compromise, and splitting-the-difference provide ways of bringing quick relief to those few decision-choices around which irritation and heat might generate. 5,5 as a marriage style is closely attuned to the 5,5 life-style prevalent in many American communities. The expectations for How Marriage Should Be Lived that a person has learned in his own home, school, and community find easy confirmation in his mate's attitudes. Because of this high stability, a 5,5/5,5 married relationship is probably the most difficult to strengthen in the sense of shifting it toward a 9,9 basis. An additional reason comes to mind. It is that people are rarely motivated to work for change unless they are dissatisfied with what they presently have. As long as a 5,5 marriage is felt to be satisfactory, there is little stimulation for thinking about how to make it more rewarding.[6]

But there's another side to it. When a 5,5 marriage does become unstable, the most probable direction of movement is a drift toward 1,1. Routine, repetition, and ritual themselves become boring. The very attitudes associated with viewing something as "boring" are likely to keep a person from putting out the same degree of effort as formerly. 1,1 requires less energy and effort than 5,5 and offers an even more relaxed basis of living. If 5,5 marriage does become dull to either or both mates, there may be less inclination to solve the cause of the dullness than there might be to seek liveliness in relationships outside the marriage.

5,5/9,1

You might think that 5,5-oriented people would naturally gravitate to each other and marry. It's undoubtedly true that many do. 5,5 pairs can make comfortable companions for each other. But if 5,5's always tried to pair off as doublets, combinations of 5,5 with mates who have other Grid styles would be rather rare. Look around you, though, and you'll find plenty.

George is married to Martha. They've just returned home at 2:00 A.M. after a party at her father's house.

Martha. Make me a drink.
George. What?
Martha. I said, make me a drink.
George. Well, I don't suppose a nightcap'd kill either one of us. . . .
Martha. A nightcap! Are you kidding. We've got guests.
George. We've got what?
Martha. Guests. GUESTS!
George. GUESTS!
Martha. Yes . . . guests . . . people . . . we've got guests coming over.
George. When?
Martha. NOW!
George. Good Lord, Martha . . . do you know what time it. . . .
   Who's coming over? [7]

As you can hear, Martha has guests coming, without even telling George she was inviting them. He only gets to know as she ridicules him for not knowing. Note George's reaction. He protests mildly by referring to a convention—the lateness of the hour, when good people should be in bed. Then he goes along with her to get along with her, changing his mind swiftly as he asks, *"Who's* coming over?" His Grid style is very evident.

5,5/1,9

What's a 5,5/1,9 relationship like? Burt and Gina have been married for about a year. He was recruited on campus for a big company's executive development program. Gina's as good as enrolled in it, too, though she'd be surprised if he told her this directly.

Burt. All right if I say something about last night's Annual Dinner?
Gina. Yes.
Burt. I mean, don't take any of this as personal criticism, although it *is* rather important.
Gina. Why of course not. But what *is* it? Is anything wrong? Did I offend someone somehow?
Burt. No, darling, at least, nothing serious. But . . . now how shall I put it? There are two worlds for married couples like us who want to get ahead and be respected. One is when we're alone together like this and can talk about anything that comes into our heads. The other is when we're in public, like last night. Then we have to be kind of discreet.
Gina. But I love you wherever we are, and there's no harm in showing it, is there?
Burt. Well, it doesn't pay to make people jealous, and there *are* some rotten marriages among those people we visited with at the top table.
Gina. I'd never have thought so. They all seemed so . . . upper-upper.
Burt. They know how to conduct themselves so as not to embarrass one another at social functions.
Gina. Darling, *did* I embarrass you?
Burt. Well, when you were talking with Mr. Bell . . .
Gina. He's such a nice gentleman—I'm so glad he's your boss. And Mrs. Bell told me afterwards I'm very sweet!
Burt. It's best to think first before you say anything to people like

the Bells. For instance, when they asked you where you were from, you said Newark.

Gina. Why sure . . . I grew up there.

Burt. If you'd said New York, it'd have sounded better. I'm not knocking Newark, but . . .

Gina. Oh.

Burt. And he asked you where you went to college and you said you never went at all!

Gina. I meant *you* were the genius in our family, I was boosting *you,* Burt! What's it matter, why are you . . .

Burt. What *does* it matter? It matters a great deal in the Corporation. Mrs. Bell and most of the executive wives are college graduates. The more you have in common with them, the more they like you. Gina, please try to *think* when you're in these situations. I enrolled you for Sunrise Semester—you *could* have said you were taking social anthropology at New York University.

Gina. I guess I'm always making you ashamed of me, but I *do* love you and I *do* try! Next time please tell me what I ought to say. I don't want to embarrass you anymore.

Burt. It'll be all right, darling. But the thing is, we must always try to make a good impression on the best people, and fit in wherever we go.

Here is an example of how Burt clearly hears the cadence of his company colleagues and follows the beat of his boss's baton. But poor Gina. She is trying hard to please Burt and get her security from his strength. Yet until becoming attuned to the same signals as he is, her efforts are likely to fall short no matter how hard she tries.

5,5 / 1,1

A 5,5 / 1,1 marriage has a wasting-away quality about it which may go unnoticed when the mates marry or when a 1,1 attitude first enters the life of one of them. This is because 1,1 behavior of taking the line of least resistance may not seem too different from the quieter side of 5,5. What is really apathy may have the outer appearance of contentment, or what was formerly contentment may become apathy without either mate noticing the transition. Over time, however, the 1,1-oriented mate usually affects the other in a way that can be summed up as "vague discouragement."

Nick, who holds office in a fraternal society, is checking out his ceremonial uniform for the upcoming state convention. Ima looks on noncommittally.

Nick. I'll have to do something about this hat. Look how the feathers got broken when it blew off during the last parade.

Ima. It blew a long way.

Nick. Yes, and then some lout stepped on it. I was so nervous, I put it back in the box and forgot to send it off for repair.

Ima. Brushing and sponging it will help some.

Nick. Hey, aren't some feathers missing?

Ima. Oh, I'm sorry. Johnny needed an Indian hat for school and he used one or two, I think.

Nick. How could you? You know I'm bucking for Grand Pasha this year. How can I face them wearing this?

Ima. But you did want Johnny to be in the play—all the other kids had feathers.

Nick. You spend more time on them than you do with me. You're taking them places and picking them up when I come home. My dinner's late half the time.

Ima. Well . . .

Nick. And you'll sew all day for Amy and not put a button on my shirt. I've half a drawerful I can't wear.

Ima. Amy needs the clothes and we can't afford to buy them all.

Nick. Yeah, I know. But that's no excuse for my buttons. You just don't care about me as much as you do the kids. I could drop off the face of the earth and your day wouldn't be disturbed.

Ima. They're your kids too.

Nick. Oh, these feathers—what am I going to do?

Ima. Maybe they'll perk up if you put them out in the sun.

Nick. What's the matter? You used to be so proud every time I made a new degree. You used to keep my uniform clean and pressed. And you've always enjoyed the conventions and stuff.

Ima. Not any more. I'd sooner stay home. You go if you want to.

Nick. But there are those people from all around the state we've been meeting for years. I'd stick out like a sore thumb if I went on my own!

So it seems that Ima is centering her attention on the children and neglecting Nick and his prized regalia. She has kept up with her 5,5 mother role but has dropped into the 1,1 corner as a wife. Whether her slow drizzle will rain out Nick's parade or whether he will react to it by becoming even more status-oriented is not yet clear. But evidently the shock of finding her so unenthusiastic has rocked his 5,5 balance.

This is an example of where the wife's intense involvements with children have a debilitating effect on her involvement with her husband. The reverse of this situation can be found where the husband is focusing his energy outside the home and the wife feels neglected and abandoned. In this way, 1,1 in a husband or wife relationship may not be characteristic of either person's interactions with other people.

We have examined the marriage assumptions that arise from moderate concerns for what happens and for one's mate. The attitudes of tentativeness and balancing, of adjustment and accommodation, of compromise and backing off have been illustrated in connection with each key element. A common theme running through many of these attitudes is the quest for social acceptability. This entails keeping in step with friends and colleagues, paying respectful attention to what established authorities prescribe, and taking the advice of revered status figures. Without these props a 5,5-oriented person feels uncertain and lacks a clear sense of direction. This preoccupation leads 5,5-oriented mates to rely on traditional or fashionable role prescriptions, however much these may fly in the face of logic.

CHAPTER 13 | 9,9—MUTUAL FULFILLMENT

It's possible to enjoy marriage in a 9,9 way when concerns for what happens and for your mate are both high. The attitudes stemming from 9,9 concerns are those which aid in really joining one's own life into another's. Two gains result. One is that each mate becomes interdependent with the other. The second is increased autonomy for each. The way mates interrelate makes it possible for each to feel more fulfilled. The expansion of autonomy within interdependence may seem paradoxical. Autonomy is independence, privateness, separateness. Interdependence means sharing, unity, togetherness, and mutual fulfillment. The truth within the paradox is that in a 9,9 relationship, independence, privateness, and separateness are rooted in and emerge from interdependence, sharing, and unity.[1] Interdependence can release unused potentials which cannot be tapped by someone who acts alone. 9,9 interdependence comes about when emotional relations and problem-solving fuse with one another in a closely integrated way.

Sabrina has been in school and working in Paris for five years. She returns home to New York after turning down Paul. She is now telling her friend Linus why she didn't want to marry Paul.

Linus. Why don't you marry him?
Sabrina. I'm afraid.
Linus. Of what?

Sabrina. Of being domesticated. That's not funny. Do you think men have the exclusive right to run from domestication? Pooh! That's a myth! Men adore it!

Linus. You've found that out.

Sabrina. Yes.

Linus. And you want no part of domesticity.

Sabrina. I didn't say that. I love being domestic. I'm afraid of being domesticated. There's a difference. . . . Do you understand that?

Linus. Yes. I do.

Sabrina. The trouble with marriage is that men want to give you the world, but it has to be the world they want to give you. And what of the other worlds outside the window? Do you know what I mean? The things he does are fun to do, and I love doing them with him, and you can't have a marriage without that. But suppose then I find that they keep me from doing all the other wonderful things I've wanted to do? Suppose I find that instead of opening up my life, I've closed it down and locked it off?

Linus. You can't do everything, Sabrina.

Sabrina. Ah, but it's important to try!

Linus. What do you want to do, Sabrina?

Sabrina. I don't know.

Linus. What *can* you do?

Sabrina. Nothing impressive. I cannot sing a song or write a poem or paint a picture, and I shall never run for Senator from Connecticut—

Linus. Why Connecticut?

Sabrina. It makes a nice sound.

Linus. That's as good a reason for running as any.

Sabrina. But I think I have a talent, all the same. I think I have a talent for living. Perhaps I'm trying to make the most of something small for want of something better, but I think a true talent for living has the quality of creation, and if that's the talent I was meant to have, I'm awfully glad I have it. I'd rather live a first-rate life than paint a second-rate picture.

Linus. So would a lot of second-rate painters. Do you know how to live a first-rate life?

Sabrina. I'm beginning to learn; I've been to school.

Linus. In Paris. And what did Paris teach you?

Sabrina. Two things! To develop my appetites; and to discipline them.

Linus. That's admirable.

Sabrina. And to want to do everything and see everything, sense everything and feel everything and taste everything; to know that life is an enormous experience and must be used. To be in the world, and of the world, and never to stand aside and watch.[2]

9,9 qualities show through in Sabrina's talk about marriage. She wants a marriage that provides interdependence, doing together, and having fun. But she recognizes that togetherness aspects are not the end-all. She wants marriage to provide opportunities for independence so that she can pursue those interests and talents unique to herself. The whole-person concept of 9,9 in marriage involves the interdependence of connectedness and sharing and the freedom to be oneself and fulfill one's own distinctive potentialities. 9,9 is a fulfillment-seeking marriage.

In a 9,9 orientation you have your mate's best interests at heart. This happens when self-interests and mate interests are so meshed that it would never occur to you to try to make a distinction between the two. You find joy or pain in an activity, not in what it does for you or what you get out of it but because of what it does for "your-mate-and-you"—the relationship. This concern comes through to your mate consistently in what you say, think, and do. It is a part of you, and there are at least three general ways in which it is evident.

One is in being *considerate,* as distinct from being just polite and surface-friendly or cloying. Part of this involves anticipation. That's when you project your thinking into the future and ask yourself, "How would my mate think or feel if I did this or that? What's a good and sound action here?" You consider your mate's thoughts, feelings, and desires so as to respond in ways that forward his or her best interests. You do not set yourself up as the better judge, but sometimes you can take steps to prevent an undesirable situation from arising and hurting your mate. Or you could perhaps be taking action to reduce a burden your mate carries.

A second way in which 9,9 concerns are apparent is this. When everything else is going well, your anticipations often lead you to do something that goes beyond practicalities, providing pleasure and fun. You spring a pleasant surprise such as choosing a gift, cooking a special dish, giving a heartfelt compliment, or making it possible for your mate to have something which had been hoped for but previously had seemed out of reach. All are actions that say convincingly that you have your mate's best interests in mind. They tell your feelings because (1) you weren't obligated to do any of them, (2) had you failed to do them no one would have been the wiser, and (3) you did them without personal gain in mind. You do them because you enjoy your mate's feelings of pleasure and happiness.

This doesn't mean that every action you take produces a radiant short-term glow. Yet, this climate of openness promotes an easiness of exchange where people can really talk about things that matter without feeling attacked or defensive. Sometimes you may be tempted to keep a secret to avoid hurting your mate's feelings. But, of course, it is a much better basis of living together if you can be open and therefore fully able to express yourself with complete frankness, in ways that promote acceptance rather than tension and defensiveness.

Acting in accordance with your mate's best interests may sometimes mean being critical. But you don't criticize out of a wish to reject or put down. Your criticism comes from a desire to help your mate take an objective look at something which needs to be better understood or changed to strengthen the relationship. Or maybe there's something in your mate's dealings with the children, neighbors, sales people or whomever, which you see as harmful or self-defeating. These can range from "Your slip is showing," or "That shirt doesn't go with your jacket," through "I think you're spending too much on fishing equipment," or "You're letting the kids ruin the rugs with their muddy shoes," and even into deeper personal matters. The common feature of all 9,9 ". . . *best interests at heart"* feelings and actions is that you have a genuine and deep concern for increasing your mate's effectiveness, pleasure, security, and gratification.

What is at the core of a 9,9 concern for what happens? Objective idealism are two words that grasp a sense of it. Taken together they mean several things. One is problem-solving. This means meeting life's dilemmas on a "what is *best* to do" basis as they develop. Another is readiness to move out, to see a new day as new, not just as a repetition of yesterday. Past events are not ignored; history is placed in its proper perspective and used for guidance and reflection. Yet a person is free to move forward according to the dictates of "here and now." Current action is cut loose from the silent control of tradition, precedent and past practice. Objective idealism strengthens the realism of a person's approach to enable creative dealing with matters at hand. The question, "What is the *best* decision, not just for now, but also for tomorrow?" leads to actions that can solve current problems and at the same time strengthen future performance. 9,9 thinking rejects mortgaging the future by temporary expedients and compromise for compromise's sake.[3]

No heritage specifically teaches people how to live together vitally, as equals, in ways that promote mutual respect and confidence. There is no ready formula for learning how to solve problems while at the same time coming to committed agreement. When mates approach problems in a 9,9-concerned way, feelings of belonging and responsibility for results can draw them toward one another in unity. Strong and valid problem-solving makes a positive contribution to rich emotional relations; just as, conversely, genuine affection provides a favorable basis for the kind of interaction that's needed for getting solutions to marriage-related problems.

The pursuit of best solutions—regardless of the problem to which the solution applies—is one of the main streams through which the values of objective idealism are expressed in daily living. Ways for finding the best solution to any given problem are varied and many, yet all share a common factor. This involves a desire by both mates to work for a solution to which they will be jointly committed. One condition for this is agreement to a decision that's based on mutual understanding, rather than a decision that is imposed, made by default, or based on impulsiveness.

One start toward achieving mutual understanding as the basis for agreement is to ensure that your mate participates in discussing and deciding issues of joint concern. This is true whether one mate is more or less expert than the other on the particular topic under consideration.

Another consideration is recognizing and responding to reservations and doubts. This is part of the basis for achieving a decision based on commitment. Debbie and Larry are discussing the purchase of a new kitchen appliance. Debbie has been investigating Larry's choice of brands.

Debbie. Everything seems to check out, the price is within our reach, and I want it as much as you. But there's something that makes me uneasy about it. I've tried and tried but I can't put my finger on what it is!

Larry. OK. Speed isn't vital. I'd rather wait till you're able to spot what's bothering you.

Debbie. Oh, let's go ahead. If I can't figure out what it actually is, I must be imagining something.

Larry. Why? You may be saving us from a mistake if you wait a little, till you're more sure. We've been through this enough to know that today's hesitation is often tomorrow's insight. Anyway, we might be able to use it on a trial basis for awhile.

Mutual respect is present. One is saying, "I don't feel right about it." The other is saying, "It's important that we wait and see what it is that doesn't fit." In contrast, think of Virginia talking with Bob about clothes for the New York trip.*

Important in decision-making is the belief that the thoughts and feelings of your mate are authentic even though they're different from your own.[4] What is seen or sought for in authenticity is:

> ... an honesty, openness, a genuineness of personal relationship; they are out to find a genuine feeling, a touch, a look in the eyes, a sharing of fantasy. The criterion becomes the *intrinsic meaning* and is to be judged by one's authenticity, doing one's own thing, and giving in the sense of making one's self available for the other.[5]

Listening to one another's imaginings, getting a laugh out of them while constructively discussing the *why,* is authentically helpful. Feelings *are* facts. And even more so, your mate's genuine thoughts and feelings are valuable, both in themselves and also for adding perspective to your own. This means "two heads are better than one." There is no intention to use the other person as one's *aide-de-camp.* Communication is two-way, and problem-solving becomes a joint effort which integrates the mates' best thinking in accordance with shared objectives.

But when choices have to be made and the best one is not self-evident, how can you go about effecting a decision in a 9,9 way? An initial step is to become clear about what the issue is. This seems self-evident! But is it really? Problems are rarely quite so obvious as they seem at first glance. If they were, people would find it pretty easy to solve them. Defining a problem is not a matter of one mate seeking to bring the other into participation with the announcement: "Here's the problem. *This* is what we need to do. Agreed? Now how do we go about doing it?" Instead, the first question for *both* to consider is: *"What is* the real issue?" You begin by taking a direct, fresh look, rather than taking for granted that you both know what it is. This is not necessarily as simple as it may appear. Problems don't describe themselves. *You*—both of you—have to describe them. Each of you may notice one or two prominent features, assuming the other person sees the same things. Yet neither of you may have a clear sight of the general scope.

Decisions made and acted upon in a 9,9-oriented way don't have to be two-person choices *every* time. When common goals and shared understandings of how best to work toward them are present, each of you, when working alone, can confidently make decisions and act on them with these objectives in mind. In this way there is no delay in grasping opportunities or in tackling problems as they arise. You keep each other informed of decisions and actions taken independently so as to continue meshing efforts. Making one-alone independent decisions isn't a matter of seeing "your area and my area" as it is under 5,5 arrangements. Nor is it doing something forced on you by a 1,1 mate's default. It is a matter of picking up the ball and heading for the goal whenever one of you can do this immediately and do it well without needing to consult the other.

Another feature of 9,9 decision-making that is unlikely to be noticed in any of the other Grid-style approaches is making use of *critique*. This means first testing the wisdom of the decision to check whether it's likely to bring the results you both anticipated. Afterwards, it also means frequent rechecking to ensure that the decision is bringing the results expected from it. Critique such as this helps ensure that problem-solving will be solution-centered rather than person-centered. A test of person-centered pet solutions is, "Did I get my way?" A test of the solution-centered solution is, "Did it solve the problem?" The conclusions reached earlier are not fixed and unchangeable; and immediate change of course in a more favorable direction can be taken when the need for it becomes evident.

Decision-making in a 9,9 way doesn't come easily. But once you have it, several benefits accrue. Both of you have a vested interest in the outcome. There develops an immediate readiness to listen for and to respond to your mate's current thoughts and feelings, expressed without being muffled by reserve. When each sees and is committed to the same goal, support to implement the decision is assured. Two minds working on any given problem can be many times more effective in getting the best solution than is one alone. When different ideas about how to solve a problem rub against one another, comparison of alternatives becomes possible. Strengths and weaknesses of each can be seen more clearly, and novelty is prompted. The very process of involvement, participation, and thinking through the problem is in itself stimulating and marriage-strengthening. It is a discovery experience in which two people find that they *can* work creatively in ways which promote innovation, heightened mutual involvement, and more effective problem-solving.

A 9,9 orientation produces strong, clear convictions, but they are not rigid. A person who has high concern for what happens, whatever his concern for the other mate, is likely to develop convictions on his own. When a person thinks and analyzes, particularly when he does so in a problem-solving way, it is inevitable that he reaches conclusions.

A 9,9-oriented person is thus confronted with a dilemma. How can he think through to convictions and yet not become trapped in false certainty? How can he remain flexible in matters of joint concern, yet stay open to other relevant facts and opinions? Only by remaining open-minded can he gain his mate's free and meaningful involvement in a cooperative search for solutions to common problems.

A 9,9 premise is that convictions rooted in feelings and emotions are of very different quality from those which are factually based. The strongest basis of certainty is found when facts, logic, and feeling all point in the same direction and give the same conclusion. (For contrast, think of a 9,1-oriented person who makes little distinction between fact-based convictions and emotion-based opinions. Both are likely to be held with the same degree of intensity. Yet most 9,1 convictions are felt to be "true.") Certainly, feelings can reinforce convictions, but they should not *produce* them.

Howard is reading the paper. The doorbell rings and Sarah answers it.

Sarah. Sorry to interrupt—there were two youngsters at the door with a petition. They left it for us to study and are coming back in thirty minutes. They'd like us to sign it.

Howard. Read it over, will you, honey?

Sarah. "We the undersigned demand a reduction in appropriations for space exploration in order to permit an accelerated effort to solve problems of the cities." I hope we'll sign it. They're such nice young people and everybody knows the cities need help. They say the ghettos are terrible.

Howard. Did these youngsters tell you who they represent? There's no indication of what—if any—group they belong to.

Sarah. No, but our neighbors signed it.

Howard. They didn't add their reasons, did they?

Sarah. No, but they usually have opinions we can agree with.

Howard. I don't think I want to sign it, at least until we talk to them more.

Sarah. Oh, dear, why not?

Howard. For these reasons. It comes through to me as vague, simplistic, maybe over-emotional and prejudiced. There's no mention of the amount of reduction demanded, or of how the funds would be reemployed. Also, we don't know what use

will be made of the petition. And then, as I see it, space exploration and solving the problems of the cities aren't incompatible.
It's not an either-or in my book. I'd like to hear these youngsters—or their sponsors—put their case. At this moment
I'm far from being convinced.

Sarah. When the doorbell rings again, could you answer it? I don't
want to tell them no.

Howard. I'll go, but let's both interview them and compare ideas.
My mind's still open but these are the kinds of reservations
they'll have to deal with.

The meaning of 9,9 convictions becomes clearer through comparing Howard's and Sarah's approaches. Howard has thought
about the larger picture and has adopted a reasoned point of view
for evaluating the wisdom of signing the petition. He has reservations, but he's amenable to listening to the other side. Sarah doesn't
hold to convictions about the petition's content. But in a 5,5 way,
she is swayed by other factors such as "The neighbors are saying,"
"It'll please the youngsters," "They say . . ."

9,9 thinking is not restricted by stereotypes—those traditional-
ized attitudes or oversimplified mental pictures that are easy substi-
tutes for real thought and observation. Instead, there is active interest in promoting the kind of involvement and participation which
will give opportunities for both to examine each other's points of
view. In this way, the convictions and reservations that each has
can be evaluated. If you are 9,9, you are open-minded. The goal is
not to win for a personally held point of view or to enforce it on
the other mate; rather it is to find assurance that the convictions
held are sound and are justified by the circumstances. If they are
not, it is time to change them. In a similar way, you do not automatically take the traditional route. Yet you don't go against it just
because it is traditional. The aim is to accept the wisdom of tradition when it's appropriate and challenge when it's not. Nor do you
necessarily adopt the majority point of view at face value. If another person's agreement with your own views seems superficial,
you will probe deeper and, if appropriate, continue discussion until
it is evident that the other person's agreement is deep-rooted and
genuine.[6]

Marriage activities can promote teamwork when a problem for one becomes a problem for both to solve. One mate does not say to the other, "You have made your bed, now sleep in it." Indeed, the opposite attitude prevails.

Libby has had "one of those days" and she begins to unburden herself on Tom as he arrives at the door.

Libby. Today was awful. Thank God you're home. I can't take it.
Tom. Tell me about it. What in the world happened?
Libby. Everything.
Tom. Like what?
Libby. I went to get some meat out for supper. The deep freeze was off. I don't know how long it's been. Maybe the food is all spoiled. I can't tell.
Tom. Is it back on now?
Libby. No, I can't find out what's gone wrong with it. But as you see, there's no power cut.
Tom. Good.
Libby. What do you mean "good," for heaven's sake?
Tom. Let's go look at it. We can see how soft the food is since there's been no refreezing. If it's spoiled we'll know it.
Libby. It'll get worse before morning if it stays off.
Tom. But if we can fix it this problem will be solved. If I can't we can ask Phil and Doris to use some of their space till we can get the repairman out.
Libby. Thanks, Tom. I know you're tired and want a drink.
Tom. Just give me a beer while I check it out. You go ahead and work on supper if you want.

Tom has taken on "her" problem as his own. He might have said:
What did you do to overload the circuit *this* time? (9,1)
Well, that's life. Too bad. (1,1)
Poor dear. I know you're *so* tired. Let me take you out to dinner. We'll get the repairman tomorrow. (1,9)
If it's spoiled, it's only on top. The bottom keeps its freeze longer. (5,5)
Here are comments researchers gathered, dealing with teamwork

in marriage. They describe bases of cooperation for both man and woman.

> The things we do together aren't fun intrinsically—the ecstasy comes from being *together in the doing*. Take her out of the picture and I wouldn't give a damn for the boat, the lake, or any of the fun that goes on out there.[7]

Joint activity may also encompass the husband's career when the wife does not have an independent outside work interest. In these circumstances, she may work with him and contribute in a synergistic way to his career. A husband's description of his wife in their 9,9/9,9 relationship gives the essence of it.

> She keeps my files and scrapbooks up to date. . . . I invariably take her with me to conferences around the world. Her femininity, easy charm and wit are invaluable assets to me. I know it's conventional to say that a man's wife is responsible for his success and I also know that it's often not true. But in my case I gladly acknowledge that it's not only true, but she's indispensable to me. But she'd go along with me even if there was nothing for her to do because we just enjoy each other's company—deeply. You know, the best part of a vacation is not *what* we do, but that we do it together. We plan it and reminisce about it and weave it into our work and other play all the time.[8]

How does this kind of relationship actually work? As we have said, one of the keys to real love in a marriage is that one mate's sense of involvement causes him to treat the other mate's problem as his own. This didn't happen in the Hugh and Dee soda-syphon incident when she promised and then forgot.* By not delivering on her commitment, she also violated his expectations. But we saw concern in Tom's immediate helpfulness in Libby's problem. This isn't meddling. It's pick-up in teamwork. The question "Whose problem is it?" isn't raised; it would seem meaningless. A knotty problem is handled by both of them even when the problem relates to only one of them.

* Chapter 7, pp. 102–103.

In marriage, the 9,9 goal is to unleash and merge the participation and involvement of both in planning activities that can be implemented through teamwork. This is how to bring into reality the future that you consider to have the richest significance for yourselves. Since your mate and you have jointly held stakes in the outcome, planning for vital aspects of your lives tends to lead to more valid expectations as to where you want to be and how you intend to get there.

This kind of two-way strengthening, which enriches interdependence while simultaneously promoting autonomy, is *synergistic*. Rules of arithmetic say that $1 + 1 = 2$. But one plus one can add up to more than two in a synergistic way when two mates relate to each other with zest through the entire marital spectrum. One plus one may equal three or five, or any amount greater than two. Thus, synergy is a mutually enhancing feature of 9,9 teamwork.

It becomes ever more evident that humankind doesn't live by thought alone. Feelings are a rich part of a full and rewarding life. A 9,9-oriented person expresses emotions in a genuine way. These feelings accord with the situation in the sense that some observer, viewing the situation objectively, would see them as sound and valid. A main factor here is the nature of 9,9 basic assumptions around which emotions arise. They are *enlivening*.

With 9,9 attitudes, your feelings and thoughts lead you to high expectations for yourself, your mate, and your marriage. If these expectations are not completely fulfilled, there's no spinning off into emotional dead ends. Instead of crying over spilt milk or driving even harder, you focus on what you and your mate might have done better and you incorporate these learning points in your next project. What you can't control hardly matters except as indicating the present limits you're operating within.

Whenever you are engaged in joint activities, your enthusiasm is likely to be catching. It adds zest and a can-do spirit to your participation. As one 9,9 husband said, "Every place I go I have a good time." His wife further explained, "It's not because we carefully pick and choose what we do; rather, it's because Jack is interested in everything, and wherever he is he can throw himself into activities and pretty soon I'm involved and enjoying them, too."

If your mate's performance is something more than you had anticipated, you're overjoyed. Often then new topics for discussion come to mind, stimulating your mate and you to aim for higher things than you've ever previously tackled.

In emotional relations, too, your expectations are high. Whenever you sense that your mate's emotional warmth toward you is less than you expected, this signifies to you that some problem is impinging on one or both of you. You wish to identify and solve it, and you say so. Whatever emerges can be discussed with a view to early reconciliation.

There's another side of this, too. When you have your self-confidence as well as respect for another person, you don't feel any need to be on guard or defensive. You have the freedom to be yourself and to respond in terms of your spontaneous feelings. You have confidence in doing this, because feelings don't lead you astray or into a blind alley, or into trouble with your mate. This capacity to trust one's feelings and to harness them creatively is *spontaneity*. This is different from impulsive action whereby emotions dictate what you do under the premise that it's better to do something than nothing.

Expectations generated within the 9,9 viewpoint have the greatest likelihood of permitting mates spontaneously to feel *for* each other and *with* each other. They can produce a bright relationship which is difficult for third parties to describe in detail, though the generalization is that a 9,9 couple is likely to be always doing something new and different. Couples like this don't seem to struggle, or deliberate painfully, or worry, but on the other hand you don't get the feeling that they act by whim, one way today and a different way tomorrow. It's a game-free relationship, within which mates don't feel compelled to score points. It's also role-free; no one acts according to protocol for its own sake. It's just fun to be alive.

Lou is talking with her sister Bette. She illustrates the kind of surprise that one mate is likely to create for the other, where the realistic expectation is that her mate will be pleased by the outcome.

Bette. What are you doing with yourself while Bob is gone?
Lou. I was sitting in the living room the other night where we

usually watch the news program before dinner. I looked
around, and all of a sudden I knew what I wanted to do.

Bette. What in the world is that?

Lou. Bob will be back next week, so I thought I would paint the
living room as a surprise.

Bette. What makes you think he'll like it?

Lou. We'd planned to do it soon anyway, but I'm going to get it
done while he's gone. I know he just hates to do the tiny
molding around the edges and work on the ceiling, although
—bless him—that's what he'd probably take on if we were
doing it together.

Bette. Gee, you must be getting awful tired.

Lou. Not particularly, since I don't have to race the clock. I'm
making progress, and I can't wait to see the look on his face
when he walks in and sees it all finished.

This behavior is based on understanding without a need to double check to get authorization or approval. It contributes to the
couple's mutual objective of having a pretty house. It doesn't put
Bob under obligation and doesn't require a lot of engineering to
bring it off. There's evidence that Lou has the best interest of her
husband at heart; but that's not all. She finds pleasure in doing it,
because it will give him pleasure; and she finds anticipation of his
pleasure adding an extra something to the activity she's engaged in.

9,9 assumptions emphasize unity of effort with mates moving in
concert in matters of joint interest. They share common stakes in
achieving success from living in the fullest way possible. That married mates cooperate in doing this is of core significance. When differences in points of view occur, conflict can result even within the
effort to cooperate. *Confronting* conflict is the approach to it in a
9,9 relationship. How is this done?

The very opposition of views generates feelings. One thing about
conflict-sparked feelings is that you have to do something about
them. You can't ignore them or hide them. Feelings need expression. They will influence your behavior, whether you like it or not.
These feelings can be channeled into competition. They can be
turned inward and directed against yourself as *self-criticism,* as in
Dorothy's wail of woe as she received Joe's comments about her

lack of punctuality from the Palm Court to Piccadilly Circus and elsewhere.* Conflict-based feelings don't just "go away." Confronting conflict means facing feelings and studying how they originated. Confronting conflict also means getting the opposing viewpoints defined so that they can be examined and evaluated by you and your mate. As you both gain more clarity, the emotions which initially gathered around points of misunderstanding tend to get worked through. Then a rational basis for solution may be discovered.

Though getting conflict out into the open constitutes the most valid approach to solving it, the thought of doing so meets strong resistance in our culture today. Such resistance springs from several sources.

9,1 reservations come from the attitude that recognizing emotions and feelings as "real" denotes weakness and makes one appear soft and spineless. Fear of personal inadequacy leads to the 9,1 mode of reacting to disagreement—suppressing conflict and seeing to it that your mate stays cowed.

1,9 reluctance to face conflict stems from the belief that married people can't possibly love one another if they feel hostile and sometimes fight. Furthermore, you think that getting into the conflict situation can result only in more damage to a relationship.

The 1,1 attitude is that conflict is something you hope to live through without getting all stirred up. "It'll pass."

5,5 resistance comes from the conviction that it is preferable to maneuver around conflict or to get an armistice-type solution. Such approaches can get conflict set aside in a quiet and sophisticated way, if both parties stay on their respective sides of the truce line.

With all these resistances, why maintain that confrontation is, in fact, the most effective way of dealing with conflict? Here's why. When people are hampered by their tensions from achieving coordinated effort, actions that would enhance the marriage are not undertaken. Much personal energy is deployed in applying patches that, at best, are temporary ways to close a torn relationship or in detouring around problems instead of resolving them.[9] These are some of the disadvantages of failure to confront conflict.[10]

Now we can consider what's possible when *both* mates approach

* Chapter 8, pp. 119–120.

potential or actual conflict with 9,9 assumptions. This route can promote true understanding, love, and respect between you almost regardless of how you've gotten along in other Grid-style combinations in the past. It provides a sound method for resolving points of disagreement. It deals with emotions and feelings in a constructive way, removing those which form barriers and replacing them with enthusiasm and commitment. It avoids pushing for your position in a way that violates and perhaps crushes your mate's expectations. Of course, initially, it may take longer to reach 9,9 agreement than it might take a 9,1-oriented mate to overwhelm and crush an objection. However, the 9,9 approach is time-conserving over the long haul, and marriage can be the longest haul possible. It's an approach which permits you to disagree and then to resolve your disagreements after searching out the full facts, data, reasoning, and understanding of emotions and feelings involved. It's what is needed for reaching a true meeting of the minds. It is an approach where *you* are as committed to your mate's high expectations being fulfilled as your mate is interested in helping you toward shared objectives.

Intimacy is a bonding agent in a 9,9 relationship. It provides the extra dimension which brings everything else into a meaningful unity. You can't really subdivide the mind-heart-body of one party from the mind-heart-body of the other in 9,9 sex-intimacy. In the final analysis there is found a oneness that would lose its coherence if you tried to divide and separate its elements. This quality of wholeness is found here in interview comments from one research study:

> You can't draw the line between being in bed together and just being alive together. You touch tenderly when you pass; you wait for the intimate touch in the morning.

> I don't quite understand these references to the sex side of life. It *is* life. My husband and I are first of all a man and a woman—sexual creatures all through. That's where we get our real and central life satisfactions. If that's not right, nothing is.[11]

Researchers studying a different group of married people heard the same attitudes expressed.

It is no fun for him unless I come across, so I try.

Sometimes he wants it when I don't and I usually let him have it. But he really don't like it so much, and he wants us to come together. He understands real good too what I need to get me going. Sometimes I don't want to start and he'll fool around until I do.

There is no enjoyment for me if she doesn't.

She wants it as much and as often as I do—I couldn't ask for anything more.[12]

Listen to this man who's been married for twenty-four years.

When I was a kid I thought it was the greatest thing, and I still do. I get a big charge out of it, yeah man! We do it about four or five times a week; I'm cagier now than when I was twenty-five. [Cagier?] I do it more now than ever. [What is your wife's feeling?] Oh, she likes it too, and will give it to me any time I want it. We are having more intercourse now than when we were first married. I feel horny all the time. There ain't nothing no better. It gives me release. I'd like it more of-tener, too. It means I got somebody to love. It couldn't be any better than it is. My wife enjoys it as much as me; she gets a thrill out of it as well as myself because she is just a sexy kind.[13]

All these are examples of mutual sexual gratification on a 9,9 basis.

One woman was asked, "Does it ever leave you feeling nothing?" She answered, "Well, even if I don't work up to going off like a factory whistle it's still almost always nice."

Why? Another woman explains.

There is more to sex than just sex. There's being together and knowing you love each other. It doesn't always have to be hot. . . . Another woman said she liked anything that made them feel so near and so good about each other.[14]

Here's a wife being interviewed.

Janice. . . . Now we have it about four times a week.

Interviewer. How are you aware of your husband's desires?

Janice. All I have to do is just look at him. All I have to do is take it off. I always wear thin gowns, and I say, "Honey, tonight's the night." It's important to me; I don't get as nervous and tensed. I think that's got a lot to do with women that are nervous. Hell, everybody else is going to the moon, I might as well go to heaven! It makes me feel I'm wanted, too.

Interviewer. Do you want intercourse more or less often?

Janice. I'll just take it any time I can get it; I like it. It reassures us of our love for each other.

Interviewer. How does your husband feel?

Janice. If I don't give it to him, you'd better believe he's mad the next day! It boosts his morale. All men feel that way; they think they are men then. My husband really enjoys it if I make it; he always waits for me.[15]

These and many other indications verify that a deep relationship exists for many so that it becomes difficult to think of separating sex from intimacy in a 9,9 setting. Margaret, whom we met in Chapter 9,* seemed to have this major goal in mind as she tried to stimulate her 1,1-oriented husband, Brick.

Here's another view of it. Remember Harriet and George, in Chapter 1? ** They were arguing about twins versus a double bed. Here's George again, sounding off about how he sees sex-based intimacy.

George. Let me tell you about twin beds. . . I tell you, the longest distance in the world is the distance between twin beds. I

* Chapter 9, pp. 134–135.
** Chapter 1, pp. 1–2.

don't care if it's six inches or six feet. It's psychological
distance. . . . In an old fifty-four, you may get into bed. You
don't know what you feel like. . . . Then you roll up
together . . . and you know . . . In twins, you've got to make
up your mind all by yourself, and then cross that damned gulf
and find out if your twin feels like it. And then if you get
there and find out you were wrong about yourself, well, it's a
lot of embarrassment retreating. Or if you find out she's not in
the mood . . . it's a big rejection. But in good old fifty-four,
you don't make a move until you're sure of yourself, and you
can pretty well sense if she's in the mood. . . . And if it still
doesn't work out, what the hell, you just fall asleep, all
wrapped around each other. No damage done.[16]

Here's another way of describing sex within a more deeply
human context.

 . . . The pleasure and experience of self-affirmation in being
able to *give* to the partner. The man is often deeply grateful
toward the woman who lets herself be gratified by him. . . .
This is a point midway between lust and tenderness . . . and it
partakes of both. Many a male cannot feel his own identity either as a man or a person in our culture until he is able to
gratify a woman. The very structure of human interpersonal
relations is such that the sexual act does not achieve its full
pleasure or meaning if the man and woman cannot feel they
are able to gratify the other. . . . What is omitted . . . is the experience of giving feelings, sharing fantasies, offering the inner
psychic richness that normally takes a little time and enables
sensation to transcend itself in emotion and emotion to transcend itself in tenderness and sometimes love.[17]

Here is a good way to sum all this up. The beginning of love

 . . . is the relationship between people which we term care.
Though it goes beyond feeling, it begins there. It is a feeling
denoting a relationship of concern, where the other's existence
matters to you; a relationship of dedication, taking the ultimate form of being willing to get delight in or, in ultimate
terms, to suffer for, the other.[18]

So there you have it. Interdependence nourishes intimacy, yet autonomy is respected. Mates complete one another with each maintaining the freedom to be spontaneous while sharing the joys of interdependence.

Here, then, is the complete Mirror for 9,9.

Problem-solving Relations. I place high value on getting sound decisions through understanding and agreement. I have clear convictions but listen for, seek out, and respond to better opinions, attitudes, and ideas by being convinced of a sounder position. I want us to gain the advantages of "two heads are better than one"; otherwise to divide things up according to who is in the best position to do what.

Emotional Relations. I have high expectations and am challenged to find ways to realize them. When conflict arises, I seek to understand our feelings and to relieve the emotions that are aroused. I try to identify reasons for differences in our positions and to resolve underlying causes. Intimacy is an expression of my love for my mate which is thoughtful and imaginative in ways that bring richness to our relationship.

CHAPTER 14 | VITAL MARRIAGES

The key to the 9,9 approach to marriage is in integrating the two high concerns for moving toward every kind of richness in the *problem-solving* dimension of marriage and for cherishing *and relating* to one's mate in the way most closely attuned to that other person's individuality. In 9,9, there is no contradiction between these two concerns; they provide a unified and authentic marriage approach.

Within a 9,9 marriage, the meaning of participation and involvement is this. A decision is presumed agreed upon only when there has been a genuine mind-meeting consensus. Then understandings and agreements between us are reinforced by shared feelings of emotional validity that the decision is right. Or you've given yourself completely to solving some problem or situation to which I have also committed my total effort. We're together on it.

9,9 / 9,9

Oliver Wendell Holmes and his wife, Fanny, provide an example of two people who are 9,9 in their orientations. The point is illustrated by the following episode. They are talking about themes for a speech Holmes is preparing for the reunion of his Harvard graduating class. Mary, the housekeeper, interrupts them.

Housekeeper. I beg your pardon, sir—but Mr. Henry Adams is downstairs asking to see you.

Holmes. What? At this hour of night? Oh no—this is too much. Fanny—help me out of this like a good girl.

Fanny. But I'm not a good girl and I'm not at all sure I'd say the right thing. Just what is on Mr. Adams' mind, Mary?

Housekeeper. I can't make out exactly, ma'am. But he seems to be worried about something.

Holmes. Oh, you can be sure. . . . Each administration brings Adams new woes and, gad, how he enjoys them! Mary, my apologies to Mr. Adams. Tell him I'm sorry that I'm in conference. . . . I can't be disturbed . . . but Mrs. Holmes will be down in just a few minutes. Tell him—

Fanny. Well, I like that—

Holmes. I thought you would. All right, Mary. Start calming Mr. Adams. And as for you, my dear—suppose you help me out with this speech.

Fanny. Oh, so I'm your secretary now, is that it?

Holmes. Fanny, what am I going to tell my old classmates? What *can* I tell them? Listen, eh—while I gather a little wool?

Fanny. Very well. But don't forget—Mr. Adams is waiting downstairs.

Holmes. Adams! Ah, don't you see, Fanny, the trouble was I was trying to add up the years the way Henry Adams would add them up. But life isn't doing a sum. It's painting a picture . . . and sometimes you have to have a little faith that the canvas will fill out as you go along. What difference does it make that I haven't reached all my objectives in my few years down here? No man ever can. We are lucky enough if we can give a sample of our best . . . and if in our hearts we can feel that it was nobly done. Well, at least I've made them see that the Constitution is a *living* thing . . . I've helped them see that the personal views of judges ought not to determine what is allowed and what is not allowed under the Constitution . . . it takes a lot of live and let live to put a republic together and keep it going. We must not be afraid to trust the people to. . . . Well, you were right, Fanny. I *am* a believer in spite of everything. I even believe in myself—and the universe I'm part of—though

I'm damned if I know yet just what it is that holds us both to-gether from one minute to the next. Oh, I know—I don't have the evidence to back all this up. But life isn't a matter of how much evidence you have . . . because you never will have enough. It's a matter of how much faith you have . . . faith in a universe not measured by your fears. Ah, there's the trick, Fanny, the real trick. Not to measure things by our fears but by our faith.

Fanny. Now you are beginning to come out from behind those beautiful white whiskers!

Holmes. Yes, and I feel naked somehow—naked but warm. You know, that's what's wrong with people like Henry Adams. They have no fire in the belly and where there's no fire, there's no hope. There's no—

Fanny. Now, Wendell, belly is *not* a nice word.

*   *   *

Holmes. Very well. If the word belly will shock the delicate sensi-bilities of the old boys at Harvard, we won't use it. But belly was what I said and belly, by heaven, is what I mean . . . it's the thing you crawl on when the bullets get too thick overhead . . . it's the thing you march on when everything else is gone . . . a belly, my good woman, is the place where a soldier's faith is born . . . a belly . . .

Fanny. I'm sorry, Wendell, really I am. But I suddenly remembered poor Mr. Adams waiting downstairs . . . and I just got to thinking. . . . I'm sure Mr. Adams never thought of the word belly in his whole life . . . and if he did . . . if he did just once . . . I'm sure he wouldn't have the stomach for it![1]

Feel the richness? The brightness? There's a depth here. There's interdependence and a mutual strengthening between them. There's autonomy, too, in the sense of each individual being a fully blos-somed person. The notion that interdependence and autonomy are mutually exclusive is little more than a self-fulfilling prophecy; a block in fancy, not in fact.

A 9,9/9,9 marriage style is by no means common. But when achieved, it has more going for it, and less going against it, than any other type of relationship.

9,9 / 9,1

Now we can compare other marriage styles with it. We've already met George and Harriet, the "double versus twin bed" pair,* and found them to be 9,9/9,1-ish. Here are Chuck and Edith. They are a 9,9/9,1 pair, too. They give us a glimpse of how these two Grid-based attitudes are likely to interact with each other. They're talking at cross-purposes about emotions and feelings which center around sex. Chuck is describing 9,9 sex; Edith, 9,1 sex. During the discussion you will notice that Chuck's conflict style shifts to 9,1 as a backup.

Edith. Don't knock my dad! He opened my eyes to a great deal about life and love and the nature of man. With Mother's "disorders" he had a woman on the side. And he told me about it quite frankly . . . about the needs of a man, et cetera. . . . He thought I should know this. . . . And I'm damned glad he told me.

Chuck. You sound as though his teaching you this . . . this matter of man's nature . . . woman on the side . . . infidelity . . . had stood you in good stead.

Edith. Well, we're not discussing that.

Chuck. I am. . . . That's the goddamndest thing I've ever heard. Do you think I haven't been faithful to you?

Edith. It's not worth discussing. It's not important.

Chuck. Not important?

Edith. It's only important *not* to discuss it . . . I think.

Chuck. You have assumed bravely, stoically, armed with your daddy's sweeping wisdom about these matters, that I have been unfaithful to you?

Edith. I find it embarrassing to discuss—

Chuck. —I find it impossible not to discuss.

Edith. I'm not making any accusations.

Chuck. You are implying very heavily, and you seem to be decking yourself with some kind of sweet tolerance which I find dis-

* Chapter 1, pp. 1–2.

gusting. . . . If you think I've been unfaithful to you, I'm appalled, frankly appalled, that you haven't stood up and shouted.

Edith. That would be pretty ridiculous, wouldn't it? After all, what does it matter?

*   *   *

Edith. Long trips, extended periods. A woman would be foolish not to expect something to happen. . . . Oh, meaningless, of course. . . . But I'm trying to tell you, it doesn't matter.

Chuck. Well, I'm sorry as hell to disappoint you, but there have been no little meaningless sexual skirmishes. . . . My life is full enough of meaninglessness not to go looking for it in outlying districts.[2]

And a little later on,

Edith. Difficult as it is for you to grasp, your virginity was not a concern of mine before we were married, and your strict fidelity is not a concern of mine now. I am not your jailer, and I am not stupid. The subject is closed as far as I am concerned.

Chuck. Jesus Christ, men are not all like your father. All men do not relish meaningless rolls in the hay—in their own beds or other beds. . . . I feel like clobbering you for assuming that I've laid every broad in every small town I've visited, all because your father gave you the lowdown. Why didn't he let you find out for yourself what your man . . . your husband would do? Because if it doesn't matter to you, it matters to me. . . . It's hard as hell trying to keep any meaning going, but here, here in the most personal and private core of me, I insist that there be meaning. I want there to be meaning. . . . I long for there to be meaning.[3]

Rough that it has turned out that way. Chuck is operating out of 9,9 assumptions toward sex, but he's up against pretty strong 9,1 rejection of sex-related intimacy and emotional closeness. Can it be expected they'll work it through? It's just possible. This conversation might be a turning point. At least Chuck now has some new key understandings coupled with knowledge of attitudes that were previously a closed book to him.

9,9 / 1,9

9,9/1,9 is a particularly interesting marriage combination. The 1,9 person has no real sense of autonomy but finds security in interdependence. The 9,9 mate, while respecting and valuing the importance of interdependence, feels a loss of autonomy because of the entwining aspect of a 1,9 mate.

Midway through a weekend afternoon, Roy begins fidgeting around, and eventually speaks.

Roy. Gayle, is anything wrong?
Gayle. Nothing that I'm aware of. Why?
Roy. You haven't said anything in a long while.
Gayle. Well, I'm reading, as you see.
Roy. I thought maybe you were mad at me.
Gayle. I wasn't. But this *is* an interesting book, Roy, and I'm trying to concentrate on it.
Roy. I'm sorry . . . er, um . . .
Gayle. Look, is something on your mind, or what?
Roy. I feel lonely, Gayle, I feel . . . you're so *distant.* Why can't we talk or do something? You don't seem to hear me.
Gayle. My thoughts were elsewhere, sure, but I wasn't reading this book in an attempt to desert you. *You're misreading me.*

Gayle probably feels that both their marriage and her reading interests will be well served if she can help Roy to shuck off his dependence on her moment-to-moment attention. This requires his finding some independent foundations for self-assurance.

9,9 / 1,1

Also in the area of sex-intimacy we've found a 1,1/9,9 relationship between Brick and Margaret.* In a 1,1 way, he has almost totally withdrawn from her. We see how she tries to deal with it. These epi-

* Chapter 9, pp. 134–135.

sodes give a real sense of her 9,9 assumptions, and her persistence in seeking to turn his 1,1 attitudes around into a stronger relationship with her. Even though her husband will have nothing to do with her, Margaret knows she is a hot number and attempts to increase her appeal to Brick by talking about her attractiveness to others.

Margaret. . . . You know, our sex life didn't just peter out in the usual way, it was cut off short, long before the actual time for it to, and it's going to revive again, just as sudden as that. I'm confident of it. That's what I'm keeping myself attractive for. For the time when you'll see me again like other men see me. Yes, like other men see me. Look, Brick! How high my body stays on me!—nothing has fallen on me!—Not a fraction! My face looks strained sometimes, but I've kept my figure as well as you've kept yours, and men admire it. I still turn heads on the street. . . .[4]

You get her sense of his 1,1 indifference in the following remark to Brick.

Margaret. . . . Of course, you always had that detached quality as if you were playing a game without much concern over whether you won or lost, and now you've lost the game, not lost but just quit playing, you have that rare sort of charm that usually happens in very old or hopelessly sick people, the charm of the defeated. You look so cool, so cool, so enviably cool.[5]

Does the situation right itself? Margaret's attempt to revive Brick by alluding to her attractiveness to other men gets nowhere, as we heard earlier,* even though it may have helped her to remain objective about her own appeal. But her leveling eventually brings a change of attitude which is sparked off when Brick bats into conflict with his sister Mae.

Brick. Mae, Sister Woman, how d'you know that I don't sleep with Maggie?

---

* Chapter 9, pp. 134–135.

Mae. We occupy the next room an' th' wall between isn't sound-
proof. . . . We hear the nightly pleadin' and the nightly refusal.
So don't imagine you're goin' t' put a trick over on us. . . .

*   *   *

Brick. . . . This girl has life in her body.

Mae. That is a lie!

Brick. No, truth is something desperate, an' she's got it. Believe me,
it's somethin' desperate, an' she's got it. An' now if you will
stop actin' as if Brick Pollitt was dead an' buried—I'm drunk,
and sleepy—not as alive as Maggie, but still alive. . . .

Brick is clewing us in here that Margaret's constant confronta-
tions about their relationship may in fact be getting through to
him; as is suggested when they converse after Mae has left. It's bedtime.

Margaret. . . . What do you say? What do you say, baby?

Brick. I admire you, Maggie.

Margaret. Oh, you weak, beautiful people who give up with such
grace. What you need is someone to take hold of you—gently,
with love, and hand your life back to you, like something gold
you let go of—and I can! I'm determined to do it—and nothing's more determined than a cat on a tin roof—is there? Is
there, baby? [6]

The striking thing here has been Margaret's maintenance of her
own morale and confidence, never feeling defeated or walking out,
but staying determined that she's going to revive her marriage.

9,9 / 5,5

A 9,9/5,5 marriage can be very strong and rewarding to both par-
ticipants much of the time. This is the case when basically different
attitudes do not arouse conflict of the sort that causes the convictions gap to become apparent. A 5,5-oriented person is flexible
and so is responsive to many 9,9 initiatives in emotional, as well as
problem-solving, activities. One mate's emphasis on fullness in living coincides, at several points, with the other's accent on commu-

nity and status considerations. When the two Grid approaches do get out of kilter, one of the most difficult conflict reactions to cope with from a 9,9 point of view is the other mate's readiness to compromise and accommodate.

Christina and David have been married six months. On a visit to David's home, it becomes evident to Christina that her mother-in-law is determined to pull David away from her. She is equally determined that her marriage will not be controlled by his mother. The mates are now alone and have an opportunity to talk in private. The conversation goes as follows:

Christina. Dave! . . .
David. Yes?
Christina. Whom do you love?
David. You. Why?
Christina. I wondered, that's all. I want to be kissed.
David. That's easy.
Christina. Such a tired girl, Dave. . . . I want to be held on to and made much of . . . I want to feel all safe and warm . . . I want you to tell me that you're in love with me and that you enjoy being in love with me. Because just loving isn't enough and it's being in love that really matters. . . . Will you tell me all that please, Dave? [7]

Christina is upset by what she is seeing in the attachment between David and his mother.

Christina. I've never come up against anything like this before; I've heard of it, but I've never met it. I don't know what to do about it. And it scares me.
David. What does?
Christina. I don't know how to tell you. But I've got to tell you, Dave. I've got to tell you. There are no two ways about that.
David. What are you driving at?
Christina. Well. . . . May I ask you a question? Rather an intimate one?
David. If you must!
Christina. Being your wife, I thought I might.

David. Shoot!

Christina. Do you look on me as apart from all other women? I
mean, do you think of all the women in the world and then
think of me quite, quite differently? Do you, Dave?

David. I'll bite. Do I?

Christina. Please answer me. It's awfully important to me just now.

David. Of course I do.

Christina. Because that's how I feel about you and all the other
men in the world. Because that's what being in love must
mean and being properly and happily married. Two people,
together by themselves, miles and miles from everybody, from
everybody else, glancing around, now and then, at all the rest
of mankind, at *all* the rest, Dave, and saying: "Are you still
there, and getting along all right? Sure there's nothing we can
do to help?" [8]

Taken together, these two interactions between Dave and Christina offer a very good illustration of her concept of 9,9 love and
affection, which contains a sense of distinctiveness in their own relationship produced by the unity that two people should feel in and
with each other. At the same time, Dave's 5,5 tentativeness shows
through in his uncertainty as to how to answer the question in a
way that would be acceptable, if not pleasing, to her.

In the following conversation, David's 5,5 attitude can be picked
up in his use of platitudes for evading a direct answer.

Christina. . . . Who comes first with you? Your mother or me?

David. Now, what's the good of putting things that way?

Christina. That's what things come to! If your mother and I ever
quarrelled about anything; if it ever came up to you to choose
between sticking by me or sticking by her, which would you
stick by?

David. I'd . . . I'd try to do the right thing. . . .

Christina. That's an evasion.

David. But why ask such a question?

Christina. Because I love you. Because I've got to find out if you
love me. And I'm afraid . . . I'm afraid.

David. Why?

Christina. Because you won't see the facts behind all this. I'm trying to tell you what they are and you won't listen. You can't even hear me.[9]

How a 5,5 husband appears to his wife can be sensed in the following remarks that come out of a discussion between David and Christina.

Christina. . . . I've been through the most awful experience of my life to-night, and I've been through it alone. I'm still going through it alone. It's pretty awful to have to face such things alone. . . .[10]

Christina was talking about the dramatic revelation of the controlling influence that David's mother exercises on him.

David. Oh, Chris!

Christina. No, don't interrupt me. I've got to get this off my chest. Ever since we've been married I've been coming across queer rifts in your feeling for me, like arid places in your heart. Such vast ones, too! I mean, you'll be my perfect lover one day, and the next I'll find myself floundering in sand and alone, and you nowhere to be seen. We've never been really married, Dave. Only now and then, for a little while at a time, between your retirements into your arid places. . . . I used to wonder what you did there. At first, I thought you did your work there. But you don't. Your work's in my part of your heart, what there is of my part. Then I decided the other was just No-Man's Land. And I thought: little by little, I'll encroach upon it and pour my love upon it, like water on the western desert, and make it flower here and bear fruit there. I thought: then he'll be alive, all free and all himself; not partly dead and tied and blind; not partly someone else—or nothing. You see, our marriage and your architecture were suffering from the same thing. They only worked a little of the time. I meant them both to work all the time. I meant you to work all the time and to win your way, *all* your way, Dave, to complete manhood. And that's a good deal farther than you've got so far. . . . Then we came here and this happened with Hester and your brother, and you just stepped aside and did nothing about it! You went to bed. You did worse than that. You re-

tired into your private wastes and sat tight. . . . I've shown
you what you should do and you won't see it. I've called to
you to come out to me, and you won't come. So now I've discovered what keeps you. Your mother keeps you. It isn't No-
Man's Land at all. It's your mother's land. Arid, sterile, and
your mother's! You won't let me get in there. Worse than that,
you won't let life get in there! Or she won't! . . . That's what
I'm afraid of, Dave: your mother's hold on you. I've seen
what she can do with Robert. And what she's done to Hester.
I can't help wondering what she may not do with you and to
me and to the baby. That's why I'm asking you to take a
stand on this business of Hester's, Dave. You'll never find the
right any clearer than it is here. It's a kind of test case for me.
Don't you see? What you decide about this is what you may,
eventually, be expected to decide about . . . about our marriage.[11]

Christina's comments provide good insight into the background
of David's 5,5 tentativeness through his inability to take a stand,
even when right and wrong are clearly delineated. He also tries to
use time to reduce pressure and to delay matters. Above all, his 5,5
approach is seen in readiness to accommodate and compromise in
order to avoid strife.

9,9 is undoubtedly a very strong and enduring basis for a mutually gratifying marriage. It makes possible the richest experience
of emotions, while creating the most valid basis for solving the inevitable array of problems two mates face. When both combine 9,9
attitudes, they can share and solve on an upward spiral of meaning-
fulness and joy. A strong 9,9/9,9 marriage is intrinsically fulfilling.

Marriages in which only one mate is 9,9 are likely to be less rewarding. The reason is that the 9,9-oriented mate might not be in
any position to operate in the two-mate 9,9 way that is seen as best,
particularly when unbridged differences or conflict prevail. One alternative posed is to abandon the 9,9 approach and embrace some
other Grid style as backup. But when 9,9 is a person's dominant
style, one naturally sees sticking with it to be the more consistent
alternative. By doing so, you can keep on challenging and encour-
aging your mate to relate with you on the same level.

CHAPTER 15 | VARIETY

If there is any single area that rises above others as an active volcano in married life, it is the question of "one-mate-for-life or one-mate-at-a-time or several-mates-at-any-time?" A striking conclusion about marriage is that, for many, passions cool and mutual interest wanes. The fire is banked, and the flames settle down or disappear. As time goes by, fewer and fewer sparks can be struck. The excitement of discovery, of having novel emotions and impressions, of conflict, of finding new ways of sharing, becomes more and more infrequent as mates come to know each other more fully. Then, too, marriage often gets dull, boring, stale, empty, deadly.

Although for some this kind of "so what" indifference comes amazingly soon, for others it's postponable for some years. Evidence indicates, however, that eventually it comes to the great majority of marriages in some degree.[1] One major research study, involving hundreds of families, showed that the longer people lived together, the less satisfied with the arrangement a mate became. This generalization held up for marriages that were thirty and more years old.[2]

Some mates separate to seek new stimulus in new marriages. Some stay under the same roof, learning with greater or lesser skill to live parallel lives together. Pursuit of each other and the fun and excitement that it entailed has wound down through matrimony into mutual boredom. Wife-capturing or husband-snaring was not where the fun began. It's where it ended. Monogamy has turned into monotony, bed's become boring, sex no longer scintillates.

What leads to staleness in marriage? Is it inevitable? What seems to be lacking as much as anything is variety—be it sexual or otherwise. You and your mate—any two people—can become so accustomed to each other, so mutually predictable, so stereotyped in your daily and nightly interactions that a time comes when few surprises ever surface. For you, there is not much new under the sun, and almost everything that is old is too well-known to seem interesting anymore or worthwhile talking about and doing. New adventures and experiences, male-female mysteries to resolve, and all the many things your marriage once provided, disappear.[3] But the hunger for freshness and variety persists. What changes is *where* it's pursued.

Monotony, treadmilling, humdrumness, are words that describe states of feeling from which people usually want to escape, things they don't like. This seems true whether tedium stems from eight hours on an assembly line, from eating the same food day-after-day, or from going through the same old motions with the same person, saying and thinking and doing similar things, endlessly. Satiation is the technical word for it.[4] "Fed up" is what the man on the street says.

A hundred years ago, when the home was a be-fruitful-and-multiply hatchery, a religious center, an educational center, a food processing and preserving center and bakery, a dressmaking and tailoring workshop, and so on, there was not much spare time left. To assure sheer survival, people had to share the home work. It might have been a boring life, but at least it was a busy one with no opportunity for idle hands.

Today, with The Pill, disposable diapers, supermarkets, washing machines, automated ovens, TV dinners, etc., it's getting to be a hard job to keep busy. More time is available now because there's less to do. Boredom in the kitchen can spread into the bedroom. Nonetheless, some people have found that more time means opportunity to pursue variety either within or outside their marriages.

Look at this matter of variety from a Grid angle. In most of the Grid styles, some sort of repetitiveness is likely to occur. For instance, both of you may have slumped over into the 1,1 "couldn't-care-less" corner. Or perhaps you have learned to "live and let live," keeping in comfortable cadence, accommodating and adjusting in a 5,5 way that ensures you both a "no surprise"—and therefore, a "no variety"—basis of being together. Or how lively is a 1,9/1,9 love nest where both are eager to be first to yield for love's sake? How satisfying is a 9,1/1,9 "I demand, you capitulate" pairing? How much joy is there in the continuous warfare of two 9,1-oriented people?

All these can make the "grass look greener" in the yards beyond, and, when it does, you may reach the conclusion "monogamy is monotony." You look around, seeking the kind of freshness you feel a stale mate can't provide. A wide range of options for real or imagined sexual variety is available. They can tell us something about this monotony problem.

First, there's vicarious variety. It comes in the form of sex fun by word, image, and fantasy. And these sources of variety are not limited to male audiences. You can prove this to yourself by picking up any three woman's magazines. If you want, you can examine for a more thorough study. Here's a summary of themes and characters that appear in this kind of magazine, month after month and year after year. The crux is captured here:

> Taken as a whole, the sexual content of our mass circulation women's magazines affords a more comprehensive and revealing description of the sexual attitudes, interests, and fantasies, of the American female than has previously been made possible through the polling and interviewing of a limited sampling of thousands.

> And what a wild assortment of interests they are!

> Fornication, adultery, exhibitionism, voyeurism, rape, incest, mate swapping, group sex, lesbianism, prostitution, flagellation, pyromania, and necrophilia are among the numerous subjects one finds recurring time and again in these prettily packaged monthlies. Considering that most of these themes and deviations involve aspects of sex that Kinsey and other well-intentioned researchers have declared to be of little or no

220   *The Marriage Grid*

erotic interest to females, how can one possibly account for their luridly titillating presence in the pages of so many of our women's magazines?[5]

What does all this add up to? The simple explanation is that if most marriages were fulfilling, such reading would hold little of its present appeal. Would people gratify themselves vicariously if they could do so directly through a full and meaningful husband-wife relationship?

On the opposite side, involving real, rather than neurotic titillation, are extramarital relationships entered into by mutual consent on a premeditated, planned, and programmatic basis. Swap clubs, where spin-the-bottle, toss-the-key, weekend and vacation musical-beds, and other mate-permuting arrangements are used, now function on an ongoing basis in many American cities.[6] Other forms of "civilized adultery," [7] and group marriages of two, three or more couples [8] are being discussed and projected.

The belief on the part of one wife that anyone who denies involvement in extramarital affairs is naïve is the topic in this conversation. April and Helen are talking about their husbands, Tom and Jack.

Helen. You mean Tom's never been off with another woman?
April. Not as far as I know. Why should he? He seems to be happy.
Helen. Why should he? That's a hell of a question. Why should my
     Jack, why should any of them, the dirty bastards?
April. Tom just doesn't seem interested in other women.
Helen. How old is he?
April. Thirty-nine.
Helen. He'll be starting any minute now.[9]

On a nationwide scale, the extent of this hunger for sexual variety is unknown. Probably there is a need for more research and documentation. However, many indicators suggest that the hunger is widespread.[10]

Outside adventure and its consequences are being described by Frank to his son Richie. Frank has learned that Richie and Joan, his wife, are breaking up, and Frank thinks it's because Richie is cheating on Joan.

Richie. That's not the reason.

Frank. Come on, you can tell me. I never told you this before, but you're grown up now. I strayed too, when I was young. Don't get me wrong.' I never went looking for it, but, you know, sometimes you're walking along and it falls in your lap.

Richie. You don't have to tell me this.

Frank. Look, it happens to everybody. I love your mother, but, you know, sometimes you need a little more stimulation . . . you know? . . . All right, thank God she never felt that way. But . . . uh . . . there was this one time when . . . uh . . . your mother found out about it. . . . She walked out on me for four days, but then she came back. Where's she gonna go? All right, she was mad and she felt very hurt and I. . . . So, your mother and I had a lot of . . . uh . . . difficulties there for awhile, and like I was telling Joan, when there's difficulties in a marriage, it's usually caused as a result of one of the parties involved causing friction. . . . but . . . she got over it, just like Joan will get over it. Women know how to take things.[11]

In a burned-out marriage, extramarital affairs often become the main involvement, while the everyday meaningless routine continues grinding along. If conversation between stale mates gets on to the topic of their marriage problems, it rarely succeeds at more than aggravating old sores.

Sometimes, rather than enjoying secrets together, couples come to hide secrets from each other. This withholding means having experiences that can't be shared. The single greatest cause of withholding is secrets about extramarital affairs. Energy has to be applied to keeping the affair from being known, and this reduces spontaneity and naturalness. A person maintaining an important secret does so by building facades and using diversionary tactics and denials. All of these bring stiffness into a relationship. Thus the requirements for secretiveness that individual mates' outside affairs create is possibly a key reason why these attempts to gain variety are so disrupting.

Even though Debra's and Curt's marriage has been unsound for several years, *her* continued suspiciousness of Curt turns out to be well-founded.

Debra. I'm glad you're home. It's late. What happened?

Curt. Let me get a drink. I'm exhausted.

Debra. But I delayed dinner for an hour. You didn't even call.

Curt. It's getting the signature on that Mansfield contract that's been so long and frustrating.

Debra. But weren't you and Bill working together all day on it?

Curt. Yeah, but we still didn't have agreement on a number of clauses. I took him out for dinner and a couple of drinks to oil him up.

Debra. Where did you go?

Curt. Delmonico's.

Debra. Did you get his John Henry on the dotted line?

Curt. Yes. When we finished up I deposited him at the hotel.

Debra. That's wonderful.

Curt. I'm tired and want to go to bed. Anything new?

Debra. Yes. Bill called two hours ago. He said you had to leave early and he wanted to tell you something else to put in the contract before he signed it in the morning.

Curt. It couldn't have been Bill.

Debra. What *did* you deposit at the hotel?

Curt labored through a massive, uninspired coverup to hide his doings. What's more, Debra led him into her trap knowing all the while that his business was more monkey than corporate. Of course, the mutual distrust is likely to become even worse than it has been up to now.[12]

Other married mates, with each other's full knowledge and consent, go outside marriage in their pursuit of fulfillment. Here's the way investigators sum up what these couples see themselves gaining from group sex.

The "swingers" believe they have found the answer to complete sexual fulfillment and to a completely satisfying marital relationship. With an occasional change of sex partners they feel they have more fruitful lives, better lives as individuals, as marrieds, and as members of society. They believe their friendships have developed in greater depths; they believe their experience has greatly magnified their capacity for

warmth and understanding; they believe their experiences
have enriched their lives. To them their experiences are not
extra-marital sexual experiences. They *share* their experience
with each other and with another couple who feel the same
way they do, and believe the only apt description would be
"comarital." [13]

What are the within-marriage circumstances whereby many
couples—current estimates vary up to fourteen million [14]—get into
the group-sex scene? It could be that tension release and intimacy,
sex's two unifiable aspects, either have been viewed previously as
quite separate [15] or haven't yet been put together in a particular
marriage. Either of these conditions can be present in marriages
where 1,1, 1,9, 5,5, and 9,1 orientations prevail. Swingers frequently report that any fears of hurting their marriage turn out to
be unfounded, and that their within-marriage sex and companionship improve more than they ever thought it could. They see this
as a bonus benefit over and above their enjoyment with other partners.[16]

One interpretation is that the experience of contrast may help
each mate to break patterns of repetitiousness in taking each other
for granted, and in this way aid both to react to each other afresh
as distinctive individuals. A second is that new ways of thinking
and feeling—to say nothing of different techniques—may be discovered and imported into the marriage where they have a vitaliz-
ing effect. A third is that frustration and boredom within the marriage may evaporate when both mates arrive at more avenues into
sexual pleasure.

But some find there is a "down" side to swinging. On the moving
assembly line of brief encounters and one-night stands one can
come to feel more anonymous, less an individual than at the beginning. Certainly you are where the action is, yet it is all becoming a
blur, and ultimately a blah. A reason for this may be that there is
no continued relationship of the kind in which the other person reflects for you your own identity.

These illustrations have provided an indication of the widespread
desire for variety. Does this kind of activity simply produce a few
bubbles of zest like soda added to Scotch, or does it have the ca-

pacity to move a marriage toward 9,9 richness and depth? Or can two people in one marriage relate in such a way that each finds the other *unendingly* fascinating, so that extramarital adventure would *reduce* total fulfillment?

There are three different answers to these questions.

The first is a flat "NO." You may think variety, excitement, and fruitful fulfillment within marriage—or even outside it—are possible, but only for a short spell. As Sophocles put it, "Show me the man whose happiness was anything more than illusion followed by disillusion." [17]

A second is a modified "NO." This is the view that fulfillment, with all the richness of variety and novel experience which go with it, is too much to hope for long-term within a monogamous arrangement. But don't lose hope. Society is freeing people for supplementary activities and enjoyments, particularly in the arena of extramarital happenings. So the answer implies a main relationship, supported by satellite relationships and individual spheres of interest.

A third answer is a qualified "YES." It rejects the "monotony's a penalty of monogamy" definition.

Feelings of monotony and boredom indicate that there has been an ebbing away of interest. But something far more important is involved. Monotony is not *inevitable*. Rather, it may reflect a slowdown in human ingenuity. According to this view, the deepest fulfillment possible from man-woman relationships is achievable *only* when two people have learned to grow together, unendingly expanding their interdependence in ways that keep each bright, fresh, fascinating, and desirable to the other.

The way two people relate together after the newness has worn off may promote dullness, drabness, despair, mutual hostility, sweet nothingness, boring accommodation, *or* continuing interest and joy. Evidence exists that some have found a way to stay vital together with no outside help.

> . . . I do know some people—not very darn many—who are our age and even older, who still have the same kind of excitement about them and each other that we had when we were all in college. I've seen some of them at parties and other

places—the way they look at each other, the little touches as they go by. One couple has grandchildren and you'd think they were honeymooners. I don't think it's just sex either—I think they are just part of each other's lives. . . .[18]

What they're doing, what they enjoy together, is not something that calls for extraordinary talent. Quite simply, they've learned how to enjoy each other on a continuing basis. Here then is evidence that *monotony,* not monogamous marriage, is the real culprit. Some men and women

. . . rarely feel sexual desire in a general way and are not aroused by casual or merely physical contact. Sex and love are so thoroughly fused and inseparable in their emotional apparatus that they experience sexual desire only when they love. For such people, casual encounters are likely to be neither immoral nor repellent, but simply unrewarding.[19]

Of course, there are still other ways of thinking about variety. In this case it's variety within the context of married intimacy. Take the following.

True familiarity . . . is forever fascinating because the human brain can, and does, meet any situation in an endless variety of ways.[20]

We are being told that to "specialize" in getting truly to know just one other person in a deep and intimate way is the ultimate challenge.

And—focusing the discussion solely on sex for a moment—just how limiting of variety is monogamy, anyway? Legal prohibitions operate in some states, but they're not a big issue nowadays. Here's a pithy statement that sums up present professional thinking on variety in sexual expression.

There is absolutely nothing wrong with it so long as guilt doesn't ensue. If guilt follows or there is great inhibition, then there is obviously conflict present that needs resolving.[21]

In effect, it says that two people in an intimate relation are like a Rorschach inkblot. What they see, and enjoy participating in and experimenting with together is limited only by their imaginations and their openness to each other.[22]

How nature might have intended men-women alliances is a moot question; but how society has arranged for these alliances is not. Biology may or may not prescribe a first-come, first-served basis, but society has historically said savor one person forever, or start relishing another person only *after* you are legally separated from the previous one.

"How nature would have it" versus "How society has it," though, is really neither here nor there. The facts seem to be these: repetition is dulling, variety is enriching. But moving from person to person is to find a kind of variety that may pall by its very impermanence. This chapter has dealt with the question of whether it is possible within the monogamous relationship to sense the tantalizing richness that variety can provide, while attaining the gratification that only a deep man-woman relationship can contribute.

The conclusion is "yes, it is possible." Two people, in all their complexity, are, or can become, capable of enriching themselves from variety with each other. At the same time they can draw upon the gratification that comes from penetrating the recesses of mixed emotions, replenishing and enlarging the wellsprings of the relationship. The likelihood is that only through a deep and continuing relationship may both these sources of fundamental human emotions be experienced simultaneously.

CHAPTER 16 | ENRICHING YOUR MARRIAGE

What is the most obvious and commonplace thing two people living together do with each other? They talk. *How* they talk together is no less important than the topics they discuss. It may even be more important. When you watch other people conversing, you can notice all kinds of dynamics: withdrawal, disinterest, resistance, support. You can see people yielding, winning and losing, compromising and accommodating, or seeking to understand. In the more constructive conversations you've heard or participated in, you may recall diagnosing and analyzing issues, taking part and becoming involved, finding agreement and then working wholeheartedly to put decisions into effect. In contrast, you will probably recall many futile conversations that ended in impasse, rancor and wrath, or sheer indifference. It is through discussion that you arrive at conclusions or fail to reach them. Also, it is *in* discussion that emotions are communicated. Much of what couples say to each other is fueled by feelings—feelings that the other mate might not notice, or might misperceive or ignore or react to negatively.

Learning to read each other's feelings is one of the best starting points in learning a fluent married language. When each of you can sense your mate's real feelings and respond to them, you can be sure you are really talking. Yet you may have come to know each other so well that there has developed an opaque film of unawareness between you. Traditions and practices have become routine. Rituals, sacred cows, shared jokes, and so on, keep you doing the same things with each other as you did yesterday and the day before. One of the finest opportunities for refreshing the marriage climate is to reawaken your moment-to-moment awareness of both your selves. Here's how.

It should be clear by now that how people talk is significantly influenced by their Grid styles. For example, the way a 9,1-oriented person talks—the basic assumptions he makes about another person—is the Mirror opposite of how a 1,9 person seeks to communicate. Thus, each Grid style has its own unique assumptions that are revealed in how one person speaks when he talks with another person.

We want to study conversation now as a way of getting started toward changing whatever it might be in your assumptions that would strengthen your marriage.

Let's be as concrete about it as possible. Perhaps the best way is this. Go back to the Mirror of yourself and your mate that you wrote down in Chapter 3. Is what you concluded at that time still accurate? Or, having completed your study of the Grid, should you now revise these pictures to make the paragraph descriptions as objective as is possible?

After reevaluating your Mirror, draw conclusions about your Grid style. Check them out with your mate. What is your dominant style? That is, what are the distinctive and characteristic ways that you approach your mate? What comes through in your relationship as your backup? As you read this chapter think about your personal Grid style and how you and your mate talk. Listen for suggestions. Actions that you can take in shifting from whatever Grid styles are typical of you to ones you would like to be characteristic of yourself are given at each point along the way.

Communicating is no simple matter in spite of the fact we all seem to do it so effortlessly. It involves at least five issues: (1) expressing your own point of view, (2) asking questions to find out what your mate thinks and feels, (3) listening, (4) responding to your mate's point of view, and (5) expressing your own emotions and feelings while reacting to the feelings of your mate. How you talk is regulated by your Grid-style assumptions. For this reason, the last four of these five major aspects of communication will be examined, style by style. As "expressing your own point of view" has been dealt with in earlier chapters, it will not be further discussed.

ASKING QUESTIONS

It is noteworthy how important questions are in good communicating. Any person gets a lot of his information from other people. Of course, there are many supplementary sources: books, TV, newspapers, and other media; remarks by boss or relatives, friends and acquaintances. But much of this information is not specifically applicable to your marriage situation. Uniquely, individually, your mate possesses most of what you need to know in that area. Yet your mate isn't as readable as an open book all the time. You have to ask questions to understand emotions, to determine facts, to evaluate desires, to test understanding, and to form expectations.

But asking questions can be an uncertain business. If you ask questions in an effective way, you get the information you seek whether it's about a factual or an emotional matter. If the questions asked are not sound, or if you use them in a tactical manner to weaken your mate, rather than for gaining information, questioning may do a great disservice to your relationship and weaken it.

9,1

A typical 9,1 way of asking questions is to pose a query but to neglect to explain why. Being 9,1-oriented, you do this because it's a speedy, direct way to get to the point. As you see it, the question is necessary. That's sufficient reason for asking it.

Sally. How much d'you have in your wallet?
Max. Eh? Why do you want to know?
Sally. Come on, how much?—I want to *know!*

Look at this from Max's standpoint. If he doesn't know why Sally wants the information, what does this kind of blunt demand do? Does it make him want to be open, free, spontaneous, and expressive? Or does it cause him to go in the opposite direction and become closed, hidden, and distrustful? It's more likely to do the latter. Under 9,1 questioning, your mate doesn't know what you're up to and is likely to feel defensive. There's no assurance you won't misuse the information. With his attention drawn brusquely to the contents of his wallet, Max might tend to think not "How many dollars?" but "What's going to happen to my dollars now?"

Questions can be asked in a way that indicates you're pumping. Just think of what pumping means: pushing down in order to lift some water from a well—or dollars from a wallet! To your mate, this kind of questioning is very suspect. It only reinforces fear of being exploited in other ways, too. Max probably feels he can escape only by dodging Sally's point-blanks. He could say "two" when the actual count is ten. Or he just might say, "None of your damn business!"

There is another angle on questioning in a 9,1 manner. You can make your mate feel weak by asking questions that can't be answered. Whether or not your mate *should* be able to answer the questions is beside the point. It's what you think about your mate's inability to answer them that counts. If your questions come through as jabs or if they seem condescending, your mate will feel humiliated and resent being grilled.

1,9

A 1,9-oriented approach is to ask questions in a vague and indirect way. You want to avoid directly asking in a fashion that might annoy your mate or seem prying or critical. Your questions allow a lot of room for your mate to find the pleasant replies you hope for.

But what are the results? Your mate is likely to feel that you are not being constructive, that the conversation is soft, oblique, and time-wasting, lacking the "brass tacks reality" quality a person has the right to expect.

Fred. These baby clothes are cute, aren't they?
Sonia. Yeah. Come on, we're looking for some new shoes for *me!*
Fred. That bassinet—aah! Can't you just see it in our bedroom?
Sonia. What the heck are we standing *here* for?

These questions, if they're hinting that Fred wants children, don't warm Sonia toward prospects of maternity. They may cool her off. More generally, vague 1,9 questions don't move your mate toward closer consideration of the project you have in mind. They tend to generate annoyance and raise barriers between you. These, in turn, create further misunderstanding.

1,1

When your attitudes are 1,1, you are unlikely to formulate questions for your mate. You don't care for, or need, information. In fact, the less you have, the better. So you leave it to your mate to ask questions if necessary, hoping they won't be hard to answer. You assume, if information is wanted, your mate will ask for it. You operate in the same spirit.

Matt. Evening paper here yet?
Lois. Dunno. Have a look.

5,5

As a 5,5-oriented mate, you *use* questions. Often you have your thoughts about a pre-set topic all worked out, and points arranged so as to move your mate indirectly toward the kind of decision you want. Your strategy is specific; your tactics are flexible. Thus the second, third, and fourth questions may very well be on different subjects. The second question asked is a function of the answer to the first. You select the third question while displaying great interest in the information your mate has given in answer to your second question, and so on.

Bernice. What did the garage bill come to?
Lyle. Ninety dollars and a few cents. The air conditioner needed fixing.
Bernice. We're spending a lot on repairs this year, aren't we?
Lyle. Yes, unfortunately.
Bernice. Y'know, that ninety dollars could be a month's installment on a new car.

Unless you're extremely subtle, your mate will realize the questions being put are not the kind that help you understand, but are intended to assist in your current maneuver. As a result, your mate might not respond positively to this kind of interrogative hinting.

9,9

How can you go about acquiring the kind of information that's vital for an effective, strong, and rewarding marriage? Prior to asking any questions, you indicate what you know or presently understand about the situation. Your mate's confidence is increased because your standpoint is now clear. Then you ask questions, letting your mate know *how* it will help you to have the answers you seek.

Leonard. I'm making an appointment for my medical check-up. I think at our ages, especially, we both need a regular going over. Like an appointment too?

Toni. I'm frightened.

Leonard. I've had them for the past five years, and each time I came out alive! It doesn't take very long, and there's nothing unpleasant or painful. Now what's scaring you, Toni?

Toni. There's no telling *what* the doctor will find.

Leonard. If there *is* something to find, would you prefer to live unaware of it for a while until you couldn't ignore it anymore?

Toni. No, but well, y'know. . . .

Leonard. How about giving it a try? We can go together and talk things over with the doctor before you make up your mind.

Your *manner* of approach, like Leonard's, communicates several things reinforcing what you *say*. One thing communicated is that you view your mate as an individual, not as a cipher or as a subordinate or as a baby. Other unspoken messages are that you appreciate your mate's ability to think, and that the forthcoming information is valued and will be used authentically.[1] The questions are not being asked as a softening-up gambit. By being open with regard to your own intentions, you create in your mate's emotions a readiness to accept you as an honest and genuine friend and partner.

There is another way to look at questions. When you and your mate are trying to make a decision, the questions you first ask of each other should be for the purpose of acquiring mainly *factual* information. Others can explore the feelings which surround the situation, and those that are posed later can be more evaluative. The latter are questions that call upon your mate to exercise judgment, to compare and combine facts, and to expose opinions. Movement from the one type to the other is traceable in Leonard's questions. There are no quick yes/no answers to evaluative questions, yet these are indispensable in sound discussion. They aid you in understanding the character of your mate's thinking and vice versa. This is important in assisting both of you to arrive at sound conclusions. Another aspect of these more thought-provoking questions is that they promote participation and involvement, which are likely to bring a more problem-solving orientation to bear.

Questions can give you greater appreciation of your mate's emotions. "How are you?" is often a social nicety, even between husbands and wives. When it's broadened to "How do you feel about . . . ?" or "Do you like . . . ?" or "What don't you like about it?" and you really care about the feelings you detect in your mate's reply, you are concerned for your mate as an entire person, whose thoughts and emotions are significant.

Asking questions, then, is a central feature of problem-solving. Yet many people seem doubtful about the possible effects of questioning their mates. Seen in the Grid framework, the positive and negative forms of questioning can easily be distinguished. Questions can cement a conviction and tie people together instead of alienating them. They can forge, rather than fracture, sound conclusions.

LISTENING AND HEARING

A good conversation is a two-way street—a sharing of thoughts and attitudes, of ideas and opinions, of feelings and emotions. It may lead to a meeting of minds and, thus, to a positive conclusion; but there are many situations in which a detour is taken, or you and your mate go down a cul-de-sac. Poor listening may be the cause.[2]

Listening and hearing can be two quite different things. From your point of view, you can gain increased acceptance of your ideas when your mate listens attentively. However sound your talking is, it can have no effect until it's listened to. The same goes for what your mate is saying. Here are some pointers about your listening and hearing skills. First, listening does not simply mean being quiet while your mate talks. Second, listening can be biased. What is heard is not necessarily what is said, and this occurs for two reasons: one is the character of talk; the other is in the character of listening.

When a person talks, he must find words to express thoughts and feelings. Words are by no means valid full statements of what a person is thinking or how he is feeling. Words only represent thoughts and emotions; but they are not these in actuality. They can be very poor approximations. Thoughts are mediated through words and expressed in words, and the expression of thoughts can be clear, obscure, or anything in between. Also, emotions are felt by a person who is expressing thoughts. The words, in themselves, may carry very little indication of these emotions across to the person who hears them, unless the receiver is very attentive to intonations and other signs.

As a result, whenever you listen to what you are being told, you are reading between the lines. You must piece together, if you can, the totality of your mate's ideas and feelings. Both of you, hopefully, are free to ask questions. Depending on how they are phrased and replied to, these may ensure that each person's interpretation of what is being said is the intended message that the speaker wants to convey.

But at a deeper level, listening is of a personal nature. No person listens in a completely objective way. It would be impossible to do this. What a person hears may be partly determined by what is said, but it may equally be determined *by what is inside the listener*. The message that comes in gets mixed in with a mass of experience, emotions, and attitudes, taking its coloration from what has gone on and is currently going on in the listener's own mind. Accurate listening is a function of how well the listener is able to sort out and separate his own opinions from what is being said.

The importance of all this is that the quality of your conversations depends as much on listening as on talking. To listen accurately, you must grasp the meaning, not just the words. You must analyze intentions, not just the language used. When you can do this, you are far more likely to respond constructively, to discern meaning in apparently irrelevant remarks, and to give sound answers to questions.

9,1

9,1 listening may take at least two forms. One is really not listening but merely pausing in the middle of speaking. This gives you a chance to catch a breath. A brief hiatus occurs and your mate can speak. It is likely that what you say next will pick up where you left off, rather than take into account anything your mate has actually said.

However, if you listen keenly, it's for signs of opposition to your will. If you can pinpoint any reservations that seem to stand in the way of agreement and compliance, you can then launch an attack on those points and win your way by disposing of them quickly. This kind of listening has its advantages. It does keep you alert to the opinions, thoughts, and attitudes being revealed, which, if not understood, could lead to difficulty. The disadvantage is that your listening may not be at all perceptive. What you hear stimulates the sensitiveness in you and is likely to trigger aggressive attitudes. Poor listening can convert your mate's emotionally neutral question into a strong objection—as *you* hear it. You then try to shoot the objection down, and your mate, not wanting to be humiliated, begins to feel emotions of resistance. Once aroused, these may, in fact, turn the initial query into a full-blown criticism, and then a win-lose battle begins. The ensuing fight may be stimulating, but it is stimulating on the emotional level, not by reason of the ideas which emerge. Even happy warriors can become weary wranglers, and eventually turn away from each other.

1,9

1,9 listening narrows reception in a different way. It is not listening to argue or waiting to present your own position. Rather, its most characteristic feature is that you try solely to read between the lines for the emotions. You may try to hear what you want to hear—the brighter, happier side. Yet you're sensitive to your mate's feelings, and you interpret the message differently, depending on whether you sense hostility or friendliness, acceptance or rejection. This is particularly so in the case of complaints which are phrased in the form of questions. You don't like to hear hostile notes; they are unpleasant and disconcerting—"Surely my mate doesn't mean that?" So your answers are likely to be off-beam, responding on the emotional level, or coaxing and wheedling toward happiness, rather than focusing on sound consideration of the complaint. Listening for what you want to hear, though, has some advantages. You can sometimes supplement an approving remark with a series of additional points of information, all of which help confirm and prolong the pleasant mood. But despite this, your mate is unlikely to find much gratification in discussions with you. When questions are posed or problems raised, your answers have a bland quality about them. Your mate seeks food for thought; you give tranquilizers.

1,1

1,1 listening is likely to be inattentive. You feel little involvement either with your mate or with what is happening in your marriage. Thus you may provide ample opportunity for your mate to talk, but you tune yourself out and think about other things. If there does happen to be something you want to settle with your mate, you give up as soon as your views are resisted. You close down the store mentally and say to yourself, "Well, that's one gone down the drain—there's nothing more to discuss." Your listening mistake is to short-circuit the entire conversation, instead of moving it forward in a sound manner.

5,5

As a person listening in a 5,5 way, you're attempting to pigeonhole each remark you hear according to your pre-established system of interpretation. If you can fit what is being said into a particular category, you then know what answer to give. You may think, "Ah, my mate's interested. Now I know where to plug in," and go on to phrase your remarks and replies in the direction that's been set. This kind of listening can lead to hearing that is good only to the extent that the pre-established framework is good. The major difficulty with the 5,5 restricted scope of listening is that it's likely to lead to answers which, while being somewhat relevant, are not completely on target.

9,9

The prime ingredient of 9,9 listening is that your respect, appreciation, and affection for your mate make you want to really take in what's being said. You know the essence of thought and feeling is never entirely caught in words. So whenever you're not sure you've picked up your mate's meaning, you give your present interpretation and try to get this clarified. In this way you can assure yourself that you genuinely comprehend, to the fullest extent possible, what your mate had in mind. Then you are well-placed to answer your mate in a full and meaningful way. Beyond that, you summarize frequently to ensure that you and your mate are on the same wavelength.

The receptivity of 9,9 listening emerges from your involvement with and commitment to your mate. Thus you are unlikely to screen or distort what is being said by mingling your own view with your mate's in such a way as to misinterpret or attach false emphases to it. While listening, you are able to keep your own feelings separate so that they don't affect your capacity to understand your mate's viewpoint.

RESPONDING TO ANOTHER POINT OF VIEW

A conversation, no matter how smoothly it flows, can never correspond exactly to the path of thought-development in a single person's mind. Many possible ideas, as well as emotions, can occur to your mate as a conversation continues. Feeling like commenting, your mate does so. These remarks, which break the continuity of your thought, may come at any time. Some of them might be directly relevant to what is being said at that time, though you may not see the connection. Others are in the nature of general objections to what you're saying. Thus, whenever your mate's point of view differs from your own, or when the topic your mate wants to pursue switches to a different track, you are likely to be interrupted. Interruptions need to be listened to. They often indicate that your mate's point of view is at variance with your own. After all, what impels *you* to interrupt?

9,1

Let's look at the pattern of 9,1-oriented reactions, rather than at any specific interruptions by either mate.

When interrupted, you react with impatience. Either the interruption slows you down or you see it as irrelevant and, therefore, not worthy of being dealt with. In either event, it's likely to be ignored, or, with a figurative swing of the arm, you brush it aside.

How does your mate, who is trying to state a point of view, respond to this treatment? Probably he or she feels rejected, resentful, and resistant. What appears to be irrelevant to you is likely to be highly relevant to your mate, even though you rule it offside. For example, your mate may have had problems with a boss or a neighbor or a salesman or with the children, and simply wants to blow off steam. Or the wish may be to tell you about something exciting. If you don't permit this pressure to be released, it remains pent-up. Then your mate may be continuing to turn that problem or topic over and over instead of listening to you.

1,9

A 1,9 way of dealing with the same kind of interruption is to treat it with the utmost appreciation and respect. You sincerely value your mate as important, so you respond warmly. The subject matter of the interruption is put in the forefront, to be fully discussed, while whatever *you* might have had in mind is set aside.

There are likely to be several results. One is that the conversation may stretch out to an indeterminable length. It wanders all over the place, having little crispness and less direction. One topic stimulates another, and so on. The conclusion that was to be reached recedes ever further beyond the horizon. Your mate runs out of time, for there are other things that must be done. Unless also 1,9-oriented, your mate is likely to realize that this kind of meandering is wasteful. Then thoughts dwell on what could have been done had there not been so much distraction. So, although your 1,9-oriented intention is to create an atmosphere of happiness and warmth, your approach tends to be self-defeating.

1,1

When, as a 1,1-oriented person, you are interrupted, you may take this as a sign that your mate is uninterested and wants to steer you off the subject so as to finish the conversation. Your response is to assume that all is lost and to start thinking of what to do when you're on your own again. While dealing perfunctorily with the interruption, you are mentally fixing your hair and buttoning your coat. You're not listening to your mate and discussing the matter; you've already done a mental walkout. By giving up, you fulfill your own prophecy and turn aside from possible consensus.

5,5

The 5,5 way of treating interruptions is to appreciate that your mate is often disposed to talk about matters that are not directly relevant to you. But you must be flexible. It is frequently possible to move the other person along your own route via these personal byways. You accept the interruption as a detour through which the conversation must pass in order to reach your desired point. So you acknowledge interruptions with a courteous pause. You listen to whatever is said, and try to connect it with some aspect of your pre-established goals. If no connection seems possible, you hear your mate out and then make some bland remark, such as "That's very interesting." Then you can shift back to your main road.

9,9

As a 9,9-oriented mate, you understand and respect your mate's feelings. Life should be guided by logic, but life is felt through emotions. You appreciate that, like yourself, your mate has needs and emotions and feelings and frustrations. These are part of the complexity of living together interdependently. The interruption certainly is important from your mate's standpoint, so you feel it is important to understand what is being said. You seek to comprehend how your mate feels and thinks about the matter, and why. Much of this information is of background value. To become irritated by apparently aimless and disconnected statements, which seem to have no bearing on the topic of discussion, is only to lose the depth that conversation may provide. Your making the effort to comprehend the *why* of the interruption and to understand your mate's point of view, shows that your mate's thoughts, ideas, opinions, and feelings are just as important to you as your own.

DEALING WITH EMOTIONS

If life were all logic, some of the biggest barriers to human effectiveness wouldn't appear; but marriage wouldn't have much of a sparkle to it or much to recommend it, either. Cold rationality is important, but it is not the strongest thread in marriage. It may be logic that indicates solutions to problems, but emotions supply the power, the enthusiasms to get things done, and the reward when achievement is reached. They are the wellsprings which motivate action. So readiness to disclose your feelings is all-important. Worries and complaints, as well as affection and warmth, lie at the very heart of feelings. Resistance, resentment, and antipathy are your way of indicating you haven't been helped, that you've been ignored, or that you've been rejected. You probably want your mate to be full, open, and meaningful when talking with you. But how willing are you for your mate to participate along with you?

Up to this point, discussion has centered on how emotions influence conversation. Now attention is turned to emotions as such—as you find them in yourself—and what you can do, constructively, in living with them. When you understand them, you are better equipped to be helpful to your mate, who, like you, is often swayed this way and that by emotion.

Where do emotions come from? Why do people have them?

Emotions are in evidence in the higher and lower forms of life. They occur in animals as well as in men. They serve a purpose. Negative emotions arise as signals to a person that things are not right, that danger may lie ahead, that risk to life—or at least to happiness—may be in the offing. In modern society the physical risks are not as great as they once were, but the complex social environment today has more than enough stimulation to provoke many of the most negative of human emotions as responses to threats to well-being. On the positive side, there are emotions of love and enjoyment of one's mate and of excitement in everyday activities. Positive emotions arise when a person feels secure, successful, sound, and effective. They come forth when he is able to master the situations that confront him. They have a bonus-benefit effect in building further confidence in his capacity to deal with life's problems and contribute to the richness of another's life. In this way a marriage can move to higher levels, as mates' problem-solving and emotional relations interact and synergize.

If your emotions are out of tune with the situation, they undoubtedly will get in the way of your initiating and maintaining a sound relationship with your mate. This is why it is important to look deeply into the whole matter.[3]

9,1

As a 9,1-oriented person, you view emotions as a source of weakness. Men don't let them get in the way of their action. Nor should a strong woman who has to battle for supremacy. So if you are acting from 9,1 assumptions, you have learned to deny and disregard your own feelings—or at least, the sentimental range within the spectrum. You may have pushed them down so deeply into yourself that you don't recognize they are there. Your emotions-based disregard for your mate and other people may slip through in your use of humor—it is hard-hitting and carries a sting for those who are its targets. You may discharge emotions by harboring intense prejudices and hates: any and all of these provide a channel for release. You have negative emotions, but you don't experience them for what they really are. Rather, you take them out on society, or on your mate, or both, in righteous indignation; all the while denying that emotions influence you. Only when you are unable to control situations are your emotions likely to break through and become apparent. Then your temper flares, and, under some circumstances, it becomes a fit of rage.

A person who controls emotions in these ways—though there are other 9,1 ways, too—may seem to be efficient. All is business:

no play, no interruptions, no irrelevancies, get to the point, drive hard, move in, get results. What gets lost is the richness of understanding, human sympathy, and the ability to sense how the other person feels. Furthermore, controlling negative emotions in this way often results in inability to enjoy the positive ones. Success is not gratifying, achievement not rewarding. Life affords few pleasures, your mate included. If you have been leaning in a 9,1 direction, you may now be able to notice that the characteristics which have been described resemble your own approach. It can be most important for you to look inward. If you find you have these emotional tendencies, you may also find they've reduced the richness of your marriage. What can you do about it?

You can learn to be more open with yourself and to recognize what you are doing, or not doing, to have produced the observable consequences. You may find you have a self-canceling way of dealing with emotions. An initial step in doing something about it is dealing with your temper. This is most likely to be damaging to relations with your mate. Look at the situations that get your dander up. What is it in these instances that makes you feel so threatened that you react with temper against your mate? You can then ask, "Do I deal with these situations better by unloading anger, or is there a different approach that might be far more constructive for myself and my mate?" Most people, when they examine what happens during and after outbursts of temper, find that this way of reacting works against their best interests rather than in favor of them. By seeing more clearly what the features are in situations that cause your temper to flare, you then can become more perceptive about how to deal with the problem itself, rather than automatically responding with a blowup. If you can develop personal insight in this way, you are likely to find that you are more capable of relating to your mate in a relaxed yet vigorous manner with all the gains of better listening, clear logic, and increased enjoyment.

1,9

1,9 ways of adjusting to emotion put the accent on the positive. Joy is found not in action or with accomplishment, but in togetherness. This means turning away from situations in which you feel your mate might reject you. Warmth and affection are the emotions with which you feel most secure. They are the very feelings that a 9,1-oriented person feels to be sticky. The emotions which make you most uncomfortable are antipathy and antagonism; yet it is these to which a 9,1-oriented person is thoroughly accustomed. You are attracted to circumstances which produce harmony and good feelings. You run away from situations that might be characterized by tension or conflict.

Some of these 1,9 emotional dispositions can be helpful in promoting marital bliss, but backing off from anxiety areas in human relationships can become a great hindrance. It makes it difficult for a person to deal with problems, even those that get worse if left unsolved. It is in dealing with objections, interruptions, complaints, and questions that so much conviction-building is achieved and from which so much marriage strength can result.

If you're a person who leans in a 1,9 direction, what can you do so as to deal with your emotions more adequately? First, you can make clear to yourself the nature of those situations that make you feel apprehensive, that make you want to escape. The 1,9 Mirror can be looked into for clues as to what's making you so anxious. Then, you can try to live with the short-term discomfort that might arise in order to gain potential long-term positive consequences. This experiment in living with the more negative and hostile emotions can give insight into how you can be more comfortable and constructive in responding to them, rather than attempting to evade them.

1,1

The 1,1 orientation to emotions is almost a contradiction in terms. If you are a person who has gravitated into 1,1 attitudes, you have disconnected your emotions from your mate. You do not even retain the interest you formerly might have had in steering clear of risky predicaments. Neither do you venture into new situations that might be emotionally invigorating.

A person who is adjusting to emotional situations in a 1,1 way *can* do something to change his reactions. It has been learned that many such people are unaware that they've sunk into a kind of emotional slumber. How people go to sleep emotionally is not too difficult to understand either. Many a person has become 1,1 about the emotions and involvements of his marriage, yet remains highly involved, committed, and challenged by community interests, hobbies, and work. Once you wake up from emotional sleep on your marriage couch, you come to see how inconsistent this aspect of behavior is and what you are missing. Then you can take steps to revivify yourself, sometimes with a sense of rediscovery. Yet it is not easy for a person to reach this point of self-awareness. You might have a flash of self-insight now and then, but unless you begin questioning your basic assumptions systematically, the fog will roll over you again. You can ask yourself the question "am I underenthusiastic?" Frequently you will find yourself concluding that you are. It looks that way by virtue of the fact that you have lost your own involvement. A perceptible gap between the emotions you feel toward a situation and the emotions you recall feeling under comparable circumstances earlier in your life offers a clue that you have been slipping toward 1,1.

5,5

As a 5,5-oriented mate, you have your own distinctive emotional disposition. A way of picturing it is to say that you avoid the intense feelings of anger, hate, and antipathy by not pushing yourself as hard as the 9,1 person. You do not let yourself slide into the soft, indulging emotions so much enjoyed by 1,9 people. Neither do you drift into uninvolvement in the 1,1 way. By positioning yourself safely in between, you avoid getting out on an emotional limb where your mate could cut you off. This mode of emotional adjustment is conservative. It is sheltered from risk; but what it also does is exclude you from the full richness of living, too. It makes you seem mechanical and feel emotionally shallow. This shows through in the sense that you seem to calibrate your emotions, almost as an engineer might set the controls of a machine to carry out some automatic process. To "fit the situation," you respond as you are expected to, rather than as you actually feel. You don't like to kiss in the street or blow your top at home. It's simply not done.

What can a person whose emotions are of the 5,5 variety do to alter them? Stretch yourself. You have more potential flexibility and emotional range than you are using. You need to undertake an emotions-building program. You can achieve this by letting yourself be challenged in hostile situations, by allowing yourself to relax and be genuine in situations that are positive, warm, and friendly. By deepening your interests and letting yourself go, you can feel the enthusiasm of being spontaneous and more actively involved with your mate.

9,9

The 9,9 appreciation of emotions is different from any of those described so far. First of all, 9,9 emotions are valid responses to situations that are being seen from as objective a viewpoint as possible. A 9,9-oriented person can feel antipathy toward unfairness. He is capable of responding with affection. He can be aware of the plight of acquaintances who are uninvolved and withdrawn, and he can comprehend with understanding the conservative "playing it safe" attitudes of the mate who tries to keep emotions always in the metered middle. He can challenge situations that are wrong and acknowledge situations that are right because he has learned that his emotions are a trustworthy source of empathy. They provide a basis of self-confidence for coping constructively.

If you experience emotions in this 9,9 way, you may be able to enrich further your own capacities for deep emotional response to your mate. There is a special way in which this help can be provided: It's when your mate feels tense, distraught, or disturbed.

Something intuitively tells us to talk to someone when we feel tense. Bottling up, swallowing or hiding feelings, or denying that they exist, seems only to aggravate the tensions in a relationship.

The greatest relief of tensions seems to come about when the person who is experiencing them can communicate these feelings to another person. This could be the one who is the "cause" of them and who can do something to reduce or eliminate the conditions that produced them. But just talking out one's feelings, by telling them to a third person, such as a neighbor, friend, or in-law, can have the effect of relieving pressure, too.

Why does talking-out seem to help? It may be that by attempting to communicate feelings, a person gains increased objectivity and insight into his own situation. Alternatively, it may be that through the sheer fact of speaking out, one is able to unload at least part of the troubles that are involved. But in the case of a marriage relationship problem, the more direct route to a solution begins with talking to your mate, rather than to your mother or some other person.

The extent of 9,9 communication in your own marriage at present can be gauged to some extent by your answer to this question: Is your mate your confidant, a person with whom you share your emotions and thoughts unreservedly? You may or may not be interacting with your mate in this way.

Many situations that a person enters provide their own reward. Getting a good result on the job, buying a new dress, seeing your team win the game, reading an enjoyable book, observing children developing, produce their own pleasures. These are self-contained events. If a contribution of thought or action is required of you, you have the capacity to provide it. No worry is involved.

But other kinds of situations are not immediately rewarding, or perhaps never can be. They are those that require your action when you don't know what to deliver or how to deliver it. After trying to "think things through," you're blocked. Try as you may, no answer comes. The issue is too complex for you to fathom. The difficulties, as you perceive them, are so great as to be practically indescribable.

To whom, if anyone, can you turn?

Some don't turn to their mates at all. This is illustrated as Betty describes the kind of marriage situation which culminated in her leaving her husband.

> ... the last couple of months we've hardly talked to each other. He comes home and I ask him what happened during the day. He always says, "Nothing." We never eat home anymore. We go to a restaurant and we just sit there, eating. He doesn't know what to do with me, do you know what I mean? I'm his wife, so he comes home for dinner. But it's nothing, do you know what I mean? There's no love or anything. Well, I

can't stand that. I want him to love me. I want him to be pleased to see me. I want him to come home and tell me all that's happened to him and how he feels about things. And I want to tell him how I feel. . . .[4]

This kind of indifference hits you hardest when you have been feeling high concern for your mate and, naturally enough, have expected it to be reciprocated. That's what marriage is *for,* if you view it in a 1,9 way. If you're 9,9, you believe it's essential. There are practical things to do in marriage; in addition, you have individual interests, so that you don't regard the personal link with your mate to be the whole of life. Nonetheless, you want it at its fullest. Betty's comments voice a 9,9-ish sense of loss, rather than 1,9 despair. If her attitudes are 9,9 across-the-board, she'll feel like confronting her mate on the subject of this conversational and emotional barrenness. But neither your affection nor your reasoning may cut much ice with a mate who's installed fixedly in the 1,1 corner.

Yet others can and do turn for help. Where, and how? The most "natural" confidant in the world is your mate. If your mate is not available, you may turn to someone else. Betty is seeking the kind of relief which one feels can be gained in the process of voicing long-pent-up thoughts in the presence of a receptive listener.

Ma, stay with me for about half an hour. Just let me talk my thoughts out. You don't have to say anything. I just want to think aloud. Please, Ma. . . .[5]

Note that she's not asking for suggestions or proposed solutions. What she wants from Ma is what, presumably, she's not getting from her husband—merely the opportunity to unwind and let go, to clear her mind of emotional static. Often you may need to express your feelings, lessening their burdening weight on you in the very act of *letting someone else know about them,* before you can gather your thoughts sufficiently to be ready to deal with whatever the difficulty is.

Yet who ought to be in a better position to calm your emotions, to listen to you, to help you to see or to redefine the current problem, to explore alternatives with you, to serve as a sounding board, than your mate? A true confidant relationship between mates can do all these things. The problem itself remains yours, of course. The solution—if the problem is wholly external to your marriage, such as one you have at work—is yours alone to decide; a responsibility that can't really be shared. But a mate who is a confidant, one who can consult with you, is able to contribute additional firmness in a synergistic marriage.

Listen to how this confidant relationship is described by several different mates.

> "They both need each other (for heart-to-heart talks). That's one of the purposes of marriage."

If the wife's behavior puzzles him, the husband says,

> "I make her clarify it . . . what goes on between my wife and I stays with us. I never talk to anyone about it. I'm supposed to be adult; that is part of adult life."

> "I can't think of anything my wife and I wouldn't tell each other that we'd tell someone else. I suppose there are some things one doesn't want to be thinking even, and so a husband wouldn't want to talk about it. But anything a husband can talk about, he can talk about to his wife, at least I think he should. If I don't get the drift of what she is saying, I'll ask her again and perhaps even again, until I do understand."

Another says,

> "If a wife can't talk to her husband (about very personal things), she can't talk to anyone." [6]

Candor means the readiness to *listen,* to receive the other person's reactions just as they occur, without selecting some and tuning out the rest. It implies sensitivity to the other person's feelings and willingness to give the support of understanding.

If you have such a relationship, both of you have the ability and readiness to put forward your own thoughts, opinions, and emotions in all their fullness. You would have the kind of a relationship Shirley is thinking and talking about to Gene. They are reminiscing about circumstances that drew them together. Here is a part of their conversation.

Shirley. Remember when we used to talk about what it was that drew us together?
Gene. But we never got very far. Every time, we drew together and stopped talking!
Shirley. That's right. I still don't know how we first became close, any better than you do. But I know why I counted on us staying together. Ever noticed how people have ways of talking *past* each other so they don't have to talk to each other?
Gene. No, I haven't, come to think of it.
Shirley. Listen around. You'll hear people talking but not getting through. It's hardly ever like that with us. When you and I talk, we hear our feelings, too, and we know we're together at the deepest level, even when we're apart on some issue.

This kind of talking is *real* communication. Expression is not muted by simply guessing about the other person's likely reactions. It is not censored by fear of criticism.[7] Feelings are revealed without the kind of exaggeration that is motivated by status-building or dominance needs. This is talking in the best meaning of the term.

Do you and your mate talk well together? It's all-important that you do.

Here's a suggestion.

If you can't answer "yes," don't try yet to do any joint planning of how to attain better teamwork or deeper intimacy. You're too likely to stumble into each other as a result of poor listening, lack of respect for the other person's point of view, failure to recognize and comprehend emotions, and so on.

Go back. Try again. Figure out what the basic attitudes are, the ones that prevent you from talking to each other in ways that permit mutual understanding and respect. Keep at it till you feel you're really getting through to each other. Then you can move forward.[8]

MARRIAGE BY OBJECTIVES

Many couples have found that setting improvement-goals offers a way of strengthening their marriage. Based on your understanding of the Grid, on the one hand, and of your self-assessment in the paragraph description, you may now see possibilities of change that might not have occurred to you before. This can form an important step.

Nobody can tell you in precise detail the best way for you to set improvement-objectives. But here's one way to go about it. Pick the element where you can see the most obvious things you can do to improve your marriage. Jot down these actions that you propose to take. Discuss them. This discussion can be valuable in two ways. It gives you a double-check on your own thinking, and it enables your mate to see how support can be given to your effort. It can foster your use of your mate as a confidant.

Also set a definite time when you want to sit down together and talk about progress.

Repeating this cycle of setting objectives, testing progress, and then resetting objectives can do much to strengthen your marriage and enrich your day-to-day living.

Earlier it was said, "Marriage is life's most vital and rewarding but also its most delicate human relationship." It is the experience most capable of satisfying emotional, social, and physical desires. It provides a foundation for continuity with the past through parents and commitment to the future through children.

Papa is talking with his son, Bibi, and telling him something of what he hopes his son will experience. Here is how he sees the good life.

Papa. Oui. And this love we speak of now, Bibi, when it is real, when it is true, it is the greatest love of all. I know; we have it here in this house, Maman and I. It is the best, it is the most natural . . . the true love for the one of your life, the only one. In this way the world comes down to a house, and a room, and a bed, and all the world is in that bed, if there, there are two people in love. This is something you will not know for many years, Bibi. It is possible never to know it. I hope you will. If you are as lucky as I am, you will.[9]

The real choice is between living with your marriage as it currently is, or setting aspirations to make your life together as rich as it might humanly become. Yet no one can tell you the best basis for a relationship between you two. That decision is yours. On it hangs the goodness of your life.

Here's a final happy thought. It's fortunate that the two concerns of the Marriage Grid can be harmonized and integrated in increasing degrees, and that more of one need never mean less of the other. When Concern for What Happens is high and joined with a high Concern for Your Mate, you are thinking and acting in ways that build toward a relationship which is not only sound, but also beautiful as a masterpiece of living.

APPENDIX | TALKING WITH A MARRIAGE COUNSELOR

The roots of certain husband-wife woes might seem to have grown too deep for the mates themselves to unearth and clear away. They can grin and bear it, or they can break the relationship off through separation or divorce. A third alternative is to seek outside help. By this is meant help from someone with specialized training *plus* an objective view of both mates. These two features make a marriage counselor's approach different from that of relatives or friends to whom you might otherwise turn for aid.

Many different kinds of marriage counseling are available. But their common feature is that help is sought from a third person—a minister, priest, or social worker; psychologist, psychiatrist, or marriage counselor. What can a third person do? Some give advice. Some meet each of the mates alone to help them talk out their frustrations and gain deeper insights into their individual selves, aiding them to grapple with their situation in a problem-solving way. Some meet with *both* mates at the same time. If the third person is a psychiatrist or clinical psychologist, he may focus their attention on hidden attitudes and unconscious motivations which may have been causing them to be unhappy with each other. These are attitudes and motivations whose sources have not yet been recognized, but which are present and influence behavior.

An outside person can cause things to happen that marriage

mates may be unable to accomplish for themselves. One reason is his neutrality to their situation. He's not locked in to their fixed positions. With his professional experience, he can bring to their attention a point of view and a method of studying themselves that can help them thaw out frozen thought patterns and destructive habits. Because he is a professional expert, they're likely to listen to him and respect his point of view enough to give it consideration.

Here is one way whereby you can sense whether a counselor may be of value to you. The following dialogues are taken from various counseling sessions with two couples. Diane and Peter are one pair, Mr. and Mrs. Mac, another. They demonstrate how outside assistance may aid couples in dealing with their problems in rewarding fashion.

Counselor. What's your beef? I see you're not getting along. I understand both of you have been dissatisfied with your relationship for some time. I want you to level with each other and confront one another directly, eyeball-to-eyeball, with your differences, no holds barred. Our purpose here is, of course, to find a road to agreement. But we have to start with the disagreements.

Peter. She likes to bitch.

Counselor. Please tell this directly to your wife.

Diane. Oh, that won't be necessary, Doctor. . . . He has told me far too often that I am a bitch.

Counselor. I believe you. But neither of you has learned very much from these repetitious harangues. I want to see how you two can learn to fight more constructively. So please address one another directly and don't complain about each other to me. Even if you say nothing new to each other, it's new to me and the fact that you are airing your differences in front of me is a new experience for you. Now please tell your wife again what your beef is.

So Peter tells Diane she bitches too much. Her response is defensive. He suggests her complaints are unjustified and irrational and claims his criticisms of her are "constructive." She becomes annoyed and calls him a pompous ass.

Diane. You ask and answer your own questions, so how can we get anywhere? You see, Doctor, he makes it impossible to communicate with him!

Counselor. Yes, in fact, I see several difficulties that the two of you have. But please leave me out of this for a while. Try to communicate directly with each other, even though you now find it difficult. You simply must practice direct contact with each other!

Peter. OK. Yes, I believe I was right: my criticism doesn't stop you from doing exactly as you please even though your bitching seriously interferes with my work! And I've had just about enough of it.

Diane. I've never interfered with your work! I know it's important to you, that you're anxious about it and very involved and ambitious. I accept all this. I love you for it and I'm proud of your work and your ambition. So how in the world can you ever say such a stupid thing, that I interfere with your work? I'm all for you, you idiot! I love you!

Peter. I know you love me, but you show it in a most aggravating manner. . . .[1]

' This is hardly much of a start, but it shows how far out of touch with each other Diane and Peter are. What is the counselor doing? He is not permitting them to bitch about each other to him directly. He is pursuing a different course, keeping them lip-to-lip, eye-to-eye. He will continue to do so until they begin *really* talking mate-to-mate about their genuine feelings toward each other. Then progress in freeing themselves from these 9,1/9,1 warrior positions can be expected.

The discussion below takes up the same couple later.

Counselor. Do you both agree that the first fight round we had in this office last week was not very constructive in its after-effects?

Diane. Well, Doctor, I don't know about your charts and all, but I think that fight was pretty good for us! We haven't stopped talking about all this ever since that first session.

Peter. Yes, but we haven't settled a damned thing. . . .

Diane interrupts to call the counselor's attention to "evidence" she thinks will incriminate Peter. She sums it all up this way.

Diane. . . . He always starts kidding or clowning when we get too close to the truth. And then he withdraws with some sarcastic exit remark!

Counselor. Why are you complaining about him to *me*?

Diane. Well, isn't that what I am supposed to be doing, airing my gripes?

Counselor. Sure, but not to me! What good is it to air your gripes to me? *He* is the one you're living with. Go ahead, address your-selves directly to one another—and fight it out with the pur-pose of locating static noises in your communication system, or other defensive strategies you use with each other. Then, after you locate them, you're supposed to negotiate a clear-cut agreement to stop using them and start leveling, zeroing in, owning up, facing and sharing what turns you on, what turns you off and what each of you can do right now, and from now on, to turn each other more on and less off!

Diane. OK, your clowning and your sarcastic exits not only turn me off, they *bug* me.

Peter. That's the idea, dear. It's my way of slapping you down when you persist in maintaining a position that's ridiculous and untenable.

His 9,1 humor is now the topic of discussion. It is clear to both that this forms part of the unpleasant marital background. Further, both can initiate conflict anywhere. In the next exchange it soon becomes obvious what Diane is listening for.

Diane. Foul! I got you! You static-maker, you! He is not supposed to assume what I know or how much I know, but find out directly from me. Isn't that right, Doctor?

Counselor. Sure, but there's something else to be considered, too. You're too delighted to be "catching" him doing something bad. Why don't you tell him how you feel right now when he does that?

Diane tries to tell Peter how she feels about his attitudes, but in doing so, she does exactly what she's just nailed *him* for. He gets furious. Then suddenly they're laughing.

Counselor. We're laughing about something that's not really funny. But maybe you should laugh and ridicule each other even harder. Maybe that would help to get you both down to brass tacks. Have you ever satirized each other? . . .[2]

What did the counselor contribute that was helpful in their situation? He was helping them recognize their broken-record fighting patterns and getting them to look at their actions from each other's point of view. He was also giving them positive suggestions about how to diagnose communication barriers and what to do to remove them.

Another therapist is working with Mr. and Mrs. McIntosh.

Mac. . . . when she asks me and I say no, I don't want to go because I don't like them and I'm exhausted, *she'll* say, "Well, very well, I'll go alone," and she *does.* And she often meets others whom she knows and comes back at midnight or later, after I've been watching the kids, and she's just had one hell of a time. But *I've* had to clean up in the goddamn kitchen, much of which had been left over from lunch and breakfast. . . .

Mrs. Mac. I don't do that very often. You make it sound like it's a constant sort of thing, but—

Mac. And I have to fix my own breakfast. . . .

Therapist. But why, why is it, that you overstate things? Because it seems to me that you ruin your argument. You . . . are obviously sore about something so you must have a good reason . . . and I'm sure your wife has a point of view too—but somehow by putting things so strongly, as if your wife is a lush and out on the town every night, you put *yourself* in the hole, you know. You strain my credulity, really. What are you being left out of that's really kind of sticking in your craw?

Mac. Well, I uh, had always looked forward to having a happy home, but I haven't gotten it—it's one *bedlam.* The house, ac-

cording to my standards, is slovenly. . . . I always look at it
that my home is where I can come and relax, but it never happens.

Mrs. Mac. But this is just *my* point and it's what I keep trying to tell
him. That if he had a different attitude toward it and saw it as
a *team* effort, so that *he* could make some contribution to the
home too? Then he *would* have what he wanted. But I get so
mad, and the reason that I have to go out—

Now Mrs. Mac is "should"-ing it vigorously. The therapist sees it
is time to focus on the difference between the actual and the possible.

Therapist. May I ask, Mrs. McIntosh, what evidence you have that
you could work in a team yourself? Uh, what is there in your
own past that tells you that you really *could* work in a team?

Mrs. Mac. I don't understand what you mean.

Therapist. . . . Well, have you really had any experience—did you
come from a home where you *saw* real teamsmanship and cooperation in practice? Are you sure that you're not just talking about a model of operating that you're not up to because
you never practiced it?

Mrs. Mac. Well, I *am* up to it . . . I *want* to cooperate and—

Mac comes in like a D.A. pouncing on a defense witness' unin-
tentioned admission of guilt. Maybe he really thinks the therapist is
going to decide who's guilty and who's innocent. And Mrs. Mac is
almost in tears.

Therapist. . . . I'm simply trying to say that maybe both of you
want something very hard and desperately, but you simply
haven't had the practice in how to go about it, so you blame
each other for not producing it and the fact is that neither of
you—

Mac. Doctor, you've had here a perfect example of what I have to
live with. You asked her a question and she says, "I don't
know; I don't understand." This is exactly what she pulls on
me. We started to fight from the first day we got married—

Therapist. We are also having an example of what *she* has to live
with—because, you see, you made a very good point and an
important observation about your wife, but you put it in such
a truculent way 'again that I'm sure she just kind of shuts her
ears and doesn't even really hear you. . . .

Mrs. Mac is mumbling something. The therapist asks her to
speak up. He remarks that she still cares enough about Mac to cry
about it.

Mrs. Mac. . . . Sometimes I just think it's not worth it and I'm
ready to just walk out and leave the whole mess, just run. And
other times, I think that if we keep working at it hard enough,
maybe we can make something out of it. But it's just—it's a
mess. Neither of us is happy; we can't get along. And it's af-
fecting the kids. . . .[3]

Incessant weary wrangling has taken its toll, and perhaps both
mates are toying with the idea of flight into 1,1 indifference or escape from marriage via divorce. For this couple, the therapist is
digging into their real attitudes and testing whether his interpretation of what is left unsaid is valid. If it is, it adds a third dimension
to their situation that may aid them to strengthen their deteriorated
marriage bond. If the Macs remain in this three-way discussion
with the therapist, both are likely to come to recognize that each
canceling the other out holds no promise for the future, and start
practicing teamwork skills that could move them forward in a more
cooperative way.

You now may have gained some insight into the kinds of communication ruts married people can get into, and how a counselor
can help these people to look at them. Does this insight qualify *you*
to take the role of a therapist toward your mate? Not likely. You
are part of your marriage problems, whether you presently realize
it or not. To interpret to your mate might only be to walk onto another battleground. Yet if your mate reads this section, you *both*
might then be in position to begin by discussing the examples. Try
to identify what was going on beneath the surface. Ask whether

you get into circular communication flight patterns. Then you might focus more directly on what's going on beneath the surface of your own relationship. Check whether you are really saying what you mean, or if your true attitudes and intentions are so camouflaged your mate cannot recognize them.

The key thing that a counselor can contribute is aiding people to break up faulty marriage habits, rather than simply continue to attack and counterattack, withdraw involvement, or become less and less interested in married living. All of this means that the counselor is assisting them in putting aside their preconceptions, convincing them to step outside their current Grid styles long enough to gain insight into either person's attitudes, feelings, and emotions that evoke mate rejection. If you do have problems in your marriage and are able, in your own interactions, to do what the counselor in these examples suggests, then you probably can benefit your own marriage. If you can't seem to get yourselves started but *can* see yourselves being helped, as these couples seem to have been, you might make a gain for your marriage by consulting a counselor. A professional third party's advice might give you a big boost toward a constructive breakout.[4]

REFERENCES

Chapter 1: The Marriage Grid

1. Anderson, R.: "The Footsteps of Doves," in *You Know I Can't Hear You When the Water's Running,* New York: Dramatists Play Service, Inc., 1967, pp. 30–31.

2. Blake, R. R., and J. S. Mouton: *The Managerial Grid: Key Orientations for Achieving Production Through People,* Houston: Gulf Publishing Company, 1964, provides a comparable analysis for business relationships, and *The Grid for Sales Excellence: Benchmarks for Effective Salesmanship,* New York: McGraw-Hill Book Company, 1970, examines salesman-customer interactions.

    Sources that are easily interpretable within the Marriage Grid framework include May, R.: *Love and Will,* New York: W. W. Norton & Company, Inc., 1969, where *love* is comparable to Concern for Your Mate and *will* corresponds to Concern for What Happens. In a similar way, in Schutz, W. C.: *Joy: Expanding Human Awareness,* New York: Grove Press, Inc., 1967, the dimensions are *affection* and *control.* See also references to the following authors: Bach, G. R. and P. H. Wyden; Bernard, J.; Berne, E.; Cuber, J. F. and P. B. Harroff; Ellis, A. and R. Harper; Farber, L. H.; Frankl, V. E.; Fromm, E.; Harris, T. A.; Horney, K.; Leary, T.; Lederer, W. J. and D. D. Jackson; Riesman, D.; N. Glazer and R. Denney; Rubin, T.; and V. Satir.

3. Taylor, R., and J. Bologna: *Lovers and Other Strangers,* New York: Samuel French, Inc., 1962, pp. 13–14.

4. A fuller examination of how present behavior may be linked to

childhood experiences can be found in Missildine, W. H.: *Your Inner Child of the Past,* New York: Simon and Schuster, 1963.

5. Stryker, S.: "Symbolic Interaction as an Approach to Family Research," *Marriage and Family Living,* vol. 21, 1959, p. 111.

6. The idea that behavior can shift from one orientation to another is coming into wider use as a basis for accounting for contradictory behavior. Both Berne, E.: *Games People Play: The Psychology of Human Relationships,* New York: Grove Press, Inc., 1964, and Harris, T. A.: *I'm OK—You're OK: A Practical Guide to Transactional Analysis,* New York: Harper & Row Publishers, Inc., 1969, discuss how people may shift between different orientations of Parent, Adult, and Child. However, Parent-Adult-Child does not discriminate 5,5 and 9,9, nor does it provide a basis for seeing 1,1.

7. Gurin, G., J. Veroff, and S. Feld: *Americans View Their Mental Health,* New York: Basic Books, Inc., 1960, p. 86.

8. Marriage behavior patterns have been analyzed by Burgess, E. W., and H. J. Locke: *The Family,* 2d ed., New York: American Book Company, 1960, Farber, B.: "Types of Family Organization: Child-oriented, Home-oriented, and Parent-oriented," in A. M. Rose (ed.), *Human Behavior and Social Processes,* Boston: Houghton Mifflin Company, 1962, pp. 285–306. Bernard, J.: *American Family Behavior,* New York: Harper & Brothers, 1942, pp. 17–18, points out that participative marriage (9,9) calls for relationship skills which are not essential in "role-oriented" (e.g. 5,5) marriages.

CHAPTER 2: GRID ELEMENTS

1. Many vivid illustrations of the qualities of conviction may be found in Frankl, V. E.: *Man's Search for Meaning,* New York: Washington Square Press, Inc., 1963.

2. For a general formulation of approaches to intimacy which can be interpreted within a Grid framework, see Fromm, E.: *The Art of Loving,* New York: Harper & Brothers, 1956.

CHAPTER 3: THE MIRROR

1. See Hunt, M. M.: *The World of the Formerly Married,* Greenwich, Conn.: Fawcett Crest Books, 1966, and New York: McGraw-Hill Book Company, 1966, Chap. 9.

2. Hart, M.: *Christopher Blake,* New York: Random House, Inc., 1947, p. 107.

CHAPTER 4: 9,1—CONTROL AND MASTERY

1. Besier, R.: *The Barretts of Wimpole Street,* Boston: Little, Brown and Company, 1949, pp. 152–154.

2. Lewis, S.: *Babbitt,* Harcourt, Brace & World, Inc., 1922; Signet edition, 1961, pp. 52–53.

3. Horney, K.: *The Neurotic Personality of Our Time,* New York: W. W. Norton & Company, Inc., 1937, pp. 162–206, gives a general description of the quest for power. See also Riesman, D., N. Glazer, and R. Denney: *The Lonely Crowd: A Study of the Changing American Character,* New Haven, Conn.: Yale University Press, 1950, in which the "inner-directed" character is presented; Rubin, T. I.: *The Angry Book,* New York: The Macmillan Company, 1969, in which the "slush fund" type of 9,1 anger is discussed; Schutz, W. C.: *Joy: Expanding Human Awareness,* New York: Grove Press, Inc., 1967, describing the "autocrat." Wheelis, A.: *The Quest for Identity,* New York: W. W. Norton & Company, Inc., 1958, traces the historical roots in American society of this kind of individualism.

4. Albee, E.: *Who's Afraid of Virginia Woolf?,* New York: Pocket Books, Inc., 1963, selected from pp. 79–84.

5. Gilroy, F. D.: *The Subject Was Roses,* New York: Samuel French, Inc., 1962, pp. 7–8. While it is often said that children can bring a couple together, the real situation is more complex than that. Children may enrich and expand a marriage, may provide mates with a topic that they can endlessly argue about with each other, may cause one mate to seek escape from the other, may lead to separations, and so on. The relationship between mates influences their parental attitudes. How you interact with your child or teenager can be looked at in terms of Grid styles, too.

6. *Ibid.,* p. 69.

7. The concept of "Parent" in Berne, E.: *Games People Play: The Psychology of Human Relationships,* New York: Grove Press, Inc., 1964, resembles the 9,1 orientation, particularly in the convictions area.

8. Komarovsky, M.: *Blue-Collar Marriage,* New York: Vintage Books, Inc., 1967 (originally published by Random House, Inc., 1962), p. 92.

9. *Ibid.,* p. 165.

10. Gardner, H.: *A Thousand Clowns,* New York: Samuel French, Inc., 1962, pp. 73–74.

11. Cowen, R.: *Summertree,* New York: Dramatists Play Service, Inc., 1968, p. 39.

12. See Lorenz, K.: *On Aggression,* New York: Harcourt, Brace & World, Inc., 1963.

13. States of apathy that can erupt into violence have been formulated by May, R.: *Love and Will,* New York: W. W. Norton & Company, Inc., 1969, pp. 27–31.

14. Various 9,1 fight strategies used by "hawks" are described in Bach, G. R., and P. H. Wyden: *The Intimate Enemy: How to Fight Fair in Love and Marriage,* New York: William Morrow & Company, Inc., 1969.

15. Carlino, L. J.: "Epiphany," in *Cages,* New York: Dramatists Play Service, Inc., 1964, p. 37.

16. Uris, L.: *Topaz,* New York: Bantam Books, Inc., 1968 (originally published by McGraw-Hill Book Company, 1967), p. 31.

17. Cowen, R.: *Summertree,* New York: Dramatists Play Service, Inc., 1968, p. 41.

18. Taylor, R., and J. Bologna: *Lovers and Other Strangers,* New York: Samuel French, Inc., 1968, pp. 14–15.

19. Carlino, L. J.: "Epiphany," in *Cages,* New York: Dramatists Play Service, Inc., 1964, pp. 38–39.

20. Komarovsky, M.: *Blue-Collar Marriage,* New York: Vintage Books, Inc., 1967 (originally published by Random House, Inc., 1962), p. 100.

21. Carlino, L. J., "Epiphany," in *Cages,* New York: Dramatists Play Service, Inc., 1964, p. 43.

22. Miller, A.: *After the Fall,* New York: Bantam Books, Inc., 1965, pp. 38–40.

23. Lindsay, H., and R. Crouse: Clarence Day's *Life with Father,* New York: Dramatists Play Service, Inc., 1948 (originally published 1939), p. 91.

24. *Ibid.,* p. 92.

25. Komarovsky, M.: *Blue-Collar Marriage,* New York: Vintage Books, Inc., 1967 (originally published by Random House, Inc., 1962), pp. 90–91.

26. *Ibid.,* p. 93.

27. Anderson, R.: "The Shock of Recognition," in *You Know I Can't Hear You When the Water's Running,* New York: Dramatists Play Service, Inc., 1967, p. 10.

CHAPTER 5: COVERUPS

1. These loving yet weak aspects of 1,9 behavior have been classified as modest, self-effacing and docile-dependent behavior of a kind that tends to provoke leadership or help from others. See Leary, T.: "The Theory and Measurement Methodology of Interpersonal Communication," *Psychiatry,* vol. 18, no. 2, May, 1955, pp. 147–161; Shostrom, E. L.: *Man the Manipulator: The Inner Journey from Manipulation to Actualization,* Nashville: Abingdon Press, 1967.

2. Chayefsky, P.: *Middle of the Night,* New York: Samuel French, Inc., 1957, p. 56.

3. Ibsen, H.: *A Doll's House,* translated by Peter Watts, Baltimore: Penguin Books, Inc., 1965, pp. 151–152.

4. *Ibid.,* pp. 223–224.

5. One-person adjustment is analyzed by Luckey, E. B.: "Marital Satisfaction and Congruent Self-Spouse Concepts," *Social Forces,* vol. 39, 1960, pp. 153–157.

6. Ibsen, H.: *A Doll's House,* translated by Peter Watts, Baltimore: Penguin Books, Inc., 1965, pp. 225–226.

7. A classic portrayal of "Mom" is to be found in Wylie, P.: *Generation of Vipers,* 20th ed., New York: Pocket Books, Inc., 1958 (originally published by Rinehart & Company, Inc., 1942), pp. 184–205.

8. De Hartog, J.: *The Fourposter,* New York: Samuel French, Inc., 1954, pp. 20–21.

9. This kind of "crisis" for a dependent husband is examined in Dominian, J.: *Marital Breakdown,* Baltimore: Penguin Books, Inc., 1968, p. 45.

10. Other excellent illustrations of paternalism are presented in Chayefsky, P.: *Middle of the Night,* New York: Samuel French, Inc., 1957, and in Allen, J. P., *et al.: Forty Carats* (adapted from a play by Barillet and Gredy; New York: Samuel French, Inc., 1969). The latter provides a study of several paternalistic husbands.

11. Kelly, G.: "Craig's Wife," in J. Mersand (ed.), *Three Plays about Marriage,* New York: Washington Square Press, Inc., 1962, pp. 23–25.

12. See Goffman, E.: *The Presentation of Self in Everyday Life,* Garden City: Anchor Books, Doubleday & Co., Inc., 1959; and *Strategic Interaction,* Philadelphia: University of Pennsylvania Press, 1969.

13. Barry, P.: *The Youngest,* New York: Samuel French, Inc., 1922, pp. 21–23.

14. *Ibid.,* pp. 27–28.

15. *Ibid.,* p. 33.

16. *Ibid.,* pp. 46–48.

17. *Ibid.,* pp. 56–57.

18. *Ibid.,* p. 103.

19. *Ibid.,* pp. 106–107.

20. For more extended treatment of games in human relationships, see Berne, E.: *Games People Play: The Psychology of Human Relationships,* New York: Grove Press, Inc., 1964; Chapman, A. H.: *Put-Offs & Come-Ons: Psychological Maneuvers and Stratagems,* New York: G. P. Putnam's Sons, 1969; Tully, G.: *Don't Be a Wife—Be a Mistress,* New York: Belmont Productions, Inc., 1968. More technical presentations include Berne, E.: *Transactional Analysis in Psychotherapy: A Systematic Individual and Social Psychiatry,* New York: Grove Press, Inc., 1961; and Goffman, E.: *Strategic Interaction,* Philadelphia: University of Pennsylvania Press, 1969.

21. Chayefsky, P.: *Middle of the Night,* New York: Samuel French, Inc., 1957, p. 31.

22. Berne, E.: *Games People Play: The Psychology of Human Relationships,* New York: Grove Press, Inc., 1964, pp. 95–96.

CHAPTER 6: FOREVER ANGER

1. 9,1/9,1 mate selection is sometimes made on a "common enemy" basis. See Freeman, L.: "Homogamy in Interethnic Mate Selection," *Sociology and Social Research,* vol. 39, 1955, pp. 369–377, Lederer, W. J., and D. D. Jackson: *The Mirages of Marriage,* New York: W. W. Norton & Company, Inc., 1968, pp. 157–158, describe the life-styles of "paranoid predator" mates.

2. *Ibid.,* pp. 135–136. These authors originated a classification system which includes the categories "spare-time battlers" (happy warriors) and "weary wranglers." These are two varieties of the 9,1/9,1 relationship. The term "conflict-habituated" is used in Cuber, J. F., and P. B. Harroff: *The Significant Americans: A Study of Sexual Behavior Among the Affluent,* New York: Appleton Century, 1965, pp. 44–46. See also Waller, W.: *The Family: A Dynamic Interpretation,* New York: Dryden, 1938, pp. 547–548; Lantz, H. R., and E. C. Snyder: *Marriage: An Examination of*

Man-Woman Relationships, New York: John Wiley & Sons, Inc., 1962; Dicks, H. V.: "Object Relations Theory and Marital Studies," *British Journal of Medical Psychology,* vol. 36, 1963, pp. 127–128.

3. Cuber, J. F., and P. B. Harroff: *The Significant Americans,* New York: Appleton Century, 1965, pp. 45–46.

4. Uris, L.: *Topaz,* New York: Bantam Books, 1968 (originally published New York: McGraw-Hill Book Company, 1967), pp. 32–33.

5. Rubin, T. I.: *The Angry Book,* New York: The Macmillan Company, 1969.

6. Bach, G. R., and P. H. Wyden: *The Intimate Enemy,* New York: William Morrow & Company, Inc., 1969. Gunny-sackers—people who store up grievances and then suddenly unload them at some point of frustration—also have this bad temper which is characteristic of weary wranglers. When the harboring of resentments is deeply hidden or when evidence that resentments have been stored away shows through only occasionally, it may be that the person's dominant characteristics are 1,9 but beneath these is a strong 9,1 backup.

CHAPTER 7: 1,9—FEAR OF REJECTION

1. The kind of behavior characteristic of a 1,9 orientation is analyzed in Horney, K.: *The Neurotic Personality of Our Time,* New York: W. W. Norton & Company, Inc., 1937, pp. 102–161, under the term "need for affection." Rubin, T. I.: *The Angry Book,* New York: The Macmillan Company, 1969, pp. 15–16, describes the "Be a nice guy—don't make waves" approach to conflict. Bach, G. R., and P. H. Wyden: *The Intimate Enemy: How to Fight Fair in Love and Marriage,* New York: William Morrow & Company, Inc., 1969, refer to "doves" who avoid fighting.

2. Miller, A.: *Death of a Salesman,* New York: Compass Books, The Viking Press, Inc., 1958, p. 13.

3. *Ibid.,* pp. 13–14.

4. Ryerson, F., and C. Clements: *Harriet,* New York: Charles Scribner's Sons, 1943, pp. 15–16.

5. Howard, J.: *Please Touch,* New York: McGraw-Hill Book Company, 1970, pp. 80–81.

6. This dynamic is illustrated in Flaubert, G.: *Madame Bovary,* New York: Grosset & Dunlap, Inc., particularly in Léon's relations with Emma.

7. Miller, A.: *Death of a Salesman,* New York: Compass Books, The Viking Press, Inc., 1958, pp. 36–37.

8. Farber, L. H.: *The Ways of the Will: Essays toward a Psychology and Psychopathology of Will,* New York: Harper Colophon Books, 1968, pp. 51–52.

9. Yale's attitudes might indicate lack of "marital aptitude." See Terman, L. M., and P. Wallin: "Marriage Prediction and Marital Adjustment Tests," *American Sociological Review,* vol. 14, 1949, pp. 497–504.

Chapter 8: Sweetness And Blight

1. Strodtbeck, F.: "The Interaction of a 'Hen-pecked' Husband and His Wife," *Marriage and Family Living,* vol. 14, 1952, pp. 305–309.

2. Winch, R.: *Mate Selection,* New York: Harper & Brothers, 1958; Dicks, H. V.: "Experiences with Marital Tensions in the Psychological Clinic," *British Journal of Medical Psychology,* vol. 26, 1953, parts III and IV, pp. 181–196.

3. Waller, W., and R. Hill: *The Family: A Dynamic Interpretation,* New York: Dryden Press, 1951.

4. Some longer-term possibilities are examined in Dominian, J.: *Marital Breakdown,* Baltimore: Penguin Books, Inc., 1968, pp. 47–52.

Chapter 9: 1,1—Apathetic Withdrawal

1. Waller, W.: *The Family: A Dynamic Interpretation,* New York: Dryden, 1938, p. 538, points out that one mate's withdrawal of concern for the other might not be an adjustment to life as lived *with* this other person, but can be an early stage in living *without* one's present mate.

2. 1,1 withdrawal from participation is examined by Horney, K.: *The Neurotic Personality of Our Time,* New York: W. W. Norton & Company, Inc., 1937, pp. 207, 212–215. "Anomic" behavior is described by Riesman, D., N. Glazer, and R. Denney: *The Lonely Crowd: A Study of the Changing American Character,* New Haven: Yale University Press, 1950, pp. 242, 243–245. 1,1 attitudinal components are identified by Seeman, M.: "On the Meaning of Alienation," *American Sociological Review,* vol. 24, December, 1959, pp. 783–791. Rainwater, L., and K. K. Weinstein: *And the Poor Get Children: Sex, Contraception, and Family Planning in the*

Working Class, Chicago: Quadrangle Books, Inc., 1960, describe how some couples drift together and begin marriage in a 1,1 way. Cuber, J. F., and P. B. Harroff: *The Significant Americans: A Study of Sexual Behavior Among the Affluent,* New York: Appleton Century, 1965, discuss "devitalized" and "passive-congenial" modes of married living which appear 1,1/1,1 with 5,5/5,5 overtones. The "mind-your-own-business" syndrome is described in Rubin, T. I.: *The Angry Book,* New York: The Macmillan Company, 1969, p. 16.

3. Komarovsky, M.: *Blue-Collar Marriage,* New York: Vintage Books, Inc., 1967 (originally published by Random House, Inc., 1962), p. 100.

4. Chayefsky, P.: *Middle of the Night,* New York: Samuel French, Inc., 1957, pp. 34–35.

5. *Ibid.,* pp. 46–47.

6. Komarovsky, M.: *Blue-Collar Marriage,* New York: Vintage Books, Inc., 1967 (originally published by Random House, Inc., 1962), pp. 150–151.

7. Cuber, J. F., and P. B. Harroff: *The Significant Americans,* New York: Appleton Century, 1965, p. 49.

8. Richardson, J. C.: *Gallows Humor,* New York: E. P. Dutton & Co., Inc., 1961, p. 83.

9. Schisgal, M.: *Luv,* New York: Dramatists Play Service, 1966, p. 25.

10. Chayefsky, P.: *Middle of the Night,* New York: Samuel French, Inc., 1957, p. 7.

11. Williams, T.: *Cat on a Hot Tin Roof,* New York: Dramatists Play Service, Inc., 1958, p. 23.

12. Miller, A.: *A View from the Bridge,* New York: Compass Books, The Viking Press, Inc., 1960, pp. 31–32.

13. Cuber, J. F., and P. B. Harroff: *The Significant Americans,* New York: Appleton Century, 1965, pp. 174–175.

CHAPTER 10: WED BUT DEAD

1. Dickson, R.: *Marriage is a Bad Habit,* New York: Award Books, 1969, pp. 32–33.

2. Lewis, S.: *Babbitt,* New York: Harcourt, Brace & World, 1922; Signet edition, 1961, p. 10.

3. For an analysis of relationship dynamics leading up to a permanent

grievance, see Rapoport, A.: *Fights, Games, and Debates,* Ann Arbor: University of Michigan Press, 1960.

4. For a case study of this kind of deterioration in a marriage relationship see Jones, W. L.: "Marriage—Growth or Disaster?" *American Journal of Psychiatry,* vol. 125, no. 8, February 1969, pp. 1116–1117.

CHAPTER 11: 5,5—SECURITY THROUGH STATUS

1. Mate selection is being influenced by parents in a 5,5 manner. The dynamics of mate selection form an independent topic of great importance. This is analyzed from a Grid point of view elsewhere; see Mouton, J. S., and R. R. Blake: *The Mate Selection Grid* (in preparation).

2. For analyses of 5,5 characteristics see Riesman, D., N. Glazer, and R. Denney: *The Lonely Crowd: A Study of the Changing American Character,* New Haven: Yale University Press, 1950, where these are described in "tradition-directed" and "other-directed" terms. Other general references are Wheelis, A.: *The Quest for Identity,* New York: W. W. Norton & Company, Inc., 1958; and Putney, S., and G. J. Putney: *The Adjusted American: Normal Neuroses in the Individual and Society,* New York: Harper Colophon Books ed., 1966; originally published by Harper & Row, 1964, under the title *Normal Neurosis.* In Blood, R. O., Jr., and D. M. Wolfe: *Husbands and Wives: The Dynamics of Married Living,* New York: The Free Press, 1960, "companionship" as described, and "balance of power" both have 5,5 and 9,9 aspects. In Lederer, W. J., and D. D. Jackson: *The Mirages of Marriage,* New York: W. W. Norton & Company, Inc., 1968, the concept of *"quid pro quo"* in marriage is mostly in the 5,5/5,5 area but has undertones of 9,9/9,9. De Beauvoir, S.: *The Second Sex,* translated by Parshley, H. M., New York: Bantam Books, Inc., 1961; first American edition published by Alfred A. Knopf, Inc., 1953; and Friedan, B.: *The Feminine Mystique,* New York: Dell Publishing Co., Inc., 1964, analyze the 5,5 orientation, particularly with regard to notions of the woman's role. The consequences of 5,5 smoothing over of differences are explored by Winick, C.: *The New People: Desexualization in American Life,* New York: Pegasus, 1969; originally published New York: Western Publishing Co., Inc., 1968.

3. Cuber, J. F., and P. B. Harroff: *The Significant Americans,* New York: Appleton Century, 1965, pp. 47–48.

4. This kind of marriage was viewed by early role theorists as success-

ful, in terms of the degree of adjustment achieved. See Cottrell, L. S., Jr.: "Roles and Marital Adjustment," *Publications of the American Sociological Society,* vol. 27, 1933, p. 109.

5. Effects of traditional influences on decision-making are analyzed in Burgess, E. W., and L. S. Cottrell: *Predicting Success or Failure in Marriage,* Englewood Cliffs, N.J.: Prentice-Hall, 1939; Goode, W.: *After Divorce,* Glencoe, Ill.: The Free Press, 1956; Rainwater, L., and K. K. Weinstein: *And the Poor Get Children,* Chicago: Quadrangle Books, 1960, pp. 68–69; Blood, R. O., Jr., and D. M. Wolfe: *Husbands and Wives: The Dynamics of Married Living,* New York: The Free Press, 1960, pp. 22–23.

6. Blood and Wolfe, *op. cit.,* pp. 47–54; Johannis, T. B.: "Conceptions of Use of Non-work Time: Individual, Husband-Wife, Parent-Child and Family—A Methodological Note," *Coordinator,* vol. 8, 1959, pp. 34–36.

7. Whyte, W. H., Jr.: "Corporation and the Wife," *Fortune,* vol. 44, 1951, pp. 109–111, and "Wives of Management," *Fortune,* vol. 44, 1951, pp. 86–88; Helfrich, M. L.: "The Generalized Role of the Executive's Wife," *Marriage and Family Living,* vol. 23, 1961, pp. 384–387.

8. For a description of typical middle- and working-class American husbands' and wives' role expectations, see Spiegel, J. P.: "The Resolution of Role Conflict within the Family," *Psychiatry,* vol. 20, 1957, p. 3.

9. Albee, E.: *Everything in the Garden,* New York: Dramatists Play Service, Inc., 1968, p. 12.

10. See Packard, V.: *The Status Seekers,* New York: David McKay Company, Inc., 1959.

11. Gardner, H.: *A Thousand Clowns,* New York: Samuel French, Inc., 1962, pp. 76–77.

12. Lewis, S.: *Babbitt,* New York: Harcourt, Brace & World, 1922; Signet Classics edition, 1961, p. 186.

13. Charny, I. W.: "Marital Love and Hate," *Family Process,* vol. 8, no. 1, 1969, p. 8.

14. Lindsay, H., and R. Crouse: Clarence Day's *Life with Father,* New York: Dramatists Play Service, Inc., 1948, pp. 22–23.

15. Bowman, H. A.: *Marriage for Moderns,* 5th ed., New York: McGraw-Hill Book Company, 1965, p. 408.

16. Bach, G. R., and P. H. Wyden: *The Intimate Enemy,* New York: William Morrow & Company, Inc., 1969, pp. 30–31.

17. Sexual problems within 5,5-like marriages are discussed by Ter-

man, L. M., with P. Buttenwieser, L. W. Ferguson, W. B. Johnson, and D. Wilson: *Psychological Factors in Marital Happiness,* New York: McGraw-Hill Book Company, 1938.

18. For a statistical study of sexual practices in marriages that appear 5,5-oriented, see Bernard, J.: "The Adjustments of Married Mates," in H. T. Christenson (ed.), *Handbook of Marriage and the Family,* Chicago: Rand McNally, 1964, p. 720.

CHAPTER 12: MARRIAGE IN THE MIDDLE

1. Schisgal, M.: *Luv,* New York: Dramatists Play Service, Inc., 1966, p. 41.

2. Lewis, S.: *Babbitt,* New York: Harcourt, Brace & World, 1922; Signet Classics edition, 1961, pp. 10–11.

3. *Ibid.,* p. 190.

4. Taylor, R., and J. Bologna: *Lovers and Other Strangers,* New York: Samuel French, Inc., 1968, pp. 39–40.

5. If success in marriage is viewed in 5,5 terms, the probability of success is relatively high. See Terman, L. M., with P. Buttenwieser, L. W. Ferguson, W. B. Johnson, and D. P. Wilson: *Psychological Factors in Marital Happiness,* New York: McGraw-Hill Book Company, 1938; Burgess, E. W., and L. S. Cottrell: *Predicting Success or Failure in Marriage,* Englewood Cliffs, N.J., Prentice-Hall, Inc., 1939. A 5,5/5,5 marriage is balanced in the sense that husband and wife roles can be routinized so as to make a smooth long-term fit. See Kelley, E. L.: "Consistency of the Adult Personality," *American Psychologist,* vol. 10, 1955, pp. 659–681; Kerckhoff, A. C., and K. E. Davis: "Value Consensus and Need Complementarity in Mate Selection," *American Sociological Review,* vol. 27, 1962, pp. 295–303.

6. Reiss, I. L.: "Toward a Sociology of the Heterosexual Love Relationship," *Marriage and Family Living,* vol. 22, 1960, pp. 139–145.

7. Albee, E.: *Who's Afraid of Virginia Woolf?,* New York: Pocket Books, Inc., 1963, p. 8.

CHAPTER 13: 9,9—MUTUAL FULFILLMENT

1. Autonomy of the 9,9 kind is described by Riesman, D., N. Glazer, and R. Denney: *The Lonely Crowd: A Study of the Changing American Character,* New Haven: Yale University Press, 1950, pp. 249–260. A different yet refreshing concept of autonomy is pro-

vided in Rand, A., and N. Branden: *The Virtue of Selfishness: A New Concept of Egoism,* New York: Signet Books, 1964. A self-fulfillment view of autonomy is available in Maslow, A. H.: *Motivation and Personality,* 2d ed., New York: Harper & Row, 1970.

2. Taylor, S.: *Sabrina Fair,* New York: Dramatists Play Service, Inc., 1954, pp. 44–46.

3. The descriptions of Intrinsic Marriages in Cuber, J. F., and P. B. Harroff: *The Significant Americans: A Study of Sexual Behavior Among the Affluent,* New York: Appleton Century, 1965, convey a sense of 9,9 relationships even though some of them carry 5,5 overtones. Patterns of relationship that have a 9,9 quality are also discussed in Komarovsky, M.: *Blue-Collar Marriage,* New York: Vintage Books, 1967 (originally published by Random House, Inc., 1962), particularly in chapters 6 and 8. Alexander, C.: "The City as a Mechanism for Sustaining Human Contact," in W. R. Ewald, Jr. (ed.): *Environment for Man: The Next Fifty Years,* Bloomington: Indiana University Press, 1967, pp. 60–109, discusses qualities of human contact and relates them to the settings in which they do or could occur. More general references are Wheelis, A.: *The Quest for Identity,* New York: W. W. Norton & Company, Inc., 1958; May, R.: *Love and Will,* New York: W. W. Norton & Company, Inc., 1969. In Lederer, W. J., and D. D. Jackson: *The Mirages of Marriage,* New York: W. W. Norton & Company, Inc., 1968, the *"quid pro quo"* concept has some 9,9 qualities mingled with larger amounts of 5,5.

4. Foote, N. N.: "Love," *Psychiatry,* vol. 16, 1953, pp. 245–251.

5. May, R.: *Love and Will,* p. 306.

6. Convictions of a 9,9 kind are examined and discussed in Farber, L. H.: *The Ways of the Will: Essays toward a Psychology and Psychopathology of Will,* New York: Harper Colophon Books, 1968 (originally published by Basic Books, Inc., 1966).

7. Cuber, J. F., and P. B. Harroff: *The Significant Americans,* p. 55.

8. *Ibid.,* p. 59.

9. Eaton, J. W.: "Social Processes of Professional Teamwork," *American Sociological Review,* vol. 16, 1951, pp. 707–713.

10. In Bach, G. R., and P. H. Wyden: *The Intimate Enemy,* New York: William Morrow & Company, Inc., 1969, the "fair fight" concept is 9,9.

11. Cuber, J. F., and P. B. Harroff: *The Significant Americans,* p. 136. For contrasting approaches to living in close proximity, see Goffman, E.: *The Presentation of Self in Everyday Life,* Garden City: Anchor Books, Doubleday & Co., Inc., 1959.

12. Komarovsky, M.: *Blue-Collar Marriage,* New York: Vintage Books, Inc., 1967 (originally published by Random House, Inc., 1962), pp. 84–85.

13. Rainwater, L., and K. Weinstein: *And the Poor Get Children: Sex, Contraception and Family Planning in the Working Class,* Chicago: Quadrangle Books, 1960, p. 98.

14. Komarovsky, M.: *Blue-Collar Marriage,* New York: Vintage Books, Inc., 1967 (originally published by Random House, Inc., 1962), pp. 85–86.

15. Rainwater, L., and K. Weinstein: *And the Poor Get Children,* p. 100.

16. Anderson, R.: "The Footsteps of Doves," in *You Know I Can't Hear You When the Water's Running,* New York: Dramatists Play Service, Inc., 1967, p. 27.

17. May, R.: *Love and Will,* pp. 55–56.

18. *Ibid.,* p. 303.

CHAPTER 14: VITAL MARRIAGES

1. Lavery, E.: *The Magnificent Yankee,* New York: Samuel French, Inc., 1946, pp. 55–59.

2. Anderson, R.: *You Know I Can't Hear You When the Water's Running,* New York: Dramatists Play Service, Inc., 1967, pp. 51–52.

3. *Ibid.,* pp. 52–53.

4. Williams, T.: *Cat on a Hot Tin Roof,* New York: Dramatists Play Service, Inc., 1958, p. 23.

5. *Ibid.,* p. 13.

6. *Ibid.,* pp. 79–81.

7. Howard, S.: *The Silver Cord,* New York: Samuel French, Inc., 1926, p. 61.

8. *Ibid.,* pp. 62–63.

9. *Ibid.,* pp. 68–69.

10. *Ibid.,* pp. 69.

11. *Ibid.,* pp. 69–70.

CHAPTER 15: VARIETY

1. Luckey, E. B.: "Number of Years Married as Related to Personality Perception and Marital Satisfaction," *Journal of Marriage and the Family,* vol. 28, 1966, pp. 44–48.

2. Blood, R. O., Jr., and D. M. Wolfe: *Husbands and Wives: The Dynamics of Married Living,* New York: The Free Press, 1960, pp. 263–266.

3. Hobart, C. W.: "Disillusionment in Marriage, and Romanticism," *Marriage and Family Living,* vol. 20, 1958, pp. 156–162; "Attitude Changes during Courtship and Marriage," *Marriage and Family Living,* vol. 22, 1960, pp. 352–359; Pineo, P. C.: "Disenchantment in the Later Years of Marriage," *Marriage and Family Living,* vol. 23, 1961, pp. 3–11.

4. Maslow, A. H.: *Motivation and Personality,* 2d ed., New York: Harper & Row, 1970, pp. xiv–xv, 49, 71–72.

5. Iversen, W.: *Venus U.S.A.,* New York: Pocket Books, Inc., 1960, p. 6.

6. Breedlove, W., and J. Breedlove: *Swap Clubs: A Study in Contemporary Sexual Mores,* Los Angeles: Sherbourne Press, 1964; Lewis, R. W.: "The Swingers," *Playboy,* April, 1969, pp. 149–150, 216, 218–222, 224, 226–228; Packard, V.: *The Sexual Wilderness: The Contemporary Upheaval in Male-Female Relationships,* New York: David McKay Company, Inc., 1968.

7. Ellis, A., and D. Mace: "The Use of Sex in Human Life," *Journal of Sex Research,* vol. 5, no. 1, 1969, pp. 41–49.

8. Rimmer, R.: *The Harrad Experiment,* Los Angeles: Sherbourne Press, 1966; *The Harrad Letters to Robert H. Rimmer,* New York: The New American Library, 1969; *Proposition 31,* New York: The New American Library, 1969.

9. Prior, A.: *The Loving Cup,* New York: Fawcett World Library, 1968, p. 20.

10. A pioneering anthropological study in this area has been made by Bartell, G. D.: *Group Sex: A Scientist's Eyewitness Report on the American Way of Swinging,* Chicago: Peter H. Wyden, 1971.

11. Taylor, R., and J. Bologna: *Lovers and Other Strangers,* New York: Samuel French, Inc., 1968, pp. 37–38.

12. Numerous examples of the marriage tensions associated with an affair are to be found in Hunt, M. M.: *The Affair,* New York: Signet Books, New American Library, Inc., 1971.

13. Breedlove, W., and J. Breedlove: *Swap Clubs: A Study in Contemporary Sexual Mores,* Los Angeles: Sherbourne Press, 1964, pp. 37–38.

14. Lewis, R. W.: "The Swingers," *Playboy,* April, 1969, p. 216.

15. Kanin, E. J., and D. H. Howard: "Postmarital Consequences of Premarital Sex Adjustments," *American Sociological Review,* vol. 23, 1958, pp. 556–562.

16. No research has been undertaken as to the correlations between Marriage Grid styles and one or the other mate becoming involved in extramarital affairs. But as a comparison of the core assumptions demonstrates, some Grid-style pairings tend to draw mates together while others are likely to push them apart. 9,1/9,1 "weary wranglers" probably are more interested in extramarital ventures than are "happy warriors." Comparative reasoning will suggest which Grid-style combinations are those most likely to knit mates into a strong mutual relationship, and which drive one or the other into affairs.

17. Sophocles: "King Oedipus," in *The Theban Plays,* translated by E. F. Watling, Harmondsworth, England: Penguin, 1947, p. 59.

18. Cuber, J. F. and P. B. Harroff: *The Significant Americans,* New York: Appleton Century, 1965, pp. 48–49.

19. Hunt, M. M.: *The World of the Formerly Married,* Greenwich, Conn.: Fawcett Publications, Inc., 1967 (originally published New York: McGraw-Hill Book Company, 1966) p. 125.

20. Bach, G. R., and P. H. Wyden: *The Intimate Enemy,* New York: William Morrow & Company, 1969, p. 23.

21. Rubin, T. I.: *The Winner's Notebook,* New York: Trident Press, 1967, p. 194.

22. Results of original research into sexual attitudes are presented in Kinsey, A. C., W. B. Pomeroy, and C. E. Martin: *Sexual Behavior in the Human Male,* Philadelphia: W. B. Saunders Company, 1948; Kinsey, A. C., W. B. Pomeroy, C. E. Martin, and P. H. Gebhard: *Sexual Behavior in the Human Female,* Philadelphia: W. B. Saunders Company, 1953; Masters, W. H., and V. E. Johnson: *Human Sexual Response,* Boston: Little, Brown and Company, 1966; and *Human Sexual Inadequacy,* Boston: Little, Brown and Company, 1970. The cross-cultural range and variety of sexual behavior is described in Mead, M.: *Male and Female: A Study of the Sexes in a Changing World,* New York: Mentor Books, 1949. Biological versus cultural factors, as related to sexual behavior, are analyzed in Bates, M.: *Gluttons and Libertines: Human Problems of Being Natural,* New York: Random House, Inc., 1958.
For suggestions as to how variety in a sexual relationship can be developed see Eichenlaub, J. E.: *New Approaches to Sex in Marriage,* New York: Dell Publishing Co., Inc., 1967; Reuben, D. R.: *Everything You Always Wanted to Know about Sex—but Were Afraid to Ask,* New York: David McKay Company, Inc., 1969; *The Sensuous Woman* by "J": New York: Lyle Stuart, Inc., 1969; Brecher, E., and R. Brecher (eds.), *An Analysis of Human Sexual Response,* New York: Signet Books, 1966; Masters and Johnson: *Human Sexual Inadequacy.*

CHAPTER 16: ENRICHING YOUR MARRIAGE

1. For a comprehensive treatment of questioning, as well as other aspects of communication, see Nirenberg, J. S.: *Getting Through to People,* Englewood Cliffs, N.J.: Prentice-Hall, Inc., 1969.

2. Nichols, R. G., and L. A. Stevens: *Are You Listening?,* New York: McGraw-Hill Book Company, 1957, is a good introductory text on this subject.

3. If you continue to have difficulties in talking and relating with each other you may want to consider getting help from professional marriage counselors or therapists who are qualified to aid you in grappling with problems you are presently unable to cope with.

4. Chayefsky, P.: *Middle of the Night,* New York: Samuel French, Inc., 1957, p. 23.

5. *Ibid.,* p. 6.

6. Komarovsky, M.: *Blue-Collar Marriage,* New York: Vintage Books, 1967 (originally published by Random House, Inc., 1962), p. 114.

7. Rapoport, A.: *Fights, Games, and Debates,* Ann Arbor: University of Michigan Press, 1960.

8. Other things you can do to strengthen your marriage include the following. Work together on completing learning exercises which have been designed for married couples. Exercises which you can do in your own home are available from Scientific Methods, Inc., P.O. Box 195, Austin, Texas 78767, as well as is information about Marriage Grid Seminars.
Additional home exercises are described in Popenoe, P.: *Marriage Is What You Make It,* New York: The Macmillan Company, 1950; Schutz, W. C.: *Joy: Expanding Human Awareness,* New York: Grove Press, Inc., 1967; Lederer, W. J., and D. D. Jackson: *The Mirages of Marriage,* New York: W. W. Norton & Company, Inc., 1968; Gunther, B.: *Sensory Relaxation,* Toronto: Collier-Macmillan Canada, Ltd., 1968; Weinberg, G.: *The Action Approach: How Your Personality Developed and How You Can Change It,* New York: World Publishing Company, 1969; Bach, G. R., and P. H. Wyden: *The Intimate Enemy,* New York: William Morrow & Company, Inc., 1969; Otto, H. A.: *More Joy in Your Marriage: Developing Your Marriage Potential,* New York: Hawthorn Books, Inc., 1969. How clear meaning contributes to the maintenance and strengthening of "self anchorages" is discussed in Frankl, V. E.: *The Doctor and the Soul: From Psychotherapy to Logotherapy,*

New York: Bantam Books, 1969; (first American edition published by Alfred A. Knopf, Inc., 1955).

Many organizations are sponsoring laboratory-type learning experiences designed to be helpful to married couples determined to live more fully together. These are typically either weekend or week-long programs. Sources of information about the laboratory approach include Otto, H. A.: *More Joy in Your Marriage,* pp. 192–196; Howard, J.: *Please Touch: A Guided Tour of the Human Potential Movement,* New York: McGraw-Hill Book Company, 1970; and National Training Laboratories Institute for Applied Behavioral Sciences, associated with the National Education Association, Washington, D.C. 20036. Religious institutions provide a context within which values can be tested and relationships strengthened.

9. Taylor, S.: *The Happy Time* (based on the stories by Robert Fontaine), New York: Dramatists Play Service, Inc., 1950, pp. 80–81.

APPENDIX: TALKING WITH A MARRIAGE COUNSELOR

1. Bach, G. R., and P. H. Wyden: *The Intimate Enemy,* New York: William Morrow & Company, Inc., 1969, pp. 170–171.

2. *Ibid.,* pp. 183–185.

3. Lederer, W. J., and D. D. Jackson: *The Mirages of Marriage,* New York: W. W. Norton & Company, Inc., 1968, pp. 420, 422, 424, 426, 428.

4. Sources of information about marriage counseling include Ellis, A., and R. A. Harper: *A Guide to Successful Marriage,* Hollywood, Cal.: Wilshire Book Company, 1968; and Lobsenz, N. M., and C. W. Blackburn: *How to Stay Married,* New York: Cowles Book Company, Inc., 1968. Both these books contain directories of marriage counseling agencies and associations throughout the United States.

More technical references are: Christensen, H. T. (ed.): *Handbook of Marriage and the Family,* Chicago: Rand McNally, 1964; Boszormenyi-Nagy, I., and J. L. Framo (eds.): *Intensive Family Therapy: Theoretical and Practical Aspects,* New York: Paul B. Hoeber, Inc., 1965; and Satir, V.: *Conjoint Family Therapy,* Palo Alto, Cal.: Science and Behavior Books, 1967.

INDEX